This is a fascinating subject. The author uses it to illuminate PR's "invisible government" working at the heart of organizations to manage perceptions and create profound social changes. It is vital that society understands how much PR shapes our world. This well written, thoroughly researched book on the corporate face, character and voice makes a big contribution to that objective.

Simon Moore, *Bentley University, USA and author of Public Relations and the History of Ideas.*

This study of *corporate persona*, particularly its focus on values and an affinitive approach, is timely given a need to address the decline of public trust in business at the same time as corporations assume an ever greater role in neoliberal capitalist societies. Also, as Burton St. John III pointedly notes, corporate persona has been largely ignored in public relations and corporate communication research. As well as creating greater affinity between corporations and their home market, an affinitive approach can reduce the negative colonizing effects of globalization by encouraging global corporate citizenship.

Jim Macnamara, *Professor of Public Communication, University of Technology Sydney, Australia.*

Professor Saint John's book is a meticulously researched, gracefully written significant contribution to PR and communications scholarship. The book borders on being an investigative report on the way in which the wooden and off-putting abstraction known as the modern corporation has been carefully fitted out with a recognizably human personality. The domestication of the corporation in the late twentieth century parallels the far more familiar current efforts of the artificial-intelligence community to produce sociable machines.

Robert E. Brown, *Professor, Communications Department, Salem State University, USA.*

Public Relations and the Corporate Persona

For much of the last century, large and predominantly U.S. corporations used public relations to demonstrate that their missions resonated with dominant societal values. Through the construction and conveyance of the "corporate persona," they aimed to convince citizens that they share common aspirations—and moreover that their corporate "soul" works as a beneficent force in society.

Through examining key examples from the last 80 years, this book argues that PR, through the corporate persona, works to create a sense of shared reality between the corporation and the average citizen. This has been instrumental in conveying, across generations, that the corporation is an affinitive corporate persona—a fellow companion in the journey of life. The construct is obviously ripe for manipulation, and the role of PR in creating and promoting the corporate persona, in order to align corporations and stakeholders, is potentially problematic. From wage inequality to climate change, preserving the corporate status quo may be negative.

This original and thought-provoking book not only critically analyzes how PR and its role in the corporate persona work to solidify power but also how that power might be used to further goals shared by the corporation and the individual. Scholars and advanced students of public relations, organizational communications, and communication studies will find this book a challenging and illuminating read.

Burton St. John III is Professor in the Department of Communication at Old Dominion University, USA.

Routledge New Directions in Public Relations and Communication Research

Edited by Kevin Moloney

Current academic thinking about public relations (PR) and related communication is a lively, expanding marketplace of ideas, and many scholars believe that it's time for its radical approach to be deepened. *Routledge New Directions in PR & Communication Research* is the forum of choice for this new thinking. Its key strength is its remit, publishing critical and challenging responses to continuities and fractures in contemporary PR thinking and practice, tracking its spread into new geographies and political economies. It questions its contested role in market-oriented, capitalist, liberal democracies around the world and examines its invasion of all media spaces, old, new and not-yet envisaged. We actively invite new contributions and offer academics a welcoming place for the publication of their analyses of a universal, persuasive mindset that lives comfortably in old and new media around the world.

Books in this series will be of interest to academics and researchers involved in these expanding fields of study, as well as students undertaking advanced studies in this area.

Pathways to Public Relations
Histories of Practice and Profession
*Edited by Burton St. John III,
Margot Opdycke Lamme and
Jacquie L'Etang*

Gender and Public Relations
Critical Perspectives on Voice, Image and Identity
*Edited by Christine Daymon and
Kristin Demetrious*

Public Relations and Nation Building
Influencing Israel
*Margalit Toledano and
David McKie*

Trust, Power and Public Relations in Financial Markets
Clea Bourne

Propaganda and Nation Building
Selling the Irish Free State
Kevin Hora

Public Relations, Cooperation, and Justice
From Evolutionary Biology to Ethics
Charles Marsh

Public Relations and the Corporate Persona
The Rise of the Affinitive
Organization
Burton St. John III

Public Relations and the Corporate Persona

The Rise of the Affinitive Organization

Burton St. John III

Routledge
Taylor & Francis Group

LONDON AND NEW YORK

First published 2017 by Routledge

2 Park Square, Milton Park, Abingdon, Oxfordshire OX14 4RN
52 Vanderbilt Avenue, New York, NY 10017

Routledge is an imprint of the Taylor & Francis Group, an informa business

First issued in paperback 2019

British Library Cataloguing in Publication Data
A catalogue record for this book is available from the British Library

Library of Congress Cataloging in Publication Data
Names: St. John, Burton, 1957– author.
Title: Public relations and the corporate persona : the rise of the affinitive
organization / Burton St. John III.
Description: Abingdon, Oxon ; New York, NY : Routledge, 2017. |
Includes bibliographical references and index.
Identifiers: LCCN 2017002733 (print) | LCCN 2017020099 (ebook) |
ISBN 9781315671635 (eBook) | ISBN 9781138945012 (hardback : alk. paper)
Subjects: LCSH: Corporations–Public relations. | Corporate image. | Social
responsibility of business.
Classification: LCC HD59 (ebook) | LCC HD59 .S728 2017 (print) | DDC
659.2–dc23
LC record available at https://lccn.loc.gov/2017002733

ISBN: 978-1-138-94501-2 (hbk)
ISBN: 978-0-367-87465-0 (pbk)

Typeset in Times New Roman
by Wearset Ltd, Boldon, Tyne and Wear

For the teachers in my life who are always provoking questions: Dana, Melissa, Joyce, Linda, Kirsten, Wie, and Joseph

Contents

Figures

Tables

Preface

On a cold evening in January 2014, 84-year-old Herbert Schmertz, former top public relations executive for Mobil Oil in the 1970s and 80s, agreed to sit down for a couple of hours in his New York City home and discuss what he attempted to accomplish for that corporation. He pointed out that he was the first senior public relations executive for Mobil and, when he moved into the job, could decide, almost unilaterally, what he wanted to focus on. The company, he said, did not have an agenda for public relations, so he was determined to portray Mobil as an entity that was distinctive from other oil companies and a leader in its industry. Moreover, he said, he saw corporations as vital within a stable of bedrock institutions—like the free market, the press, the government, education, and religion—that needed to all be healthy. "I set out to make Mobil a voice and a force in reinforcing these institutions," he said, pointing out that a corporation like Mobil that had assets "should help to stimulate and foster other institutions that may not have the resources." This was not about getting the public to like Mobil, he said, but to earn respect as an entity that had the right and duty to participate in public-policy debates. Looking back on his tenure, Schmertz said the company pursued high-profile efforts (e.g., its long-running advertorials in major newspapers) because the government often revealed antipathy toward oil companies or plain incompetence concerning energy policy and the regulation of the industry. Calling his overarching strategy "creative confrontation," he emphasized that Mobil projected an attention-getting personality that called for admiration, especially for setting the record straight and fighting back against those who would undermine Mobil, the free market, or other bedrock institutions.

"Corporations have personalities," said Schmertz, but he noted that, too often, public relations people were resistant to leverage that reality and help the organization assert its character and presence in the public sphere. Sometimes, he said, this was due to fear or that "by and large [public relations people] are not competent to do it, or they have a management that doesn't want it done." Still, he said, it is essential in the public relations business to "figure out the personality of your client, *or what you would like your client's personality to become*" (emphasis added). It was essential to communicate the corporate persona the way a politician communicates in an ongoing campaign, he said, otherwise the corporation runs the risk of being ignored or abused. During his time at Mobil, he found that projecting a corporate persona, especially through the opinion-editorial pages of major daily newspapers, made it easier to talk directly to the public and, at the same time, cast a reassuring presence to both employees and stockholders.

Near the end of the conversation, Schmertz lamented that today's corporations appear to have lost their way in asserting their personas—very few seem interested in mounting the ongoing campaign that allows them to rightfully proclaim themselves and their interests in the public milieu. He said, with disgust, that the persona message that occasionally does come through is simply "Please love me because I'm a nice guy."

Schmertz's observations about the corporate persona are intriguing because, while the corporate persona approach has deep roots within public relations, its use appears to be overshadowed by recent trends in the profession. The modern understanding of public relations is often weighted down with many concepts and words that, on the surface, associate the field with a mechanistic approach to dealing with people. Public relations practitioners, according to major public relations trade magazines like the *PRWeek* and the Public Relations Society of America's *Public Relations Tactics*, are encouraged to be more strategic about message channels and audience selection, to develop evaluation metrics like social media analytics, and to help their organizations construct and execute digital approaches to reaching multiple audiences. For example, the April 2016 edition of *Public Relations Tactics* offered pieces on how practitioners could help their clients disseminate their success stories on Snapchat, how public relations people could develop the "Ultimate Social Media Contest," and how they could use live video (like Periscope) to build awareness of clients' products or services. If one knew little about the field, or had never been a practitioner, one could get the impression from such articles that practitioners were all about having the right answers for the client, at the right time, and with the right tools to act upon those answers. But the reality of how effectively individuals and groups can be influenced is more complicated than having good analytical abilities and up-to-date technical skills. Granted, such attributes assist public relations people in their quest to help clients meet their needs, but we need to be careful about a certain tactical determinism that trumpets the instrumentality of public relations. That is, if public relations people build their bevy of strategies and tactics and then execute them, that does not necessarily mean that the audiences will come to the realization that the public relations client desires. Public relations lore is full of low points that signal the failure of tactical determinism, particularly in the product arena: the failure of the MP3 player Zune, customer hostility to New Coke, and Starbucks' 2015 "Race Together" campaign (which, amazingly, attempted to place baristas in the position of encouraging discussions with customers about racial issues) are all striking examples.

So, having a ledger of particular public relations strategies and methods is not necessarily indicative of the likelihood for success in achieving constructive influence with an audience. Here, I offer a personal account that dramatizes, instead, another very real dynamic that we must consider more carefully. After working in public relations for 10 years and receiving numerous accolades (both inside and outside my organization), I was interested in what new opportunities I could find in the field. I approached an executive consulting group, paid $3,000 and, as part of the services they provided, did a mock interview with Mike, one of the consultants. Interviewing had never been one of my overriding worries; I had had good experience with successful job interviews, and I was confident that I could point out well how I could meet the needs of the interviewer. I came in prepared, and, when the interview was completed, I asked Mike for feedback. "Well," he said, "you clearly have the skills, but you need to work on being more likable."

Of course, such feedback is never easy to hear; but now, over 16 years later, Mike's comment points to something about public relations this volume is concerned about: *the importance of personality.* That is, the ability to influence others positively (or negatively) is not as coldly analytical and systematic as public relations professionals often profess. Rather, resonance between characters is important. To go further, the way a corporate character, or *corporate persona*, is presented to the message recipient has more than an intermediary power; in fact, it can be the essential grounding that allows the sender's messages the chance to get careful consideration. To clarify, this book is not concerned about the personality of individual public relations practitioners or the general personality traits of what could be considered essential for doing public relations, but how public relations, especially since the late 1930s in the United States, has, particularly in times of crisis, facilitated the arrival of corporate personas in the public sphere—constructs that are designed to display an allegiance with the concerns of the average person.

In 1994, a corporate environmental consultant noted that there were only two corporate personas prevalent throughout the 20th century—the authoritarian, task-oriented personality, and the "John Wayne" type that, while displaying more sensitivity to human values, communicates with "infallibility, decisiveness and unswayable self-assurance" (Frankel, 1994, p. 24). This book, however, shows that the arrival of the corporate persona and the potential for its continuing appearance are more complex. Readers are encouraged to look at how public relations, through the corporate persona, attempts to appeal to one's well-established values, all in an effort to confirm the individual's commonality with corporations, rather than merely assert it.

Reference

Frankel, C. (1994). "The green-person's guide to credibility." *Public Relations Journal*, January, p. 24.

Acknowledgments

This book has been many years in germination. Many folks have been sources of support and encouragement for it to come to fruition. I am especially grateful to the staffers at the Hagley Museum and the Briscoe Archives. John Harper and Peder Hash at the Chevron Archives were helpful, as was Ron Davis at the Norfolk and Western Historical Society. Barry and Shelly Spector at the History of PR Museum helped facilitate the interview with Herbert Schmertz, who generously gave of his time, both in person and on the phone.

Kirsten Johnson, a frequent collaborator and friend, was instrumental in assisting with Chapters 8 and 9, particularly with co-developing research design and insuring quality control of data analysis. Meg Lamme, another friend and collaborator, served as a good source for support and reality-checking various facts, forces, and people at work in public relations history. Larry Atkinson provided support for the trip to the Briscoe Archives, and Old Dominion's Office of Research, through a grant, did the same for the trip to the Chevron Archives. Department chair Stephen Pullen has been a source of encouragement. I am also grateful for students Germaine Lee, Claire LeBar, and Todd Haggard, who engaged in this subject in various ways and provided helpful literature and observations.

I am also grateful to the *Journal of Communication Inquiry*, which allowed me to keep copyright to my work on reality TV and the corporate persona that appeared as "The top executive on Undercover Boss: The Embodied Corporate Persona and the Valorization of Self-Government," *Journal of Communication Inquiry 39*(3), pp. 273–329. Portions of this work appear in this book's Chapter 7.

Deep gratitude goes out to the anonymous reviewers of the original proposal. I also appreciate Kevin Moloney's enthusiasm for the project. Thanks are also due to Nicola Cupit, Jacqueline Curthoys, Laura Hussey, and Sinead Waldron.

Lastly, my deep appreciation to my wife, Dana St. John, who marvels about why I spend time on writing projects but is supportive and affectionate just the same.

1   A basis for a distinctive personality in the public relations realm

The corporate persona

In 1944, Americans were offered a slim, illustrated volume designed to serve as a reference to the fundamentals of its capitalist system. The book, *How We Live*, offered a straightforward, stockholder-focused definition of the corporation. A corporation, it said, is the "legal name for a group of persons owning the tools of production used in a given business undertaking" (Clark & Rimanoczy, 1944, p. 9). This entity, it said, essentially came about for two reasons: (1) it was a way for people to earn money (e.g., stock dividends) beyond the income they received for work, and (2) it was a way to store up that money (by holding on to stock) so as to "guard against the time when they cannot work" (Clark & Rimanoczy, 1944, p. 9).

However, even for that time, that understanding of the corporation tended toward the simplistic, emphasizing inordinately the role of the corporation as a center of transactions that could benefit stockholders. Seven years earlier, Thurman Arnold noted, in his book *The Folklore of Capitalism*, that Americans, barely 100 years into the industrial age, were already willing to see the corporation less as a financial entity and more as a human-like presence. He noted that American society had this "ideal that a great corporation is endowed with the rights and prerogatives of a free individual" and that such a valorization of the corporation as a person "is as essential to the acceptance of corporate rule in temporal affairs as was the ideal of the divine rights of kings in an earlier day" (Arnold, 1937, p. 184). His observation was particularly telling because the American legal system long held that corporations had individual rights, many of them parallel to those that the average citizen held under the Constitution. In fact, several legal decisions by the Supreme Court, most notably the 1886 *Santa Clara County v. Southern Pacific Railroad Company* case, established legal precedent for likening a corporation to a person (Allen, 2001; Krannich, 2005). Experts maintain that the court used the *Santa Clara* case as the basis for recognizing that corporations had, like American individuals, protections against unreasonable seizure, double jeopardy, and violations of religious liberty, along with rights to free speech, trial by jury, and equal protection under the law (Gans & Shapiro, 2015; Pollman, 2011).

This volume briefly examines that legal aspect of the corporate personality in Chapter 2 but is more concerned with the arrival of the corporate persona in

20th-century America as a construct used by the public relations field to help shape meanings, especially during times of stress for corporations. Definitions of the words "corporate" and "persona" abound, but this volume finds two descriptions more apt. Dutch communication scholar Cees Van Riel defined "corporate" by pointing out it "should be interpreted in the context of the Latin word *corpus*, meaning body, or in a more figurative sense, relating to the totality" (1997, p. 305). Philosopher Carl Jung described a persona as a representation of a "collective psyche" that is "nothing real: it is a compromise between individual and society as to what a man should appear to be" (Jung, 1953/2014, p. 158). Hopcke, in his collection of Jung's work, described the persona as a projection that is "used to give form to our outward sense of self" while also acting as a "container, a protective covering" for one's inner self (Hopcke, 1999, pp. 88–89). Joining both Van Riel's and Jung's understandings, a "corporate persona" is a selected projection, especially in times of stress, of key attributes of the totality of a corporation (e.g., effectiveness, helpfulness, patriotism, etc.) into a human-like face that is designed to build affiliation with individuals while also protecting from public view the self-interested goals of the organization. As such, this work explores how the corporate persona arose in times when prevailing values of Americanism, like progress and individualism, were viewed as under siege by such developments as the rise of the labor movement, the increase in the size of the American government after the onset of the Great Depression, the ascendance of fascism in the late 1930s, and the international spread of communism and socialism. As Arnold pointed out, there are prevailing American ideologies that loom behind the rise of the corporate persona, viewpoints that "put the corporate organization ahead of the governmental organization in prestige and power, *by identifying it with the individual*" (1937, p. 186, emphasis added). This work shows how several corporations have been aware of this American disposition and have attempted to convey themselves as "larger-than-life" individuals who share, and attempt to amplify, common beliefs and a sense of direction held between the citizen and the corporation. This, then, is the affinitive aspect of the corporate persona—a projection of the corporation as a friendly, fellow human-like being that wants to help all realize desired constructive ends.

Across the early to middle decades of the 20th century, one can see the corporation using a mix of rhetoric, symbol making/symbol understanding devices, and appeals to prevalent values systems to offer a relatable corporate persona designed to lead and advise Americans in times when business perceived stressors (e.g., the rise of the New Deal, labor unions, and American receptivity to socialism). Indeed, the ability of corporations to successfully affect such a capitalist "fellow traveler" approach needs careful consideration. Fones-Wolf (1994), in reviewing business' efforts during the 1950s, noted that polls revealed a marked public affiliation for business' message touting individualism instead of reliance on the state. Smith (2000) noted that, in 1953, about 56% of Americans held a favorable view of business (p. 101). By 2016, approximately 60% of Americans indicated they viewed capitalism favorably, with 85% holding a positive opinion of the free enterprise system (Newport, 2016). This volume contends that the enduring American affinity for capitalism and free enterprise is about more than how Americans see the marketplace and the benefits they perceive come from the logics of capitalism. That is, Americans, even when voicing skepticism of business, have come to see their routes toward good fortune as conjoined with the journey of the corporation, an entity that affirms that it is a fellow person that shares a common ambition of Americans: to freely achieve a self-made life.

Theoretical groundings for the rise of the corporate persona

Surprisingly, the power of the organizational persona has not been given sustained, careful, and thorough study in public relations scholarship or in the broader scholarship on organizational identity (which is discussed in Chapter 2). However, the importance of personality, generally, had been particularly well-established by Erving Goffman in his 1959 study *The Presentation of Self in Everyday Life*. Goffman's depiction of the personality is essentially focused on how one constructs a persona that allows one to achieve private gains while attempting to convince the audience that what one is striving for is also in the audience's own interest. Similar to Kenneth Burke's dramaturgical approach (discussed in Chapter 2), Goffman stressed that the presenter of personality is essentially performing and, therefore, must offer a consistency in performer appearance and performer manner that also aligns well with the setting (or context). With these consistencies established, the performer stresses a "social front" full of "abstract standards" that the audience can relate to like integrity, competence, and modernity (Goffman, 1959, p. 26). Goffman further maintained that this link between personality and the social front

> tends to become institutionalized in terms of the abstract stereotyped expectations to which it is given rise, and tends to take on a meaning and stability apart from the specific tasks which happen at the time to be performed in its name.
>
> (1959, p. 27)

The weight of the association between the proffered personality and societal values allows performers to assert that their personalities are indicative of the larger field of endeavor they are engaged in and reflect the value the performers bring to society at large. This, said Goffman, is a "collective representation" that is seen as "a fact in its own right" (1959, p. 27). Moreover, he noted, the performer's presentation "will tend to incorporate and exemplify the officially accredited values of the society, more so, in fact, than does [the presenter's] behavior as a whole" (Goffman, 1959, p. 35). Based on how much the presentation amplifies "common official values of the society," the presentation may be seen as a ceremony or as "an expressive rejuvenation and reaffirmation of the moral values of the community" (Goffman, 1959, p. 35). For Goffman, alignment of the presentation with societal values and expectations is key to the personality falling within the audience's range of acceptability; this, indeed, is a hallmark of the appeal of the corporate persona as detailed in further chapters in this book. All personalities have some degree of boundaries; the grocer, the tailor, the auctioneer all have a "dance" that conveys their personality—but a grocer who appears to be a dreamer, noted Goffman, "is offensive to the buyer, because such a grocer is not wholly a grocer" (1959, p. 76). So, in an attempt to work through such restrictions and achieve their aims, performers, rather than "attempting to achieve certain ends by acceptable means ... attempt *to achieve the impression* that they are achieving ends by acceptable means" (Goffman, 1959, p. 250, emphasis added). In fact, personality can overwhelm the audience's ability to assess the presenter's actions because of the keen alignment of the presenter's character with the audience's values. "The very obligation and profitability of appearing always in a steady moral light, of being a socialized character," said Goffman, "forces one to be the sort of person who is practiced in the ways of the stage," carefully cultivating an association with the viewers' values (1959, p. 251).

Goffman's observations about the power of the performer's personality to overshadow audience perceptivity of performer actions are an important consideration for examining the corporate persona. As the chapters in this book show, corporations use the corporate persona to communicate more about who they claim they are than what they do. Furthermore, many of Goffman's fundamental observations about the performance of personality appear to be a useful grounding for exploring how the corporate persona pursues value alignment between the performer and the audience. More closely aligned to the concept of a corporation conveying its persona, however, is Karl Weick's late-1960s work on how organizations enact their environments. Weick (1969) observed that humans in organizations work to create an enacted environment that has four properties: (1) the focus is on what has already occurred; (2) what is happening now influences how that past is understood; (3) both retention and reconstruction of those past events influence how we construct meaning today; and (4) stimulus from the past is only realized, identified, and defined after people have responded to it (p. 65). Weick's observation that organizational communication often serves as signaling determinism appears useful for the study of the corporate persona and how it attempts to shape and reinforce meaning:

> Even though a plan appears to be something oriented solely to the future, in fact it also has about it the quality of an act that has already been accomplished. *The meaning of the actions that are instrumental to the completion of the act can be discovered because they are viewed as if they had already occurred ...*
>
> (1969, p. 66, emphasis added)

With these comments, Weick asserts that, when one offers a plan, one senses that part of it is already a fait accompli—even if one's sense of certainty is not inevitably accurate. Weick's observation appears to resonate with popular business scholar Stephen Covey's (1989) admonition that communicators need to begin "with the end in mind." Weick stressed that the actor sets out the plan of action with a visualization of reaching the finish line, but not necessarily picturing the component parts necessary to get to that final state. These are some crucial observations because, as the cases in this volume show, the corporate persona, used by corporations to manage perceived threats or stressors, customarily reaches out to citizens in language designed to reverberate with long-established prevalent values. As Weick said, there is a certain continuity between past actions and the planned view of the future. This work finds his observation in play as the corporate persona, rather than accentuating details, attempts to build cohesion with audiences, emphasizing to audiences that it shares a sense of an incessant "already occurred" aspect of what it means to be an American (e.g., constant progress, continual assertion of freedom, the inevitability of opportunities for personal advancement, etc.).

But to assert the sense of what is inevitable about being an American (and how that links to what is also inevitable about a "fellow" corporation) requires, as Goffman pointed out, a mannerism on the part of the persuader. Yiannis Gabriel (2000) has pointed to storytelling as the ideal way to reach multiple audiences in modern societies. Gabriel's work tends to focus on questions of internal organizational communication and relationships with consumers; nevertheless, his observations about storytelling address a more macro context that is conducive to the rise and continuing presence of the corporate persona. Gabriel, noting how social science and its fact-based imperative ran into the headwinds of an increasing late-20th-century postmodernism, asserted that there was an ascendant movement to better understand man as "an animal whose main preoccupation is not truth or power or love or even pleasure, but meaning" (2000, p. 4). The storytelling lens, he said, calls for examining how stories are performances that show the organization attempting to make links to audiences in the areas of "unconscious wishes and fantasies" while also revealing "expressions of political domination and opposition" (Gabriel, 2000, p. 4). Accordingly, he said, truth is understood through the story meanings that command the audience's attention and not through the facts that the story offers. Still, *the facts are important* because they must be reliable amplifiers of the story. Gabriel stresses that a storyteller can spoil a good story if the listener, upon hearing it, can reasonably challenge the accuracy of facts mainly because "narratives and experience must be treated as having a material basis, even if this material basis is opaque or inaccessible" (2000, pp. 5–6).

These observations by Goffman, Weick, and Gabriel offer a point of entrée to seeing the corporation acting as a discernable personality in the public sphere. Occasionally, authors have hit upon this dynamic. In Arnold's book-long critique of capitalism, he devoted a chapter to "the personification of corporation," asserting that, since the industrial age, the U.S. populace developed a quasi-religious reverence for the corporation. Indeed, he said, it was relatively easy for Americans to develop the sense that corporations were much like them because these companies, making their way through the vicissitudes of the marketplace, were emblematic of the American pioneer encountering and overcoming the obstacles of untamed terrain. Companies building wealth were much like the westward explorer who "accumulated wealth by trading," he said, "which later became the mystical philosophy that put the corporate organization ahead of the governmental organization in prestige and power, *by identifying it with the individual*" (Arnold, 1937, p. 186, emphasis added). The entrenching of industrialism (which, through bureaucracies, depersonalized the workplace and eventually set the stage for a collective corporate individualism), court decisions which affirmed that corporations were like individuals, and the ascent of a laissez-faire mentality only furthered a receptivity to corporations as people. So, by the early 20th century, Arnold had already asserted, but only briefly and with few specifics, that "[t]he corporate personality is part of our present religion," where Americans "…refer to corporations as individuals in public discourse so long as the words have emotional relevance" (1937, p. 205).

But Arnold's observations about the corporation as a venerated citizen lay largely unexplored until 1960, when scholar Richard Eels observed that the 1950s revealed the corporation appearing to act as if it were a person. During that decade, he said, business encountered continual criticisms from labor organizations and was stressed by the advance of communism and escalating societal expectations that business not only be successful but also be a constructive force in society. The corporation, he asserted, was about more than making profits, delivering value to shareholders, and living up to legal obligations. Corporations were getting involved in political processes, supporting education initiatives, and even acting, at times, like a fraternal organization. "The bloodless and fictional corporation … turns out to be a most lifelike person," he said. "It has a character all its own, and it does things and exhibits purposes that cannot be explicated from the legal and economic texts" (Eels, 1960, p. 98).

Still, it took about another 20 years before more scholars touched upon the corporate persona. Crable and Vibbert's (1983) study of Mobil Oil's op-ed columns was a notable step, as that work examined how Mobil used paid space over numerous years to do more than construct arguments about public issues; it also attempted to relay a relatable, credible personality (Chapter 5 offers more on the oil industry and the corporate persona). That study was soon followed by other scholarly works into the early 21st century that touched upon aspects of the corporate persona (Brown, Waltzer, & Waltzer, 2001; Cheney, 1991, 1992; Christensen, Morsing, & Cheney, 2008; Gurãu & McLaren, 2003; Heath & Nelson, 1986; Marchand, 1998; Meech, 2006; Smith & Heath, 1990; St. John III, 2014a, 2014b; St. John III & Arnett, 2014; Zhang, 2011). As such, it comes as no surprise that Stuart (1998) observed that "corporate personality is at the heart of the organization…" (pp. 359–360) and that any attempt to understand who the corporation is, and what it is attempting to manage in the public arena, necessarily means studying what, if any, corporate persona the company is affecting (ibid.). With this much dispersed scholarship that relates to the corporate persona, scholars, students of public relations, and public relations practitioners may wonder what these varied findings point to. These works, collectively, indicate there is a logic at work, a basis for a corporation to affect a person, especially in times of societal stress.

The rationale for the corporate persona

One of the overriding reasons that a corporate persona construct would be offered by an organization is that the entity is striving to provide some semblance of grounding in the midst of turbulent times. It is no accident that, as this book shows, the National Association of Manufacturers (NAM) is likely the first large-scale progenitor of a corporate persona: offering, by the late 1930s, a helpful, beneficent visage for the collective known as "industry." NAM, as this book details in Chapter 3, made a concerted effort to express an affinitive corporate personality in the midst of the lingering Great Depression, a period that featured the rise of labor unions, the ascendancy of the federal government in daily life, and persistent skepticism toward big business. Arnold, writing during this era, noted that, in contrast to the largely pro-business 1920s, power brokers now saw that there was a world forming that was in contrast to their beliefs in the supremacy of the free market. Still freighted with "symbols or beliefs that had no relations to what [they] see before them," powerful actors "of a permanent character" have much invested in insuring existing systems serve their interests, and want to maintain the status quo without exhausting themselves by using force (Arnold, 1937, pp. 192–193). Instead, "they do it by identifying themselves with the faith and loyalties of the people," making sure to not stray from the "little pictures in the back of the head of the ordinary man" (Arnold, 1937, pp. 193–194, 199).

Although Arnold did not elaborate on specifics, it was clear by the mid-century in the U.S. how the "little pictures" appeared in American visions of what life should be—commonly referred to as the "American Dream," a phrase first coined in 1931 in historian James Truslow Adams' book, *The Epic of America*. Adams' work claimed that the values of the common man were essential to understanding how America developed and that the country was propelled, in great part, by a cultural belief in the power of individual aspiration and accomplishment. The centrality of the common man as the nexus for America's development was a given, he said, and some subsequent works in the mid-20th century carried forward the American Dream as a framing device. Most notable was Lynd and Lynd's *Middletown in Transition* (1937), which discussed, for example, how some families, through hard work across generations, progressed from the lower class toward positions of great wealth, exemplifying a core tenet of the myth. Historian Harold Davis (1946), in an essay on the significance of Americanism, asserted that the American Dream signified that all men "had an inborn right to achieve" and that government was but a facilitator of those aspirations (p. 191). The American Dream essentially meant that "a man is a fellow and a fellow has some rights" (Ascoli, 1941, p. 279), especially the right to succeed and advance to his or her highest station (McGuire, 1950, p. 200). To further dissect those values, the Advertising Council sponsored a round table of distinguished, prominent citizens (almost all of them men, none serving in government) from the world of business, journalism, arts, and academe to gather their observations. The resulting 1954 book, *What Is America?*, offered this consensus: America is classless, egalitarian, individualistic, forward-leaning, and full of ambitious individuals who are competitive yet cooperative, and who want to advance themselves through their own hard work. America was exceptional, noted Russell Davenport, managing editor of *Fortune* magazine, because Americans emphasize "the development in private hands of social goals which elsewhere people have turned over to government" (Goodfriend, 1954, p. 37). The enterprising everyday man was key, with management consultant Peter Drucker adding that "the individual is the central, rarest, most precious capital resource" for the country (Goodfriend, 1954, p. 57). Vidich and Bensman (1958), though specifically studying society in small rural communities, offered a resonating statement that was iconic Americanism, highlighting the pre-eminence of individual effort and persistence: "Work ... is the great social equalizer," they said, and when individuals fall short it is because they are either too young to have yet accumulated meaningful work, or they have suffered bad fortune (p. 42). The measure of a man, they said, is "the diligence and perseverance with which he pursues his economic ends" (Vidich & Bensman, 1958, p. 42).

Adams' 1931 book claimed that the American Dream emphasized that every individual had "the hope of opening every avenue of opportunity to him" (p. 198). Subsequent scholars (Bercovitich, 1978; Cullen, 2003; Ellis, 1993, Lipset, 1996; Samuel, 2012) have pointed to how this strong focus on the importance of the actions of individuals developed from American roots that stretch back past the Revolutionary period to the Puritan ethos of self-sufficiency and striving as a way to honor a sense of spiritual purpose. Rojecki (2008) discussed this focus as a belief in individuals working to assure the flowering of perpetual progress because the "improvement of the human condition was taken as a given" (p. 69). Cullen (2003) similarly noted that Americans, over time, held strongly to the notion that they could, with their individual efforts, "shape their fates," a belief that "seems to envelope us as unmistakably as the air we breathe" (p. 10). Over time, this valorization of the individual moved from disinterest in the state to an aversion toward government interference, making the U.S. one of the most anti-statist countries of the modern industrialized world (Lipset, 1996). Not surprisingly, one former government official said, "Americans don't want government to come in and cure their ills ... Ours is a paradox of a society of individuals manifesting collective responsibility" (Galantiere, quoted in Goodfriend, 1954, p. 111).

These mid-20th-century descriptions of the American Dream reveal that Arnold offered prescient observations about the little pictures in Americans' heads. Not only did scholars later analyze these cultural values in detail as societal myths about the predominance of the individual (Cullen, 2003; Lipset, 1996; Rojecki, 2008) but other scholars were to explore a related aspect: the exercise of corporate power to leverage these myths and associate the corporation with individuals in an attempt to help shape meaning and action during times of uncertainty. As Weick (1969) noted, actors (which includes corporations) "live in situations" that are continually undergoing change. However, the best way to manage change is to envision a collective approach that (1) focuses on past action, (2) attaches a retrospective meaning to that action and (3) offers prospective understandings that point to the need for a projected act (Weick, 1969, pp. 66–67, 70). Storytelling, not chronicling, is an effective way to emphasize a collective approach because it asserts power over the individual's meaning making and, thereby, disposition to act. This is because storytelling is about interpreting "events, infusing them with meaning through distortions, omissions, embellishments, and other devices, without, however, obliterating the facts" (Gabriel, 2000, p. 6). In fact, the chaotic nature of the world is what makes stories necessary, particularly for powerful actors. When corporations face existential threats, they can marshal narratives that provide "motive, agency, or purpose to our human predicaments" (Gabriel, 2000, p. 240), offering a sense of hope that turbulent times can be endured and overcome.

Business, then, through the corporate persona, offered itself as a stabilizing agent during turmoil. As Chapters 3–6 in this book show, the ascendancy of the corporate persona was particularly notable during the Cold War. Christopher Lasch (1984) additionally noted that consumerism rose markedly during this time and contributed to a deficit in the American individual's sense of identity and in how that identity could inform self-direction. In fact, the rise of the corporate persona was a logical development for these decades because individuals' tendency to see themselves as realized through mass consumption revealed they were more concerned with how they *appeared*, not with how their identity was realized. Power centers, said Lasch, enjoyed more authority because the American fixation on the appearance of identity promoted dependency on interlocking systems (the state, the marketplace, etc.) that they could not control. Americans, he said, increasingly exhibited a loss of confidence in their individual "capacity to understand and shape the world" so as to provide for one's own needs (Lasch, 1984, p. 33). In a description that sets a context for why corporations sensed the usefulness of projecting an affinitive persona, Lasch noted that the average American was increasingly receptive to images that "seem to refer not so much to a palpable, solid, and durable reality as to [one's] inner psychic life, itself experienced not as an abiding sense of self, but as reflections glimpsed in the mirror of his surroundings" (1984, p. 34). He maintained that a cultural narcissism was evident and that Americans were unmoored from their own sense of self and needed a reference point for developing ways to navigate their society. For the purposes of this volume, what is most interesting about his observations is his pointing to the rise of progenitors of "survival strategies," singling out the ascent of a self-help counseling industry that stressed introspection and behavior modification, so that people could "piece together a technology of the self, the only apparent alternative to personal collapse" (Lasch, 1984, p. 58).

What Lasch observed continues to put a spotlight on a cultural factor that allowed for the ascent of the corporate persona. In times of stress in the U.S., both the corporation and the individual harken to the mythical value of conquering challenges through individualism. Such an approach allows corporate interests to reassure and reorient individuals toward approaches that both the company and the individual believe make good sense—a dynamic which is explored particularly at length in Chapters 5–7 in this book. Michel Foucault has discussed this display of corporate power extensively (1977, 1988, 1997), examining the advance of marketplace imperatives in the West, coupled with an eclipse of the state. Corporations put in place rhetoric, practices, and rules that signal to Americans there are market-informed ways to govern oneself so as to maximize one's potential and pursue one's goals without needing interference from the state. Although Foucault's works on this subject tend to avoid detailed examples of the transmission of such corporate self-governing messages, he delineated stages that the individual goes through to realize his or her need for self-governance. Calling it a "metaphor of navigation," Foucault, in an extended college lecture, identified five elements: (1) the individual senses a need to progress; (2) the individual identifies a particular aim or objective; (3) the individual confirms that this objective reflects a "place of safety," a destination where one can find rootedness; (4) the individual realizes that the journey will include danger, which makes the journey even more attractive; and (5) that journey calls for "a knowledge, a technique, an art" (normally a practice that meets marketplace needs) so that it can be successfully completed (2006, p. 248). Frederic Gros observed, in editing this lecture, that Foucault laid out how the individual needed to learn, through being informed by "the other," how to be a more rational and effective actor (2006, p. 536). Gros remarked that the other serves "as the guide to one's life," assisting as "the correspondent to whom one writes and before whom one takes stock of oneself, [seeing] the other as helpful friend, benevolent relative" (2006, pp. 536–537). Although Gros' language appears to situate this mentor figure within an interpersonal context, a corporate persona acting as an institutional mentor is certainly appropriate; Foucault addressed how self-governing acted both within the realm of daily social relations and the wider institutional imperatives that bounded those daily actions.

Arnold, Weick, Gabriel, Lasch, and Foucault collectively offer a complex picture of individual identity in the 20th-century U.S. First, that individual identity is a malleable and sometimes subconscious construct, subject to pressures from power centers in society that seek to overcome or reduce destabilizing factors or occurrences. Furthermore, attempts to discern a fruitful individual identity in times of crisis may be weighed down by nuances inherent in the multiplicity of actors (e.g., corporations, the state, social activists, generational cohorts, familial relations) and the variance in values associated with these actors. Second, and more specifically, power centers, concerned about how these dynamics may play out, may exert appeals to help shape the directions of, as Foucault puts it, the "metaphor of navigation" used by various publics. Further complicating the picture, shifts in society may only add to a corporate drive to assert a sense of common purpose with individuals. For example, increasing demographic changes in the U.S. enhance the likelihood of varied cultural, generational, and socio-economic understandings of how American core values (e.g. self-reliance, progress, freedom) should be realized. At the same time, these often disparate viewpoints circulate and, at times, come into conflict with the commanding—and status quo-seeking—territory of marketplace imperatives (e.g., preserving market practices, enforcing workplace norms, encouraging materialism as self-expression). With such a muddled vista, it makes sense that a "more real than real" collective corporate person can appear to help steer individuals. Indeed, individuals may see such a simulation as important, for it allows individuals to bypass concerns about the power centers that circumscribe their sojourns. Jean Baudrillard (1983) referred to the environment that makes the corporate persona possible as a hyperrealist society. Such a world features attempts to persuade others to confuse the real with a model; the emphasis is on deterring one from contemplating mundane experiences—and the power that constrains and enforces those experiences—in favor of focusing on associations that edify the individual. For example, he said, news, propaganda, and publicity, through hyperrealism, says to the individual: "YOU are [the] news, you are the social, the event is you, you are involved, you can use your own voice, etc." (Baudrillard, 1983, p. 53). When individuals accept a loss of distinction between what is (the actual event, which one observes) and the affirmed simulation (where one is the event), such individuals lose the ability to "locate an instance of the model, of power, of the gaze of the medium itself" because they are already assimilated into the model (Baudrillard, 1983, pp. 53, 57–58). The corporate persona offers such a promise of seeing the individual and the corporation as a collective "you." This approach, ideally, allows the individual to be more receptive to the corporation's sensibilities concerning what actions should be pursued to overcome shared challenges and, thereby, progress toward a mutually valued end.

What of the corporate persona?

Having established some theoretical groundings for the arrival of the corporate persona and particular rationales for how it operates, the question of significance lingers. If the corporate persona appears, especially when businesses perceive threats or turmoil, what are we to make of its importance, especially given the limited scholarly works on this subject?

In 1990, George Cheney and Jill McMillan offered an exhaustive analysis of the state of scholarship about organizational rhetoric, making a case for how the corporation had begun to assume the stance of a person that spoke to prevailing issues in the public sphere. Cautious of what this development meant for the exercise of concentrated power in society, they called for continued theory and criticism regarding how this corporate person offered texts that shaped our understanding of society. They urged that such scholarly critiques could allow us to "better comprehend … how we conduct our 'life space,' structure our interactions, and exercise control over one another" (Cheney & McMillan, 1990, p. 108). However, in the 27 years since their observations, public relations scholarship has largely left unexplored the power of the corporate persona. Across these decades, the scholarship has been greatly influenced by the need to show that public relations has demonstrable effects. In great part, this need to display how PR has significant measurable influence has, historically, been rooted in the field's attempt to show how it shapes audiences' attitudes and behaviors in ways that are distinctive from other interlocutors within such fields as marketing and advertising. The rise of the Internet has added impetus to a quantitative approach to discerning public relations' weight in modern society, as new web-based platforms (particularly in the social media realm) allow both researchers and practitioners to measure various stakeholder environments, track message distribution, and measure audience reactions. These developments have led to a perfectly understandable undertone in public relations research: PR is often best understood through a transactional prism. Major arenas of public relations research, such as community relations, integrated communications, employee communications, and crisis communications, feature studies that examine how a theoretical premise is exhibited through transactions (exchange of messages, products, and/or services) between a company and its stakeholders. As such, it is not surprising that there are limited works on the corporate persona. In fact, aside from more recent work offered by Swenson (2016)—who examined how Betty Crocker acted as a corporate persona to signify the importance of narratives and rituals to key audiences—rhetorical scholarship on public relations, which would appear to be ideally suited to examine the role of the corporate persona, has in large part elided the subject. This is likely because critical/cultural studies of public relations, which have attempted to identify PR as a force that assists power centers in shaping audiences' worldviews, have not sufficiently moved beyond the influence of the transactional. One of the most prolific public relations scholars, Robert Heath (2006), has stated that public relations critical scholarship is particularly valuable when it explores the "courtship of identification" (p. 87) between corporations and their audiences. Borrowing from Burke (1950), Heath characterizes this courtship as taking place within a society that features ongoing wrangles in the marketplace of ideas (Heath, 1992). While useful, this concept of public relations amplifying corporate interests within an ideological marketplace of ideas resonates a bit strongly with the transactional strain in PR scholarship. Instead, this book aligns more with Stoker and Stoker's (2012) observation that public relations professionals attempt to situate the corporation within a spectrum of public interest when they act in such a way as to "promote individual freedom, growth and development and *strengthen harmonious interconnections among individuals, groups, and publics*" (p. 42, emphasis added). However, as Cheney and McMillan (1990) pointed out, organizations tend to convey their personas in ways that are protective of their interest in the status quo while not necessarily representing wider interests in society. Informed by their critiques and the concerns of others about the power of the corporate persona (e.g., Crable & Vibbert, 1983; Livesey 2002; St. John III & Arnett, 2014), this book posits that "harmonious interconnections" are not self-evident and that corporate actors use the affinitive corporate persona both to solidify connections between their interests and the concerns of their key audience(s), and to attempt to shape the worldviews of audiences about emerging societal concerns. As such, it offers a unique focus that is designed to stimulate more research on public relations' sense-making role across different times and cultural contexts.

Moreover, the study of how the corporate persona works is valuable because it reveals how public relations attempts to work *beyond the transactional to reify a sense of shared reality* between the corporation and the average citizen. That is, public relations has been instrumental in conveying to the American populace, most notably in turbulent times, that the corporation is an affinitive corporate persona, a fellow traveler in the journey of American life. As artificial and simulated as it may well be, this strategic public relations approach needs careful study, for several reasons. First, such an approach has a layer of sophistication that is not typical of conceptualizations regarding public relations' attempts to persuade. As Heath pointed out, much of public relations rhetoric and symbol making is about courting the public, a description that carries with it the connotation of attempting to "win over" audiences. The corporate persona approach, however, relies more on asserting that there is already a link between corporation and citizens—in areas like values, goals, and beliefs—that merely needs to be brought to the fore, so as to allow the corporation to assert actions that it maintains are in a common interest.

Second, the corporate persona construct offers an intriguing window into how stasis has come to dominate arenas of contestation in modern life. For example, in an era where individuals have come to value simulations (e.g., pseudorelationships on social media, approximations of real life through reality programs, and role-playing online platforms) as ways to cope with or avoid systemic stresses (e.g., wage stagnation, climate disruption, fractured racial and ethnic relations), how can such receptivity for the artificial impinge upon opportunities to find solutions? In the spirit of Lasch's (1984) and Baudrillard's (1983) observations, there are real concerns that simulation unduly amplifies a self-focus, resulting in a deadening of individuals' abilities to see systemic forces that offer these simulations, rather than enter into dialogue on redressing problems. Accordingly, it is one of the concerns in this work that the corporate persona attempts to connect with such a self-focus, participating in an artificial heightening of American values that stress a "do-it-yourself" view of life. A 2014 Pew Research survey of seven European nations and the U.S. found that Americans lead when it comes to individualistic viewpoints—57% disagreed that their success in life was mostly determined by forces outside their control, and 73% said it is very important "to work hard to get ahead in life" (Wike, 2016). Such a worldview reflects a certain unwillingness to acknowledge how power centers work to, for example, signify to Americans what "success" looks like.

Accordingly, a third major reason to understand the importance of the corporate persona is that, especially in times of crisis, it attempts to encourage Americans to pursue *self-governance*. Foucault maintained that one develops a sense of self, and situates oneself in society, by interacting with persons, places, and institutional forces (Foucault, 1988; McGushin, 2011). Through these interactions, an individual makes choices that ostensibly further a sense of self-construction. However, "these practices are ... not something that the individual invents by himself," said Foucault. "They are patterns that he finds in his culture and which are proposed, suggested and imposed on him by his culture, his society and his social group," he said (Foucault, 1988; p. 11). As the individual pays attention to these patterns and begins to co-create his sense of self—what Foucault called the "care of self"—privatized forces, like the experts and authorities that are proffered through public relations, inform that person of the choices that will allow him or her "to become a well-adjusted, happy, healthy, productive member of society" (McGushin, 2011, p. 133). These patterns of behavior that provide one with a sense of self-direction and self-construction are often informed by privatized power centers in modern democratic and capitalistic societies that stress the importance of the individual charting his or her own course, with limited interventions from the state (McGushin 2011; Paras, 2006). Sending messages of self-government, these actors stress that, rather than relying on the state, individuals should embrace ongoing self-inspection of their actions with an eye toward inventorying all possible behaviors that may increase their roles as productive citizens in the marketplace (Foucault, 1977; McGushin 2011). Therefore, borrowing from both Burke (1969) and Heath (2006), who discussed rhetorical appeals as "courtship of identification," this book maintains that, with a Foucauldian understanding, one can see that the corporate persona moves beyond that to a *courtship of re-affirmation*. That is, the corporate persona provides accounts to Americans that assert common values and perspectives in an effort to amplify how Americans can self-govern so as to share in mutual success with its fellow corporation. There is no need to work for *identifying* a commonality between the corporation and the individual. Such a commonality exists, says the corporate persona, because of mutual values and aspirations; instead, it says, let me *affirm* that commonality by offering you insights on the best way to thrive through the American private enterprise system.

Finally, critically examining the actual presence of the corporate persona allows for careful delineation of what appears to be the effects of such a construct. For example, while there may be a concern about how the corporate persona may work as a graduated exercise of corporate power through innocuous appeals to shared values, more recent developments point to public cynicism about U.S. power centers and the country's socio-economic order. One non-partisan-sponsored 2015 poll found that 64% of Americans had moderate-to-very high mistrust of business corporations, news organizations, and the federal government—and only 46% of respondents had any measurable confidence in business corporations (Jones, Cox, Cooper, & Lienesch, 2015). This same report found some chinks in Americans views of individualism and the benefits of self-reliance, as only 36% indicated that hard work was the key to success. So, in any attempt to analyze what appears to be the reality-shaping power of rhetoric, one must be wary of making undue claims. As such, Chapters 8 and 9 offer some initial observations and findings concerning a quantitative tracking of the presence of the corporate persona—the data suggest some preliminary routes toward gauging the contemporary effects of the corporate persona. Finally, Chapter 10, the conclusion of this book, offers that examining the case studies in this book can inform a deeper understanding of "substantive social phenomena" (Alvesson & Karreman, 2000, p. 1128) that signal societal conditions conducive for the re-appearance of the corporate persona (e.g., societal unrest about wage stagnation, friction due to demographic changes, and increasing hostility toward the viability of the state). For example, examining these conditions in the U.S. as being potentially conducive to re-appearance of the corporate persona may also signal how multinationals could embrace an affinitive approach in other countries to effect "global corporate citizenship" (Thompson, 2012). While it may be difficult discerning clear outcomes regarding the various proffers of the corporate persona detailed in this work, this book offers evidence of some enduring trajectories regarding the power of public relations to help shape our sense of the world in the midst of societal stressors and crisis. These routes are described across the following chapters, with the aim that, by the conclusion, one may have a heightened awareness of the potential of public relations to appeal to our sensibilities and, in doing so, assist powerful forces in structuring the horizon.

References

Adams, J. (1931). *The epic of America.* New York: Little, Brown & Co.

Allen, D.S. (2001). "The first amendment and the doctrine of corporate personhood: Collapsing the press-corporation distinction." *Journalism 2*(3), pp. 255–278.

Alvesson, M., & Karreman, D. (2000). "Varieties of discourse: On the study of organizations through discourse analysis." *Human Relations 53*(9), pp. 1125–1149.

Arnold, T. (1937). *The folklore of capitalism.* Yale, CT: Yale University Press.

Ascoli, M. (1941). "War aims and America's aims." *Social Research 8*(3), pp. 267–282.

Baudrillard, J. (1983). *Simulations.* New York: Semiotext.

Bercovitch, S. (1978). *The American jeremiad.* Madison: University of Wisconsin Press.

Brown, C., Waltzer, H., & Waltzer, M.B. (2001). "Daring to be heard: Advertorials by organized interests on the op-ed page of the *New York Times*, 1985–1998." *Political Communication 18*, pp. 23–50.

Burke, K. (1950). *A rhetoric of motives.* Berkeley: University of California Press.

Cheney, G. (1991). *Rhetoric in an organizational society: Managing multiple identities.* Columbia, SC: University of South Carolina Press.

Cheney, G. (1992). "The corporate person (re)presents itself." In E.L. Toth, & R.L. Heath (Eds.), *Rhetorical and critical approaches to public relations*, pp. 165–183. Hillsdale, NJ: Lawrence Erlbaum.

Cheney, G., & McMillan, J. (1990). "Organizational rhetoric and the practice of criticism." *Journal of Applied Communication Research 18*(2), pp. 93–114.

Christensen, L.T., Morsing, M., & Cheney, G. (2008). *Corporate communications: Convention, complexity and critique.* Thousand Oaks, CA: SAGE.

Clark, F., & Rimanoczy, R. (1944). *How we live: A simple dissection of the economic body.* New York: D. Van Nostrand Co., Inc.

Covey, S. (1989). *The seven habits of highly effective people.* New York: Simon and Schuster.

Crable, R.E., & Vibbert, S.L. (1983). "Mobil's epideictic advocacy: 'Observations' of Prometheus-bound." *Communications Monographs 50*, pp. 380–394.

Cullen, J. (2003). *The American Dream: A short history of an idea that shaped a nation.* New York: Oxford University Press.

Davis, H. (1946). "The epic of the Americas." *World Affairs 109*(3), pp. 190–196.

Eells, R. (1960). *The meaning of modern business: An introduction to the philosophy of large corporate enterprise.* New York: Columbia University Press.

Ellis, R. (1993). *American political cultures.* New York: Oxford University Press.

Fones-Wolf, E. (1994). *Selling free enterprise: The business assault on labor and liberalism, 1945–60.* Urbana, IL: University of Illinois Press.

Foucault, M. (1977). *Discipline and punish: The birth of the prison.* New York: Pantheon.

Foucault, M. (1988). "The ethic of care for the self as a practice of freedom." In J. Bernauer, & D. Rasmussen (Eds.), *The final Foucault*, pp. 1–20. Cambridge, MA: MIT Press.

Foucault, M. (1997). *Ethics: Subjectivity and truth* (Vol. 1). New York: The New Press.

Foucault, M. (2006). *The hermeneutics of the subject: Lectures at the College De France, 1981–82.* (F. Gros, Ed., & G. Burchell, Trans.) New York: Picador.

Gabriel, Y. (2000). *Storytelling in organizations: Facts, fictions, and fantasies.* Oxford, UK: Oxford University Press.

Gans, D., & Shapiro, I. (2014). *Religious liberties for corporations? Hobby Lobby, the Affordable Care Act and the Constitution.* New York: Palgrave Macmillan.

Goffman, E. (1959). *The presentation of self in everyday life.* New York: Anchor Books.

Goodfriend, A. (1954). *What is America?* New York: Simon & Schuster.

Gurău, C., & McLaren, Y. (2003). "Corporate reputations in UK biotechnology: An analysis of on-line 'company profile' texts." *Journal of Marketing Communications 9*, pp. 241–256.

Heath, R.L. (1992). "The wrangle in the marketplace: A rhetorical perspective on public relations." In E.L. Toth, & R.L. Heath (Eds.), *Rhetorical and critical approaches to public relations*, pp. 17–36. Hillsdale, NJ: Lawrence Erlbaum Associated.

Heath, R.L. (2006). "A rhetorical theory approach to issues management." In C. Botan, & V. Hazelton (Eds.), *Public relations theory II*, pp. 55–87. Mahwah, NJ: Lawrence Erlbaum Associates.

Heath, R.L., & Nelson, R.A. (1986). *Issues management: Corporate public policymaking in an information society.* Beverly Hills, CA: SAGE.

Hopcke, R. (1999). *A guided tour of the collected works of C.G. Jung.* Boston: Shambala.

Jones, R.P., Cox, D., Cooper, B., & Lienesch, R. (2015). "Anxiety, nostalgia, and mistrust: Findings from the 2015 American Values Survey." *Public Religion Research Institute.* Retrieved from www.prri.org/wp-content/uploads/2015/11/PRRI-AVS-2015-1.pdf.

Jung, C. (1953/2014). *Two essays on analytical psychology* (2nd ed.). (H. Read, M. Fordham, G. Adler, Eds., & R. Hull, Trans.) London: Routledge.

Krannich, J.M. (2005). "The corporate 'person': A new analytical approach to a flawed method of constitutional interpreation." *Loyola University Chicago Law Journal 37*, pp. 61–109.

Lasch, C. (1984). *The minimal self: Psychic survival in troubled times.* New York: W.W. Norton & Company.

Lipset, S. (1996). *American exceptionalism: A double-edge sword.* New York: W.W. Norton.

Livesey, S.M. (2002). "Global warming wars: Rhetoric and discourse analytic approaches to ExxonMobil's corporate public discourse." *The Journal of Business Communication 39*(1), pp. 117–148.

Lynd, R.S., & Lynd, H.M. (1937). *Middletown in transition: A study in cultural conflicts.* New York: Harcourt, Brace & Company.

Marchand, R. (1998). *Creating the corporate soul: The rise of public relations and corporate imagery.* Berkeley: University of California Press.

McGuire, C. (1950). "Social stratification and mobility patterns." American Sociological Review *15*(2), pp. 195–204.

McGushin, E. (2011). "Foucault's theory and practice of subjectivity." In D. Taylor (Ed.), *Michel Foucault: Key concepts*, pp. 127–142. Durham, NC: Acumen.

Meech, P. (2006). "Corporate identity and corporate image." In J. L'Etang, & M. Pieczka (Eds.), *Public relations: Critical debates and contemporary practice*, pp. 389–404. Mahwah, NJ: Lawrence Erlbaum Associates.

Newport, F. (2016). "Americans' views of socialism, capitalism are little changed." *Gallup*, May 6, 2016. Retrieved from www.gallup.com/poll/191354/americans-views-socialism-capitalism-little-changed.aspx.

Paras, E. (2006). *Foucault 2.0: Beyond power and knowledge.* New York: Other Press.

Pollman, E. (2011). "Reconceiving corporate personhood." *Utah Law Review 4*, pp. 1629–1674.

Rojecki, A. (2008). "Rhetorical alchemy: American exceptionalism and the war on terror." *Political Communication 25*, pp. 67–88.

Samuel, L. (2012). *The American Dream: A cultural history.* Syracuse: Syracuse University Press.

Sennett, R. (1977). *The fall of public man.* New York: Alfred A. Knopf.

Smith, G., & Heath, R.L. (1990). "Moral appeals in Mobil Oil's op-ed campaign." *Public Relations Review 16*(4), pp. 48–54.

Smith, M.A. (2000). *American business and political power: Public opinion, elections, and democracy.* Chicago: University of Chicago Press.

St. John III, B. (2014a). Conveying the sense-making corporate persona: The Mobil Oil 'Observations' columns, 1975–1980." *Public Relations Review 40*(4), pp. 692–699.

St. John III, B. (2014b). "The 'creative confrontation' of Herbert Schmertz: Public relations sense-making and the corporate persona." *Public Relations Review 40*, pp. 772–779.

St. John III, B., & Arnett, R. (2014). "The National Association of Manufacturers' commmunity relations short film 'Your Town': Parable, propaganda, and big individualism." *Journal of Public Relations Research 26*(2), pp. 103–116.

Stoker, K., & Stoker, M. (2012). "The paradox of public interest: How serving individual superior interests fulfil public relations' obligation to the public interest." *Journal of Mass Media Ethics 27*, pp. 31–45.

Stuart, H. (1998). "Exploring the corporate identity/corporate image interface: An empirical study of accountancy firms." *Journal of Communication Management 2*(4), pp. 357–373.

Swenson, R. (2016). "Building Betty Crocker's brand community: Conversations with consumers, 1940–1950." *Journal of Communication Management 20*(2), pp. 148–161.

Thompson, G. (2012). *The constitutionalization of the global corporate sphere?* Oxford, UK: University Press.

Van Riel, C.B. (1997). "Research in corporate communication: An overview of an emerging field." *Management Communication Quarterly 11*(2), pp. 288–309.

Vidich, A., & Bensman, J. (1958). *Small town in mass society.* Princeton: Princeton University Press.

Weick, K. (1969). *The social psychology of organizing.* Reading, MA: Addison-Wesley Publishing Co.

Wike, R. (2016). "Five ways Americans and Europeans are different." *Pew Research Center*, April 19. Retrieved from www.pewresearch.org/fact-tank/2016/04/19/5-ways-americans-and-europeans-are-different/.

Zhang, P. (2011). "Corporate identity metaphor as constitutive discourse in miniature: The case of New China Life." *ETC: A Review of General Semantics 68*(4), pp. 375–394.

2 The corporation as person

Four perspectives

Shortly after World War II, management theorist Peter Drucker observed that the corporation has a significant role in American society. Ideally, he said, corporations should be representative of American values, holding out "the promise of adequately fulfilling the aspirations and beliefs of the American people" (Drucker, 1946/1972, p. 14). These include promises of equal opportunity, rewards for producing, dignity for each individual, the chance of individual fulfillment, and an emphasis on business and individuals being "partners in a joint enterprise rather than opponents benefitting by each other's loss" (Drucker, 1946/1972, p. 14). Drucker said that one of the reasons that American business needs to be cognizant of its connection to the individual is that, "while not confined to America, the dogma of the uniqueness of the individual is nowhere else emphasized so strongly, or made so exclusively the focus of social promises and beliefs as in this country" (1946/1972, p. 136).

Drucker's observation, particularly about the need to see business *as a partner with the individual*, is apt but appears to underestimate how the corporation was already evolving into *becoming like an individual*. There are at least three established areas of understanding corporate identity which help set a foundation for the arrival of the corporate persona, none of which, however, directly acknowledge the corporate persona construct as evidenced in this book. First, U.S. law has asserted, over 130 years, that corporations *have rights that mirror individual rights*. Second, marketing understandings of the corporation have *articulated a corporate personhood that is normally linked to products and services*. Third, constructivist observers examine how corporations *build an often-shifting identity* that is designed to appeal to a multitude of internal and external audiences. All three perspectives are valuable for situating the appearance of the corporate persona, but none of the three are sufficient for exploring how the corporate persona construct signifies a different kind of appeal to the individual. As such, this chapter offers a fourth perspective—that of the reification of the corporate persona through storytelling that appeals to enduring American values.

The corporate persona—the legal perspective

In the early years of the 20th century, observers noted that under the law corporations were increasingly seen as persons. In 1916, Harold Laski noted in the *Harvard Law Review* that courts saw them as "persons who are not men" and increasingly were approximating the corporation's position "to that of an ordinary individual" (p. 408). Machen noted that the law technically described the corporate personality as a "fiction founded upon fact." This was because the court found it natural to "personify a body of men united in a form like that of the ordinary company as it is to personify a ship" (1911, p. 266). Another legal observer offered a similar description, maintaining the courts struggled to articulate in concrete terms abstract notions of an association of people within a corporation, so addressing an organization as a person was yet another example of men "stretch[ing] old words to new uses" (Smith, 1928, p. 285).

This evolution of the corporation into a legal person was not a sudden development. Legal scholars have pointed out that legal conceptions of the rights of corporations have evolved, since the early 19th century, across three stages: (1) the corporation as an artificial person; (2) the corporation as an aggregate person; and (3) the corporation as a real entity (Allen, 2001; Blair, 2013; Krannich, 2005; Mark, 1987; Millon, 1990). All stages, said legal observers, continue to be a factor in legal decisions, with courts displaying some inconsistencies in application. Still, the body of legal analysis regarding the corporate person points to a gradual progression from that of a construct (the artificial person) that was only acknowledged as a convenience to the state to the contemporary understanding of the corporation as a person that can claim particular rights.

The corporation as an *artificial person* was a natural outgrowth of the rise of corporate-like structures in 16th-century Europe, noted Blair (2013). Ruling entities (e.g., monarchies and churches) and other institutions like hospitals, convents, and universities held assets and debts that needed to be seen as legally separate from those of individuals who owned and managed the enterprise. With an artificial-person charter from the state, these institutions could ensure perpetual succession so that property and wealth were protected from excessive taxes or even reversion to the state upon death of the administrators. By the 17th century, such charters began to arise in the business world, notably for trading companies, at first for limited periods of time, but gradually some companies received charters in perpetuity. The artificial person construct for business in the U.S. started slowly. In the early 1800s, only 335 American businesses were chartered corporations but, by 1890, 500,000 businesses were chartered, the most in the world (Blair, 2013, pp. 794–795). Several factors contributed to this particular growth of the legal corporate person. First, an 1819 U.S. court decision *(Dartmouth College v. Woodward)* articulated that a corporation is "an artificial being, invisible, intangible, and existing only in contemplation of the law" (p. 636). Subsequently, the state increasingly saw that such a legal construct not only protected property interests of those invested in companies, charters also allowed for quasi-public organizations (e.g., the railroads, ferry operators) that served a public good (Pollman, 2011). Moreover, the growth of charters happened in large part because the ascent of industrialization called for businesses to have a distinct and identifiable corporate person for purposes of visibly demarcating property rights, but also for establishing a clear entity "which became extremely important ... to support mass production and mass marketing" (Blair, 2013, p. 795).

By the late-19th century, U.S. courts began to move away from seeing corporations as artificial persons that existed only by virtue of state designation and, instead, conceptualized businesses as a distinct form of a legal individual—the *aggregate person*. Although some legal scholars debate the depth of the significance of the case, most regard the 1886 Supreme Court *Santa Clara County v. Southern Pacific Railroad* decision as a key marker for the rise of legal corporate personhood (Allen, 2001; Blair, 2013; Mark; 1987; Pollman, 2011). This case centered on a dispute concerning whether the state could treat railroads differently than other corporations and individuals regarding property tax. Pollman (2011) pointed out that the case brought into question whether corporations, like individuals, were entitled to equal protection under the law. In a pre-argument pronouncement, Supreme Court Chief Justice Waite said:

> The court does not wish to hear argument on the question whether the provision of the fourteenth amendment to the Constitution, which forbids a State to deny any person within its jurisdiction the equal protection of the laws, applies to these corporations. We are all of the opinion that it does.
>
> (*Santa Clara County v. Southern Pacific Railroad*, p. 396)

This pronouncement was not placed explicitly in the ruling, nor was there any "discussion, reasoning or authority" offered that would provide the grounding for this assertion (Pollman, 2011, p. 1644). Mark (1987) observed that the pre-argument pronouncement was not a "self-consciously radical innovation" about the nature of the corporate personality; instead, he said, the decision "merely affirmed that corporate property was protected as property of the corporators" (p. 1463). Blair similarly remarked that Waite's statement acknowledged how charters had become so readily available that, de facto, express permission from the state for a corporation to exist was no longer necessary. Instead, corporate charters were only conferring what was happening: corporate persons, which were "created by the people who came together to form them," were the driving force for corporate existence (Blair, 2013, p. 802). Charters were increasingly only important as the umbrella for agreements between a corporation and its investors, said Blair, so Waite's statement was asserting that these shareholders had rights within that chartered association with the corporate person. Finally, Waite's statement appeared to resonate with James Madison's comments in the first Congress that a charter "creates an artificial person previously not existing in the law" (Madison, 1791/1906, p. 32). Still, just 2 years after the *Santa Clara* case, the Supreme Court offered language that proffered an emerging aggregate-person view of corporations:

Corporations are merely associations of individuals united for a special purpose … The equal protection of the laws which these bodies may claim is only such as accorded to similar associations within the jurisdiction of the state.

(*Pembina Consolidated Silver Mining & Milling Co. v. Pennsylvania,* 1888, p. 125)

Despite these rulings, economics professor Evan Osborne (2007) maintained that the legal conception of groups of individuals acting as a collective personality had already been well-established in the United Kingdom by the mid-18th century. In fact, he said, "The only possible innovation in *Santa Clara* is the extension of rights that were themselves novelties in American as opposed to English law…" (Osborne, 2007, p. 30). Still, he asserted, consonant with other legal scholars (Allen, 2001; Blair, 2013; Mark; 1987; Pollman, 2011), that Waite's statement was seen as "binding law" that other court decisions mistakenly amplified "beyond what even the Court had then intended" (Osborne, 2007, p. 202). Therefore, the *Santa Clara* pronouncement was seen by subsequent courts as a precedent for granting what were normally seen as individual rights to a corporate entity (Allen, 2001; Pollman, 2011; Torres-Spelliscy, 2014), all within an emerging framework of the late-19th century and into the early 20th century that saw the corporation as an aggregate person (Krannich, 2005).

As the 1900s began, the scale of corporate activities in areas like mining, the railroads, tobacco, sugar, and steel were so large that the courts' thinking began to move beyond the aggregate-person construct. The vastness of corporate enterprise called into question a legal conception of a corporate person as merely a structural umbrella that contained contracts between the organization and its investors. Instead, with the arrival of the Supreme Court's 1905 *Hale v. Henkel* and its 1910 *Southern Railway v. Green* decisions, legal thinking had advanced to conceiving of the organization as its own thriving entity, with "claims, much like those of a natural person, that extend beyond both circumstances of its legal creation by the state and the claims or interests of its shareholders" (Blumberg, 1990 p. 50). Witnessing organizations apparently "taking on attributes such as character and purpose and reputation, similar to those of individual persons," courts began to embrace a *real entity* concept about corporations (Blair, 2013, pp. 809–810). A combination of the massive scope of these organizations, increased concerns about the "inevitability of economic concentration" (Millon, 1990, p. 212), plus the earlier legal understanding that such structures came from the collective efforts of individuals helped make both the corporate person and the real entity approach seem "to be a natural way of conducting business" (Krannich, 2005, p. 81). Blumberg (1990) noted that, by the late-20th century, conservative and libertarian sensitivities in legislative and court arenas contributed to the real entity approach being used as a way to also thwart increasing governmental regulation and intrusions into the marketplace.

Accordingly, the real entity legal understanding of the corporation has led to court decisions that have recognized that corporations have, like legal citizens in the United States, several rights under the Constitution. Court decisions have asserted that corporations have first-amendment free-speech protections, fourth-amendment protections against unreasonable seizure, fifth-amendment protections against double jeopardy, sixth- and seventh-amendments rights to trial by jury, and fourteenth-amendment rights to equal protection under the law (Allen, 2001; Pollman, 2011). The real entity approach to corporations has only magnified in the 21st century. More recently, the 2010 *Citizens United v. Federal Election Commission* Supreme Court decision affirmed that corporations (along with unions and associations) could exercise their free speech rights through political donations, and that the government was barred from encroaching on such actions. Then, in 2014, the Supreme Court, in the *Burwell v. Hobby Lobby* decision, asserted that a closely held, for-profit corporation (particularly, its ownership) has an ability, like a person, to exercise its claim of a religious belief. In this case, the owners of Hobby Lobby maintained that it was a violation of their religious beliefs to force the company to comply with the Affordable Care Act's requirement that employer-based health insurance plans offer contraceptive coverage. David Gans, of the non-profit Constitutional Accountability Center, noted:

> The opinion's reasoning is that a corporation is simply the artificial embodiment of its owners and shareholders, and must have the same free exercise rights as individuals. That's a sweeping pronouncement … While this was not a constitutional ruling … it is still an extremely significant decision that doubles down on corporate personhood…
>
> (Gans & Shapiro, 2014, p. 64)

The legal perspective of the corporate persona, therefore, reveals that, increasingly, courts conceive of corporations as entities that are like people. Mark (1987) claimed that this development was about more than changes in economics and the law; rather, American society tended to see business activities as a "collection of collectivities," with each collectivity having its own life, "dedicated to its purposes and not divisible, either actually or theoretically, among its members" (p. 1469). This societal view that the corporation was autonomous from the state—and that the state needed to be restrained in its interventions—contributed to a wider "psychological assimilation of the corporation to the individual" (Mark, 1987, p. 1477).

Still, legal scholars are, at times, cautious about assigning too much momentum to the more recent rise of legal assertions that the corporation is like an individual. Some point out that courts still make decisions that, in aggregate, show that all three perspectives—artificial person, aggregate person, and real entity—are evident in court decisions regarding corporations and the law (Blumberg, 1990; Krannich, 2005; Millon, 1990). As such, the legal understandings of the corporate person are not settled. Pollman (2011) offered that, even though the real entity approach appears ascendant, the public would more likely think that "[large] corporations are neither individuals nor the government: they are in their own category" (p. 1662). Adding to the confusion, she said, is the legal under-standing of the corporate person "recognizes that corporations are human endeavors capable of holding rights, but does not explain which rights they have or how to make this determination" (Pollman, 2011, p. 1675).

From this progression of the legal understanding of the corporate persona, one can see that, much like in other areas like technology and science, develop-ments precede legal rulings. This dynamic appears to be at work as regards the law and the corporate persona—recent rulings like *Citizens United* and *Hobby Lobby* have indicated some incremental movements to increase the legal person-ification of the corporation; however, legal scholars are doubtful that there is an accretion of rulings that clarify exactly what is a legal corporate person. This is a particularly intriguing tension as, more than 100 years ago, legal historian Laski noted that American society, as a whole, was compulsive about personalizing corporations. "We do it because we feel in these things the red blood of a living personality," he said. "Here are no mere abstractions of an over-exuberant imag-ination" (Laski, 1916, pp. 404–405). Laski's observation is prescient as the chapters ahead will offer some evidence that, at a minimum, powerful organiza-tions believe that Americans have a receptivity to viewing corporations as fellow individuals. However, in the legal realm, the picture of the corporate person is still to be more fully sketched.

The corporate persona—the marketing perspective

Marketing views of the corporate person tend to be more centered on how a cor-poration is seen at the point of transactions. This perspective stresses that cus-tomers do not just purchase a product or service; rather, their decision to interact with a company is greatly influenced (and then either positively or negatively reinforced) by how the customer views the personality associated with the com-modity or service. The shorthand in marketing parlance for this aspect of the corporate person is the *corporate brand personality*, what is defined as the "human characteristics or traits that can be attributed to a brand" (Keller & Richey, 2006, p. 74). What is often simply called the *brand*, marketing and busi-ness scholar John Balmer said, stands for a "unique identity construct," one that is, to the customer, often emotional and based on an "informal, albeit powerful corporate contract between the firm and its stakeholders—a corporate brand 'covenant'" (2012, p. 6). Balmer's semi-sacred tone regarding the nature of this relationship between the corporation and the customer is a bit incongruous, however, as he also accurately points out that this kind of association is transient as "corporate brands can be bought, sold, and borrowed by firms and can be owned (or shared) by multiple entities" (2012, p. 7). Indeed, brands can be "divisible" from the corporate entity (Balmer, 2012, p. 8). This occurs even while consumers "often imbue brands with human personality traits" (Aaker, 1997, p. 347), what others have called "brand anthropomorphization." This trig-gers in audiences' minds that brands are "living entities with their own human-like motivations, characteristics, conscious will, emotions and intentions"

(Puzakova, Kwak, & Rocereto, 2013, p. 81). Indeed, customer fixation with brands may often be more about how customers see an ideal image of themselves reflected in an association with a human-like aspect of the brand (e.g., the glamor associated with a certain handbag; the ruggedness associated with a particular motorcycle). However, this particular marketing perspective concerning the corporate person is constrained because its concept of corporate identity limits its conveyance to people as *customers*, not as *members of society* who care about a variety of issues. As Olins (1989) pointed out, a corporation lives in a world that involves "a tangled web of relationships" (p. 203), and interactions with various stakeholder groups are not going to always be about marketplace transactions.

Branding, however is only a portion of the marketing view of the corporate person: the wider vista includes conceptualizations of a *corporate identity* (CI), as is visible to both the wider marketplace and to employees. Melewar (2003), in a review of the marketing literature on CI, described it as "the set of meanings by which a company allows itself to be known and through which it allows people to describe, remember and relate to it" (p. 195). His view, however, also reveals marketing's transactional overtones; he emphasized that the CI is a "central force" that fosters employee enthusiasm, helps consumers get a better picture of the company's product quality, and allows the marketplace to better assess the financial strengths of the organization (Melewar, 2003, pp. 195–196). Others have offered a similar message about the CI, asserting that it is a construct that is: (1) informed by a need for differentiation in the marketplace (Cheney & Christensen, 2001; Gray & Balmer, 1998); (2) often full of images, shaped by consumer research, and designed to boost sales (Gregory & Wiechmann, 1995; Gurău & McLaren, 2003; Johansen, 2012; van Riel, 1997); and (3) influenced by strategy signals (e.g., breadth of product offerings), institutional signals (e.g., ownership predilections, demands for social responsibility), and responsiveness to the material and psychological needs of customers, investors, and employees (Cheney & Christensen, 2001; Fombrun & Shanley, 1990; Schmitt, 2012; van Riel, 1995, 1997). In fact, the marketing understanding of CI is so common that Charles Fombrun's well-regarded 1996 book on business reputation asserts that the corporate image is wedded to the transactional. One chapter, called "Identity Traits," maintains that the corporation is understood through how it treats its employees (e.g., promoting trust, empowering workers), how well it invests (e.g., generating good stock earnings), how well it offers great products, and how well it operates as good citizens (e.g., going green). He ends the chapter by asserting that such activities display the CI, and that "internal practices ... must also correspond [to] a set of external practices to convey a set of images coherently outside the company" (Fombrun, 1996, p. 137). All of these markers of CI are about levels of transactions with internal and external audiences—providing something so as to earn something in return.

More recently, much of the marketing perspective of the corporate person is greatly exemplified by an upswing in research in the area of corporate social responsibility (CSR). In fact, this arena of corporate identity research is burgeoning to the point of obscuring any singular definition of the concept of CSR. Moreno and Capriotti (2009) maintained that CSR started in the 1950s as a way for businesses to demonstrate that they were adhering to the law while also meeting essential ethical standards. Over time, that understanding of CSR changed toward emphasizing that organizations have duties to society (Coombs & Holliday, 2012; Luo & Bhattacharya, 2006; Nazari, Parvizi, & Emami, 2012). Significantly, a core conceptual framework for CSR is that it asserts "that the corporation exists in society and has rights and responsibilities as a member (or citizen) of that society" (Carroll, Lipartito, Post, & Werhane, 2012, p. 7); increasingly, scholars tend to frame this understanding within the concept of "corporate citizenship" (Ihlen, Bartlett, & May, 2014; Moreno & Capriotti, 2009).

CSR studies that focus on company–consumer (C–C) identification are particularly notable (and examined further in Chapter 8) for attempting to delineate how the corporate person can be made real to the customer. The C–C identification approach stresses that the company projects an identity that is suffused with pro-social values that are consonant with the values of most of the citizenry (Lichtenstein, Drumwright, & Braig, 2004; Marin & Ruiz, 2007). However, befitting the marketing perspective, scholarship on C–C identification tends to emphasize that the transaction between the corporation and the consumer serves as a vehicle through which the customer can see the corporate person. Vlachos (2012, p. 1573) called this an "emotion-laden process" where a "strong cognitive and affective bond connects a brand to an individual in such a way that the brand is an extension of the [customer]" (quoting Park, MacInnis, & Priester, 2007, p. 7). Corporations that use CSR communication often work on this emotional level by casting their products or services as beneficial within several dimensions, including such areas as environmental stewardship, economic development, or societal improvement (Carroll et al., 2012). This approach can be potent because, as Bhattacharya, Korschun, and Sen (2009) have noted, when customers embrace the usefulness of a corporation's products or services, they also are drawn to an affirmation of their individual pro-social values and their personal sense of well-being. The effect, they said, is that the "I" of the individual customer can become the "we" of the corporation and the consumer.

Concurrently, some public relations scholarship has begun to articulate that CSR is more than a vehicle for attempting to meet organizational obligations to society. It is an arena that is potentially fruitful for corporations to offer flattering self-portraits, especially for companies who "handle economic, social and/or environmental issues … [CSR] is the corporate use of symbols and language regarding these matters" (Ihlen et al., 2011, pp. 7–8). In this way, CSR "is a societal narrative" that shows corporations creating and disseminating their own stories, offering a "sensemaking process" for both themselves and their stakeholders (Wehmeier & Schultz, 2011, p. 477).

However, the lion's share of CSR-related research reflects the marketing perspective of the corporate person—that the CI is a sum of its marketing activities, internal corporate culture, and socially conscious behavior. Of course, all three of these areas, based on the imperatives of management and the vicissitudes of the marketplace, and the societies which impact upon that marketplace, can widely diverge. Take, for example, Apple, a corporation which has appeared to clearly define itself as a trendsetter in electronic offerings but also encourages a workplace penchant for competitive secrecy and is also seen as out of touch concerning the foreign labor it relies upon (St. John III & Pearson, 2017). Does Apple have one CI or three? Not surprisingly, the marketing perspective allows for differences about who is the corporate person—it is any attribute that can be aligned with a particular transactional behavior of the company. Melewar (2003) pointed out that this rather dispersed notion of the corporate person—that is, one can know it primarily when one sees it—leads to uncertainty about identifying aspects of the corporation. "Corporate identity is often confused with interrelated concepts such as corporate image, personality, reputation, corporate communications and public relations," he said, when, ideally, the CI should refer "to the individual characteristics by which one organization can be differentiated from another" (Melewar, 2003, p. 196). Clearly, identifying a corporation *only* by its transactions is not as easy as it may seem. Still, while Melewar accurately describes the difficulty of the marketing perspective's often-scattered take on the corporate person, his prescription, by focusing on marketplace differentiation, only doubles down on the constrained marketing set of tools for identifying "who" the corporation is.

Looming behind the confusion within the marketing perspective about the corporate persona is the imperative that an effective corporate identity is one that helps the organization attain and sustain profitability. Olins (1989) asserted that the CI is "the most significant factor in [an individual] making a choice between one company and its products or another" (p. 9). Gregory and Wiechman (1995), in their book on corporate-image advertising, asserted that how the public perceives the CI is so important that an organization's leadership must insure that initial messages toward customers should be "molded into a positive force to enhance business prospects" or at least changed to enhance customer understanding of the corporation's current situation (p. 2). That advice appears to precisely summarize the overall limitation of the marketing perspective of the corporate persona—it is too focused on fashioning an alignment of individuals to corporate understandings and behaviors. A fuller understanding of the corporate persona, however, calls for examining how the organization uses such an entity to demonstrate that what it stands for and what it does *already comports* with what most Americans believe are essential for the country's well-being.

The corporate persona—the constructivist perspective

The constructivist view of the corporate persona is also greatly shaped by a focus on the corporate identity. Scholars in this arena are concerned with how the signals sent between multiple actors—both within and outside the organization—contribute to the construction of a CI, the varied ways the CI is understood, and how the understanding of the significance of the CI is ever-changing. Much of corporate identity research and theorizing accelerated in the 1980s, said

Cornelissen and Harris (2001), driven by: (1) more interest in how companies linked their personalities to attempts at product differentiation; (2) the ascendancy of sophisticated design, public relations, and advertising industries; (3) the upswing in merger and acquisitions; and (4) increasing views of corporations as "human-like" (p. 51). They noted, however, that these CI studies were often fuzzy, lacking clear theory development. Still, they found that, by the dawn of the 21st century, these studies had advanced three main conceptions of the CI: (1) that it is an expression of an inherent inner self or corporate personality; (2) that it is a series of brand displays (logos, slogans, product offerings, etc.) that reveal the company's personality; and (3) that of the constructivist view— that the CI is a result of language, enactments, and social interaction (Cornelissen & Harris, 2001, pp. 56–61). The first view, that a company has an inherent self, appears to suffer from a mistaken notion of likening the psychological make up of a person—the individual's character, predispositions, temperament, and interpersonal communication styles—to the development of a corporate person. Indeed, recent scholarship by Coombs and Holladay (2015) points out that studying a corporation as if it were engaged in interpersonal communication overemphasizes the corporation acting as if it had personal, strong ties to audiences, when second-order, weaker ties may be more important. Not surprisingly, while Corneliessen and Harris (2001) may well have found strains of the "inner self" conception, it does not appear to be a prominent standpoint in CI studies. The limitations of the second view, or the branding-marketing perspective, were detailed earlier in this chapter, leaving the constructivist position for further discussion.

The constructivist view that the corporate identity is shaped so as to address multiple audiences appears to be well grounded. In fact, the need for corporations to make effective links to different publics has been a pressing issue for corporations since the 20th century, especially since the Great Depression. Martineau noted, some 30 years after that economic calamity, that the world had become much more complex, with a variety of stakeholders increasingly more vocal about asserting their interests. "May it not be, then, that there is not only too much for the modern corporation to say, but also too many different people to say it to?" he asked (Martineau, 1958, p. 52). Martineau asserted that our minds

> …can only handle so many complexities…. Simple symbolic images act as a rough summation or index of a vast complexity of meanings. We personalize them and like them or dislike them because this is the only way we can interact with things—*to endow them with the attributes of people.*
>
> (1958, pp. 52–53, emphasis added)

But to be able to see the corporate identity, to visualize a corporation as a fellow human, forces within the organization needed to engage in, essentially, creating the persona. Scholars have asserted that this attempt at persona building arises from a strategic mindset; that is, it stems from a concerted effort by management (which, at times, can include the founder) to relay to all employees across the corporate infrastructure, to investors, and to the broader public that the corporation has a distinctive, helpful presence, or "soul" (Cornelissen and Harris, 2001; Olins, 1978; Zhang, 2011). Some scholars (Albert & Whetten, 1985; Whetten, 2006) have argued that this presentation of the CI is, out of necessity, normally consistent. These observers—who are of the "constant identity" school—asserted there is a "claimed central character" that over time offers a sense of sameness (Albert & Whetten, 1985, p. 265; van Riel, 1997), conveying a central and enduring identity (Whetten, 2006). Still, even the constant identity school allows that there may be imprecisions and ambiguities regarding the CI because, for one part, exactness and constancy in image projection may not be possible or even desirable (Albert & Whetten, 1985). Even with that admission, however, these scholars are outnumbered by those in the "shifting identity" school, which asserts that the CI is subject to notable modifications over time. These changes happen because there are a multiplicity of storylines that represent different contexts and voices within and without the organization, and organizations are notoriously concerned with allying their accounts with swings in public views (Cheney & Christensen, 2001; Hatch & Schultz, 2002). Johnson (2012) similarly noted that continuously developing (and sometimes eroding) narratives result in polyphonic storytelling that calls for an organization to "navigate amongst the different stories that seek to define it" (pp. 242–243). She and Zhang (2011) said that ambiguity characterized much of these attempts at articulating the CI, allowing, said Zhang, the corporation to bundle "the desirable with the less than desirable" ideological freight of the organization (p. 389). Alvesson (1990) along with Hatch and Schultz (2002), typical of this line of thought about the CI, assert that such projection of a corporate presence cannot be constant, is often loosely tied to the reality the corporation is addressing, and is often shaped by the context and stakeholders it refers to.

This shifting identity school, then, claims that the presentation of the corporate identity is informed, in large part, by corporate management taking the temperature of the internal and external environment. This assertion appears to have more support than the claims of the constant identity school. For one, scholars (Cheney & Christensen, 2001; Hatch and Schultz, 2002; Russell-Loretz, 1995) observe that organizations engage in a process known as *mirroring*, where organizations assert the viability of their CI by identifying how well, for example, it is reflected in the values, behaviors, and aspirations of their stakeholders. Commenting further, Hatch and Schultz (2002) said that the process leads to either reinforcement or adjustments in CI because management will, at times, feel a need to reflect on the identity and how well it corresponds to intra- and extraorganizational "deep cultural values and assumptions" (p. 1000). Russell-Loretz (1995) further unpacked the fluidity of the CI by pointing out that organizations may have to adopt multifaceted faces to "appease interests that, while important to one's identity, may be in conflict" (p. 162). For example, a large company like Costco may attempt to tout its better wages and family-friendly policies as a way to appear more connected to its local community, while also pointing out to profit-focused shareholders that its nationwide presence allows it to work with suppliers to bring in large bundles of materials at lower cost. As Martineau (1958) observed, there is not a singular corporate person and "there cannot be because every firm has different publics" that need to have their specific need addressed by a particular manifestation of the CI (p. 58).

Understanding that corporations appear, over time, to show fluidity in the projection of their personality does not mean, however, that such changes are taken lightly. Indeed, said the shifting identity school, the CI construct is asserted exactly because changing conditions in society signal to corporate management that some type of control needs to be exerted by the organization. Among the many disturbances corporations fear are societal unease about capitalism and corporations (Olins, 1978), societal fragmentation and the rise of a service economy (Alvesson, 1990), the decrease in manufacturing positions (ibid.), the loss of distinctiveness in an overcommunicated public sphere (Cheney & Christensen, 2001), and the resultant need for corporations to "preserve for tomorrow what has made them what and/or who they are today" (Whetten, 2006, p. 224). However, as Olins (1978) remarked, American culture is not normally receptive to didactic institutions, so corporations need to send messages and images that stress notions of joint participation between the corporation and the individual. These kinds of messages—claims about the commonality between the CI and an individual's sense of self—are most commonly asserted during times of crisis, said Cheney and Christensen (2001). They note that, for well over 6 decades, corporations have used the corporate identity as a "creative reaction" to societal turbulence and the "related reduction of predictability" that marks the modern industrial-technological era (Cheney & Christensen, 2001, p. 253). Corporate attempts to assert their personhood in the public sphere are attempts to address "precariousness of meaning" and reduce "identity-threatening anxiety" by conveying "a picture which is appealing, familiar and reduces uncertainty" (Alvesson, 1990, p. 385). But there is an inherent tension here, said Zhang (2011): if the organization was already the person it claimed it was, it would not have to "use metaphors and imagery to convince audiences" (p. 389). So, he claimed, the organization would always fall short of realizing its particular assertion of a corporate persona.

Across these observations, it is apparent that, like the marketing perspective, the constructivist view of the corporate person can lead to a "big tent" approach. That is, varied understandings of the clarity, constancy, and aims of corporate identity lead to some blurriness about how the corporation, through relaying its personhood, can amplify a sense of allegiance with the individual. Still, one of the clearest and most helpful insights from the constructivist school is the description of the role that crisis plays in magnifying the corporation's need to project its persona. In fact, this is a central precept across years of constructivist commentary on the corporate identity: it is a larger-than-life construct designed to overcome stressors that would fracture society and the corporation's footing among the people.

A fourth route—the corporate persona through storytelling

As this chapter has shown, prevailing modes of identifying the corporate persona have provided legal, marketing, and constructivist views that, separately and as a whole, provide solid insights but also a sense of disjointedness. That is, legal imperatives to assert corporate personhood are constrained by legal precedence, ownership interests, and compelling necessities or opportunities to prevail in the courts. From the legal view, appealing to broader audiences beyond the courts is of limited concern or value. The marketing approach is similarly circumscribed because it centers on a transactional understanding: the corporation's character is best understood through how *customers* (not diverse stakeholders) view, and interact directly with, the corporation's product and services. Within the marketing view, however, is a strain—company–consumer identification—that parallels some public relations scholarship on the corporate persona (Cheney, 1992; Heath & Nelson, 1986; St. John III, 2014; St. John III & Arnett, 2014). But the limitation of C–C identification is there in its mode of analysis: it, too, focuses on stakeholders as consumers (see Chapter 8 for more on company–consumer identification). However, there are many clusters of individuals within a society that do not interact directly with the goods and services of a company and yet are affected by how the organization goes about its mission and how it takes a stand on issues of compelling public interest (e.g., how fracking companies attempt to influence energy policy, how pharmaceutical organizations lobby for changes in health care laws, etc.). Finally, the constructivist view offers important considerations regarding the corporation's attempt to put forward a corporate identity that, in large part, helps the company address the disruptions in society. Collectively, the constructivist perspective maintains that the CI is a compensatory device: when the corporation senses internal and/or external changes that could imperil the company's livelihood, an ambiguous, often-shifting CI is asserted so as to dampen turbulence within and without the organization. This view, in contrast to the legal and marketing perspectives, offers more of a societally imbedded take on the corporate person. However, it tends to emphasize, by its focus on CI ambiguity (and even polyphony), a certain level of high variability regarding how the corporate person is projected. It is true that corporate strategic needs, marketplace pressures, legal concerns, and societal unrest may all play, at different times, a role in shifts of tone voiced through the corporate person. However, the constructivist view tends to ignore an important factor that works to limit wide variances of the corporate persona projection: dominant, persistent American value sets that trumpet the supremacy of individualism (e.g., self-reliance, initiative, liberty, etc.). As such, the constructivist view, with its emphasis on shifting CI representations, tends to downplay how corporations are keenly aware of enduring, core values of American individualism and how they hone their corporate personality in such a way as to show that the corporation is in alignment with that orientation.

Those persistent Americanist orientations are the essential grounding for the corporate ability to simulate a personal relationship with individuals. In fact, this desire to be seen as a beneficial corporate "good citizen" was particularly strong by the mid-20th century. Rex Harlow (1942), writing of the promise of public relations as a constructive societal force, said that public relations, in the years after World War II, would need to serve as a promoter of "individual dignity, free inquiry, and love of truth" (p. 208). This would be accomplished, he said, through an emerging crop of PR professionals who would encourage management to keep in mind that any corporate decision must resonate with "the deep social values inherent in all human relationships" (Harlow, 1942, p. 214). Harlow was apparently in tune with this increasing inclination by corporations to be seen as embracing values that were in alignment with the citizenry. Eells (1960), reflecting on the 1950s, noted that mid-century businessmen were troubled by any perceptions that they were uncaring about their fellow citizens. They wanted their corporations to be understood as an "integral part of the community," an essential institution that is "just as important to people as churches and schools and fraternal organizations" (Eels, 1960, p. 131). But Eels added that it was even more than that: the corporation, he said, wanted to be known as a neighbor, "an association of human beings who share with their fellow citizens a conscientious interest in the commonweal" (1960, p. 261).

With this desire by corporate leaders to relay to individuals that the corporation was an entity who shared the daily life space came approaches that emphasized the corporation as a fellow actor facing life's challenges. In the increasingly industrialized and hypercommunicated mid-20th century, with an ever-increasing pace of life and escalating emergence of social issues (civil rights, the Cold War, militarization, etc.), it became clearer, said Heath (2000), that institutional actors like the corporation had more persuasive opportunities than did most individuals. As modern society presented a cacophony of events, issues, and crises, individuals sought out stories that offered a sense of groundedness, displaying a receptivity to reality-affirming narratives that helped make sense of the world around them. Boorstin (1962) pointed out that the times were ripe for such narratives because Americans were already too willing to accept stories that were actually illusions and that acted as "the very house in which we live," helping to define our very existence (p. 240).

During such a time of susceptibility to illusion, public relations was well-positioned to use storytelling to amplify the corporation beyond the limited notions of a legal actor or product/service purveyor to that of a fellow actor in the walk of life. Kent (2015) called this approach "reifying organizations, and organizational members, as trusted and beloved community members"—using stories to appeal to people's experiences, values, and attitudes so as to elicit audience identification with the institution (p. 1). Jackall (2010) similarly observed that public relations people are uniquely equipped to offer such a corporate appeal to the individual as they "have a fine appreciation of how the drama of social reality is constructed because they themselves are usually the playwrights and the stage directors" (p. 175). These scholars' observations follow in the tradition of Burke's dramatistic view of persuasive communication in *A Grammar of Motives* (1945), which described entities as actors on the stage of life, behaving within the bounds of act, scene, agent, agency, and purpose. In discussing these aspects, Burke was interested in how rhetors engaged in "out-witting or cajoling" others (p. xvii), but his observations in the latter *A Rhetoric of Motives* (1950) allow for a more sophisticated take on the corporate persona. In a discussion of identification, Burke pointed out that actors, especially in times of stress, seek to assert a consubstantiality, or an acting together, with their audience. In other words, a sense of identification between the actor and the audience needed to be asserted precisely because there was a perceived division between the two. As this book shows, corporations detected threats to their ability to operate at key points in 20th-century America and used the corporate persona to effect a consubstantiation with others, attempting to magnify that it was an affinitive presence in Americans' lives.

Burke (1950), however, noted that the internal monologue within the individual is a complicated item to address and that only the voices "that speak in the lan-guage of the voice within" will be effective (p. 39). Decades later, Walter Fisher's (1989) narrative paradigm added more insights into how narratives resonate with audiences—stories are judged by how well they are credible (the degree to which the story holds together) and whether they display fidelity (the degree to which the story appears to be truthful). Fisher's paradigm states that facts and data are important, but individuals judge the worthiness of the story through the prism of their character, status, lived experience, and culture, as well as the nature of the text presented in a multidimensional "historically situated moment" (Moffitt, 1994, p. 46; see also Fisher, 1989; Heath, 2013). All of these story-validation factors can be broadly construed to fall either within the context of the event-driven existential or the realm of the ideologically driven temperamental. Both necessarily come into play in mid-20th-century United States where business believed that audiences needed to hear that the free market was struggling under government regulations and policies and that free enterprise was threatened by the spread of communism and socialism (the existential realm). Corporations complemented these messages with a soothing appeal to the temperamental realm: Americans needed to avoid reliance on the welfare state and reassert, with corporations, a mutual adherence to self-reliance and independence.

Business worked to project a credible and truthful story that proclaimed to Americans the need to resist threats in both the existential and temperamental realms. Moreover, it conveyed to Americans that corporations shared the values of the individual and that returning to those values (e.g., a faith in the free market, trust in the constructive force of business) would allow the country to thrive in the midst of its challenges. The arrival of the human-like corporate persona in the mid-20th-century United States is notable because of the story it offered: a call to Americans to come home to what they already believed. As discussed in Chapter 1, scholars (Gabriel, 2000; Goffman, 1959; Weick, 1995) said that personalities offer fact-based stories as sense-making, placing frames around information so as to direct the story recipient to *comprehend and develop a sense of consistency/harmony* with what has already been authored. This corporate bent for accordance is something that Heath (2000) noted in public relations' tendency to offer visions of organizations and individuals acting in concurrence, mainly by proffering statements of values that "foster or frustrate the growth of a community" (p. 84). The corporate persona, as detailed in this volume, magnifies the "foster" aspects, specifically by offering a window into the corporation that is about displaying the organization's adherence to dominant myths and rituals (Trujillo & Toth, 1987). Public relations people, working to assert bridges between the corporation and the individual, know how to leverage dispositional tendencies to hold onto mythical notions of Americanism because they study the roads that Americans walk and then offer supportive narratives. Said Jackall:

> Men and women in public relations simply utilize their own intuitive and experiential understandings of the quandaries, negotiations, and brokered and bungled solutions of private lives as the stuff to shape the scripts of public drama. They succeed precisely when the stories they fashion have emotional resonance in the private lives of broad sectors of the public, even though such resonance might precipitate a recoiling jolt of self-recognition and consequent antagonism toward the storyteller.
>
> (2000, p. 201)

Curiously, Jackall elides discussion of how such storytellers avoid blowback from their audiences. Dervin and Foreman-Wernet (2013), however, provide through a discussion of their sense-making methodology (SMM) some insights as to why public relations messages, and the corporations that offer them, often avoid such hostility. SMM, they assert, allows organizations to building "lasting and viable intersections between institutions and internal and external constituencies" and that a corporation is likely to be seen as a fellow striver when it communicates to audiences that it, too, is attempting to "make sense of changing circumstances" (Dervin & Foreman-Wernet, 2013, pp. 147, 153). More recently, Coombs and Holladay (2015) pointed to individuals' receptivity to parasocial relationships with corporations. They stated that "people can deliberately cultivate close relationships with organizations they perceive are already similar to them in addition to developing close relationships with organizations that reflect an identity they wish to become" (Coombs & Holladay, 2015, p. 4). This book, however, offers evidence that the nature of the corporate persona is more about asserting an existing affiliation—a claim that the corporate persona is already in the web of societal structures that, when heeded, can assist one's inclinations to maximize oneself and realize one's values and aspirations. The story already exists, and a relationship does not need to be cultivated; the corporate persona need only be allowed to assist.

What of the corporate persona?

As pointed out in Chapter 1, Lasch (1984) referred to a mid-20th-century rise of consumerism, accompanied by Americans turning to corporations for more than products or services. Corporations addressed the inherent insecurity of American narcissism, he said, by offering them orientations that can help them manage daily life. Foucault (1977, 2006) went further, asserting that consumerism was not necessarily an important element in this ascendancy of the corporate voice. Instead, he said, power centers within capitalism emphasize that individuals view the marketplace, and not the state, as the way to maximize who they are and what they can achieve. Indeed, in times of unrest, such an appeal to American individualism seems to be a logical fit, said Sennett (1977), because when people are faced with complexity they "reach for some inner, essential principle…" rather than extensive, rational analysis (p. 219). An appeal to the insecurities inherent within a culture's narcissism can work, he noted, because complex and messy facts and elements of a public issue can be converted into "symbols of personality" (Sennett, 1977, p. 219), which encourages recipients to suspend their judgments about their own best interests in favor of "images that bind them together" (ibid., p. 222). What happens, said Sennett, is that such a collective presentation works toward entrenching societal views of what it is to be an American, with the culture robbed of dialectic discourse about what Americans are or how they should aspire to certain ways of living.

Such an emphasis on a harmonious view of what it is to be an American has been readily proffered in the United States since the rise of the New Deal, calling into question that, when it comes to core corporate appeals to American sensibilities, there are significant variations in corporate persona messages over time. This book offers signs of the durable corporate person. Its drive to declare an alliance with deep-seated American values does not shift as widely as scholars of corporate identity maintain. In fact, the corporate persona's endurance is greatly attributed to the fact that it does not attempt to convince Americans of certain arguments or positions; rather, the corporate person simply signals to Americans that it is a fellow citizen that shares the frustrations and aspirations of the average individual. David Finn, founder and chairman of public relations firm Ruder Finn, wrote in 1961 that the corporate person needs to be "individual and distinctive," offering an image that compensates for the average person's lack of knowledge of the organization (p. 136). Finn's statement points to how public relations practitioners in the mid-20th-century United States were uniquely positioned to convey that the corporation was more than a point of exchange for products and services: it was a larger-than-life affinitive corporate citizen, something that, in the next chapter, is seen in the National Association of Manufacturers' assertions in the turbulent years just prior to World War II.

References

Aaker, J. (1997). "Dimensions of brand personality." *Journal of Marketing Research 34*, pp. 347–356.

Albert, S., & Whetten, D. (1985). "Organizational identity." *Research in Organizational Behavior 7*, pp. 263–295.

Allen, D.S. (2001). "The first amendment and the doctrine of corporate personhood: Collapsing the press-corporation distinction." *Journalism 2*(3), pp. 255–278.

Alvesson, M. (1990). "Organization: From substance to image?" *Organization Studies 11*(3), pp. 373–394.

Balmer, J.M. (2012). "Corporate brand management imperatives: Custodianship, credibility, and calibration." *California Management Review 54*(3), pp. 6–33.

Bhattacharya, C., Korschun, D., & Sen, S. (2009). "Strengthening stakeholder-company relationships through mutually beneficial corporate social responsibility initiatives." *Journal of Business Ethics 85*, pp. 257–272.

Blair, M. (2013). "Corporate personhood and the corporate persona." *University of Illinois Law Review 3*, pp. 785–820.

Blumberg, P.L. (1990). "The corporate personality in American law: A summary review." *The American Journal of Comparative Law 38*, pp. 49–69.

Boorstin, D. (1962). *The image: Or what happened to the American Dream.* New York: Atheneum.

Burke, K. (1945). *A grammar of motives.* Berkeley: University of California Press.

Burke, K. (1950). *A rhetoric of motives.* Berkeley: University of California Press.

Carroll, A., Lipartito, K., Post, J., & Werhane, P. (2012). *Corporate responsibility: The American experience.* Cambridge: University Press.

Cheney, G. (1992). "The corporate person (re)presents itself." In E.L. Toth, & R.L. Heath (Eds.), *Rhetorical and critical approaches to public relations*, pp. 165–183. Hillsdale, NJ: Lawrence Erlbaum.

Cheney, G., & Christensen, L.T. (2001). "Organizational identity: Linkages between internal and external communication." In F.M. Jablin, & L.L. Putnam (Eds.), *The new handbook of organizational communication*, pp. 231–269. Thousand Oaks, CA: SAGE.

Coombs, W.T., & Holladay, S.J. (2012). *Managing corporate social responsibility: A communication approach.* Malden, MA: Wiley & Sons.

Coombs, W.T., & Holladay, S.J. (2015). "Public relations' 'relationship identity' in research: Enlightenment or illusion." *Public Relations Review 41*(5), pp. 689–695.

Cornelissen, J., & Harris, P. (2001). "The corporate identity metaphor: Perspectives, problems and prospects." *Journal of Marketing Development 17*, pp. 49–71.

Dartmouth College v. Woodward, 17 U.S. 518 (Supreme Court 1819).

Dervin, B., & Foreman-Wernet, L. (2013). "Sense-making methodology as an approach to understanding and designing for campaign audiences: A turn to communicating communicatively." In R. Rice, & C. Atkin (Eds.), *Public communication campaigns* (4th ed.), pp. 147–162. Thousand Oaks, CA: SAGE.

Drucker, P. (1946/1972). *Concept of the corporation.* New York: The John Day Company.

Eells, R. (1960). *The meaning of modern business: An introduction to the philosophy of large corporate enterprise.* New York: Columbia University Press.

Fisher, W. (1989). *Human communication as narration: Toward a philosophy of reason, value and action.* Columbia, SC: University of South Carolina Press.

Fombrun, C. (1996). *Reputation: Realizing value from the corporate image.* Boston: Harvard Business School Press.

Fombrun, C., & Shanley, M. (1990). "What's in a name? Reputation building and corporate strategy." *The Academy of Management Journal 33*(2), pp. 233–258.

Foucault, M. (1997). *Ethics: Subjectivity and truth* (Vol. 1). New York: The New Press.

Foucault, M. (2006). *The hermeneutics of the subject: Lectures at the College De France, 1981–82.* (F. Gros, Ed., & G. Burchell, Trans.) New York: Picador.

Gabriel, Y. (2000). *Storytelling in organizations: Facts, fictions, and fantasies.* Oxford, UK: Oxford University Press.

Gans, D., & Shapiro, I. (2014). *Religious liberties for corporations? Hobby Lobby, the Affordable Care Act and the Constitution.* New York: Palgrave Macmillan.

Goffman, E. (1959). *The presentation of self in everyday life.* New York: Anchor Books.

Gray, E., & Balmer, J.M.T. (1998). "Managing corporate image and corporate reputation." *Long Range Planning 31*(5), pp. 695–702.

Gregory, J.R., & Wiechmann, J.G. (1995). *Marketing corporate image: The company as your number one product.* Lincolnwood, IL: NTC Business Books.

Gurău, C., & McLaren, Y. (2003). "Corporate reputations in UK biotechnology: An analysis of on-line 'company profile' texts." *Journal of Marketing Communications 9*, pp. 241–256.

Harlow, R. (1942). *Public relations in war and peace.* New York: Harper and Brothers.

Hatch, M.J., & Schultz, M. (2002). "The dynamics of organizational identity." *Human Relations 55*(8), pp. 989–1018.

Heath, R. (2000). "A rhetorical perspective on the values of public relations: Crossroads and pathways toward concurrence." *Journal of Public Relations Research 12*(1), pp. 69–91.

Heath, R. (2013). "The journey to understand and champion OPR takes many roads, some not yet well traveled." *Public Relations Review 39*, pp. 426–431.

Heath, R.L., & Nelson, R.A. (1986). *Issues management: Corporate public policymaking in an information society.* Beverly Hills, CA: SAGE.

Ihlen, Ø., Bartlett, J., & May, S. (2011). "Corporate social responsibility and communication." In Ø. Ihlen, J. Bartlett, & S. May (Eds.), *Handbook of communication and corporate social responsibility*, pp. 3–22. Oxford, UK: Wiley-Blackwell.

Jackall, R. (2010). *Moral mazes: The world of corporate managers.* Oxford: Oxford University Press.

Johansen, T.S. (2012). "The narrated organization: Implications of a narrative corporate identity vocabulary for strategic self-storying." *International Journal of Strategic Communication 6*, pp. 232–245.

Keller, K.R., & Richey, K. (2006). "The importance of corporate brand personality traits to a successful 21st century business." *Brand Management 14*(1/2), pp. 74–81.

Kent, M. (2015). "The power of storytelling in public relations: Introducing the 20 master plots." *Public Relations Review 41*(4), pp. 480–489.

Krannich, J.M. (2005). "The corporate 'person': A new analytical approach to a flawed method of constitutional interpreation." *Loyola University Chicago Law Journal 37*, pp. 61–109.

Lasch, C. (1984). *The minimal self: Psychic survival in troubled times.* New York: W.W. Norton & Company.

Laski, H.J. (1916). "The personality of associations." *Harvard Law Review 24*(4), pp. 404–426.

Lichtenstein, D., Drumwright, M., & Braig, B. (2004). "The effect of corporate social responsibility on customer donations to corporate-supported nonprofits." *The Journal of Marketing 68*, pp. 16–32.

Luo, X., & Bhattacharya, C. (2006). "Corporate social responsibility, customer satisfaction, and market value." *Journal of Marketing 70*(4), pp. 1–18.

Machen, A. (1911). "Corporate personality." *Harvard Law Review 34*(4), pp. 253–267.

Madison, J. (1791/1906). *The writings of James Madison* (Vol. 6), G. Hunt (Ed.). New York: G.P. Putnam's Sons.

Marin, L., & Ruiz, S. (2007). "'I need you too!' Corporate identity attractiveness for consumers and the role of social responsibility." *Journal of Business Ethics 71*, pp. 245–260.

Mark, G.A. (1987). "The personification of the business corporation in American law." *The University of Chicago Law Review 54*(4), pp. 1441–1483.

Martineau, P. (1958). "Sharper focus for the corporate image." *Harvard Business Review 36*, pp. 49–58.

Melewar, T. (2003). "Determinants of the corporate identity construct: A review of the literature." *Journal of Marketing Communications 9*, pp. 195–220.

Millon, D. (1990). "Frontier of legal thought: Theories of the corporation." *Duke Law Journal 2*, pp. 201–262.

Moffitt, M. (1994). "A cultural studies perspective toward understanding corporate image: A case study of State Farm Insurance." *Journal of Public Relations Research 6*(1), pp. 41–66.

Moreno, A., & Capriotti, P. (2009). "Communicating CSR, citizenship and sustainability on the web." *Journal of Communication Management 13*(2), pp. 157–175.

Nazari, K., Parvizi, M., & Emami, M. (2012). "Corporate social responsibility: Approaches and perspectives." *Interdisciplinary Journal of Contemporary Research in Business 3*(9), pp. 554–563.

Olins, W. (1978). *The corporate personality: An inquiry into the nature of corporate identity.* London: Design Council.

Olins, W. (1989). *Corporate identity: Making business strategy visible through design.* Boston: Harvard Business School Press.

Osborne, E. (2007). *The rise of the anti-corporate movement: Corporations and the people who hate them.* Westport, CT: Praeger.

Park, C., MacInnis, D., & Priester, J. (2008). "Brand attachment and management of a strategic brand exemplar." In B. Schmitt, & D. Rogers (Eds.), *Handbook of brand and experience management*, pp. 3–17. Cheltenham: Edward Elgar.

Pembina Condolidated Silver Mining Co. v. Pennsylvania, 125 U.S. 181 (1888).

Pollman, E. (2011). "Reconceiving corporate personhood." *Utah Law Review 4*, pp. 1629–1674.

Puzakova, M.K., Kwak, H., & Rocereto, J.F. (2013). "When humanizing brands goes wrong: The detrimental effect of brand anthropomorphization amid product wrong-doings." *Journal of Marketing 77*, pp. 81–100.

Russell-Loretz, T. (1995). "Janus in the looking glass: The management of organizational identity in corporate recruitment videos." In W. Elwood (Ed.), *Public relations as rhetorical criticism: Case studies of corporate discourse and social influence*, pp. 156–172. Westport, CT: Praeger.

Santa Clara County v. Southern Pacific Railroad, 118 U.S. 395 (1886).

Schmitt, B. (2012). "The consumer psychology of brands." *Journal of Consumer Psychology 22*, pp. 7–17.

Sennett, R. (1977). *The fall of public man.* New York: Alfred A. Knopf.

Smith, B. (1928). "Legal personality." *The Yale Law Journal 37*(3), pp. 283–299.

St. John III, B. (2014). "Conveying the sense-making corporate persona: The Mobil Oil 'Observations' columns, 1975–1980." *Public Relations Review 40*(4), pp. 692–699.

St. John III, B., & Arnett, R. (2014). "The National Association of Manufacturers' commmunity relations short film 'Your Town': Parable, propaganda, and big individualism." *Journal of Public Relations Research 26*(2), pp. 103–116.

St. John III, B., & Pearson, Y. (2017). *Crisis communication and crisis management: An ethical approach.* Thousand Oaks, CA: SAGE.

Torres-Spelliscy, C. (2014). "The history of corporate personhood." *Brennan Center for Justice*. Retrieved from www.brennancenter.org/blog/hobby-lobby-argument.

Trujillo, N., & Toth, E.L. (1987). "Organizational perspectives for public relations research and practice." *Management Communication Quarterly 1*(2), pp. 199–281.

Van Riel, C.B. (1995). *Principles of corporate communication.* Essex, UK: Pearson.

Van Riel, C.B. (1997). "Research in corporate communication: An overview of an emerging field." *Management Communication Quarterly 11*(2), pp. 288–309.

Vlachos, P. (2012). "Corporate social performance and consumer-retailer emotional attachment: The moderating role of individual traits." *European Journal of Marketing 46*(11/12), pp. 1559–1580.

Wehmeier, S., & Schultz, F. (2011). "Communication and corporate social responsibility: A storytelling perspective." In O. Ihlen, J.L. Bartlett, & S. May (Eds.), *The handbook of communication and corporate social responsibility*, pp. 467–488. Oxford, UK: Wiley-Blackwell.

Weick, K. (1995). *Sensemaking in organizations.* Thousand Oaks, CA: SAGE.

Whetten, D.A. (2006). "Albert and Whetten revisited: Strengthening the concept of organizational identity." *Journal of Management Inquiry 15*(3), pp. 219–234.

Zhang, P. (2011). "Corporate identity metaphor as constitutive discourse in miniature: The case of New China Life." *ETC: A Review of General Semantics 68*(4), pp. 375–394.

3   The corporate persona and industry

The National Association of Manufacturers walks with you

In the years before the Great Depression, business in the United States, as a whole, was seen as a hero. Dumenil (1995) pointed out that, by the end of World War I, business was well-positioned to assert itself as a powerful force: progressivism (which criticized concentration of private power and wealth) was in eclipse while anti-statism was ascendant. Business could claim it helped America win the war, and it began to use more advertising and public relations to assert it had a service role in society. Industry was seen as a potent force that was on its way to "banish[ing] poverty, war and injustice," noted history writer Robert Goldston (1968, p. 13). Americans demonstrated their faith in the corporation with their pocketbooks—in 1920, 2 million Americans owned stock; as 1929 ended, that figure had ballooned to 10 million shareholders (Hawkins, 1963, p. 145). Historian Thomas Cochran noted that this time period showed business enjoying "a degree of public approval unique in American history" (1957, p. 140). John Kenneth Galbraith quoted one professor who, in 1929, proclaimed good feeling toward business:

> The common folk believe in their leaders. We no longer look upon the captains of industry as magnified crooks. Have we not heard their voices on the radio? Are we not familiar with their thoughts, ambitions and ideals as they have expressed them to *us almost as a man talks to his friend*?
>
> (1954, p. 170, emphasis added)

To a certain degree, business had achieved such approval because it had helped bring Americans products and services that society needed and wanted. Between 1900 and 1930, the nation's manufacturing output had quadrupled, thanks in part to widespread factory electrification. The introduction of mass production, the automobile, mass broadcasting, consumer credit, and advertising produced in the U.S. the world's first mass-consumer economy (Goldston, 1968; Wall, 2008). The 1920s, in particular, were marked by large production increases in manufacturing, mining and agriculture, expansion in construction, and the roll out of chain stores—all signs of a "triumphal march of American industry and business," noted *Harper's* editor Frederick Lewis Allen (1952, p. 122). Many middle-class families already had some trappings of modernity, such as washing machines, refrigerators, telephones, and automobiles. But there were those who made the case that corporations had a humanistic bent to them—that they owed something to society more than material goods. Advertising executive Bruce Barton wrote, in the bestselling *The Man Nobody Knows* (1925), that business was developing a spirit that took into account individual and societal needs, and that, in fact, this was a compassionate orientation that followed the legacy of Jesus' teachings. That same year, public relations pioneer Ivy Lee wrote that organizations should direct their public relations and publicity efforts with "an attitude of citizenship rather than a merely selfish relation to the community at large" (1925, p. 54). Companies engaged in advertising that went beyond touting products and services, projecting the corporation as a good citizen (Marchand, 1998). Other organizations interacted with local clubs while simultaneously deluging newspapers and magazines with pro-business information—all designed to show the corporation as a "friendly giant" (Ewen, 1996, p. 216). Indeed, business leadership in the 1920s increasingly saw itself in the role of balancing the private, profit-making interests of the corporation against community and societal interests—sometimes even getting actively involved in public charities and causes (Heald, 1961; Tedlow, 1976). In sum, prior to the Great Depression, employers had already started making links between the corporate character and individuals in the area of shared traditional American values that centered on individualism, freedom, and social harmony (Fones-Wolf, 1994). Wecter (1971) noted that, by the end of the 1920s, Americans were "never more loyal … to the doctrine of individualism and unhampered private enterprise" (p. 8).

However, the crash of the markets in 1929 and the onset of America's economic depression significantly eroded this store of goodwill. In fact, past business practices that asserted connections between companies and individuals became dated because the Great Depression was unprecedented. In October 1929, when the bull market collapsed, almost 40% of the value of U.S. stocks disappeared within a matter of weeks. Plunging share prices caused more than 100,000 American businesses to fail between 1929 and 1933 (Galbraith, 1955, p. 127). By early 1932, the nation's industrial production was less than half what it had been just 3 years earlier (Ewen, 1996, p. 233; Goldston, 1968, p. 61). The following year, unemployment soared to almost 25%, leaving approximately 17 million people—nearly one third of the American workforce—jobless (Bird, 1966, p. 35). Among those still employed, many witnessed large wage cuts, while others held tenuous part-time jobs. Farm income, which had been flat throughout the 1920s, was devastated even further; between 1929 and 1932, the price of farm goods fell by 50%. Banks collapsed, taking with them a multitude of life savings. Millions of Americans were evicted or lost heavily mortgaged houses and farms, and at least one million Americans took to the road to find means of support (Ewen, 1996, p. 233; Watkins, 1993, pp. 54–55, 57).

The failure of laissez-faire capitalism, and the resultant economic and social upheaval, helped propel Democratic candidate Franklin Delano Roosevelt into the presidency in the 1932 national elections. Promising relief, recovery, and reform, Roosevelt had run on a pledge of a New Deal for the American people

(Ritchie, 2007). The president later summarized the deal as the "use of the authority of government as an organized form of self-help for all classes and groups and sections of our country" (Roosevelt, 1937, p. 8). From the beginning, FDR stressed collectivism, asserting that it was the government's responsibility to serve Americans' *communal* interest. Roosevelt pointed out the importance of unity, in thought and action, of the American people. "I assume unhesitatingly the leadership of this great army of our people dedicated to a disciplined attack upon our common problems," he said in his inaugural address in 1933 (quoted in Wall, 2008, p. 36). This war metaphor stressed a sense of urgency and solemnity and sought to unify all citizens in the drive to restore economic stability. The Roosevelt administration believed in the power of government to facilitate a harmony of interests; it pursued legislation that created work projects, established new labor laws, and raised taxes on industry. As business and political interests increasingly accused the White House of working to establish socialism or communism, FDR countered that his efforts to rehabilitate a sense of security might be new and revolutionary, but the times required such methods (Ewen, 2006).

The National Association of Manufacturers' challenge

Just 9 months after Roosevelt took office, Robert Lund, president of the National Association of Manufacturers (NAM), asserted that business interests needed to move past their old tendencies toward self-satisfaction and begin to articulate the value that business offered to society. "We must come back to the fundamental fact that, unless we reach the people, others will, and the prejudice they create is more than likely to be injurious," he said (Lund, 1933). Starting in 1934, NAM had $36,000 budgeted for public communication and engaged in some preliminary efforts—primarily sending out news materials, editorials, and cartoons for use by local NAM chapters (Fones-Wolf, 1994, p. 25; St. John III, 2010). Despite these initial efforts, it appeared that business as a whole was not well-prepared to articulate the value it brought to society. In 1934, one Texas manufacturer said that "the capitalist system can be destroyed more effectively by having men of means defend it than by importing a million Reds from Moscow to attack it" (quoted in Perkins, 1934, p. 619). Batchelor (1938) noted that the days of thinking of business' influence as "impregnably entrenched" were over, as "the American people today regard industry with suspicion and distrust" (p. 4). That concern appeared to be well-founded. By 1935, a *Fortune* magazine survey revealed that over 80% of the lower-middle class, the poor, and African Americans believed that government should ensure that every American who desired to work should have a job ("The Fortune survey," 1935, p. 67). A 1936 poll by the Psychological Corporation found that nearly 75% of the public was not sensitive to business' concern that government policies might have been hurting free enterprise (Batchelor, 1938, p. 48). In fact, NAM's own polling in 1937 found, rather, that citizens cast a cynical eye on business' role, with over 65% of Americans saying that the business sector had not done enough to attack unemployment (NAM, 1937, p. 4). So it is not surprising that NAM ramped up its public relations budget in 1937 to $793,000, more than half of NAM's income for that year (Fones-Wolf, 1994, p. 25). That figure is a modest indication of NAM's willingness to engage the public about the benefits of business—it also received more than $3 million combined in free radio, newspaper, and outdoor advertising in 1937 alone (Tedlow, 1976, p. 33).

NAM, a pro-industry trade group founded in 1895, did not come to this effort naturally; for decades the association saw itself as primarily dedicated to thwarting unionism, with no need for a concomitant high-visibility, public role (Ewen, 1996; Tedlow, 1976, 1979). But NAM realized that the advent of the New Deal was about more than the issuance of laws and policies that enabled the growth of unions: it also brought about a heightened role for the state in the average American's life. There was a shift in the public's definition of what it meant to be an American. That sense of self-definition increasingly moved away from the individualistic and harmonious tones that business maintained was a cornerstone of the country. Instead, Americanism, among workers in particular, was becoming associated "with such terms as economic equality, social justice, and human rights, in particular the right to a decent wage and to security from poverty, ill health, unemployment, and old age" (Fones-Wolf, 1994, p. 17).

NAM's decision to ramp up its public relations program in 1937 was, in large part, propelled by several turns in events. For one, the 1936 elections saw Roosevelt returned to the presidency with an overwhelming majority in the electoral college, and the Democrats holding an almost a 4:1 majority in the House of Representatives and almost a 5:1 majority in the Senate. The president was not hesitant about leveraging such a mandate, encouraging Americans to be skeptical of business interests which insisted that the public should return to seeing corporations as the heroes they once were. America's salvation, he said, does not come from "the vesting of power in the hands of a select class"; instead, the will of business elites, like NAM, should never be allowed to rule and supersede "the principle of the greater good for the greater number, which is the cornerstone of democratic government" ("Text of," 1937, p. 21). While FDR amplified criticism against business as economic royalists, critics noted that corporations focused too much on appearances and not on building relationships with communities (Walker & Sklar, 1938). NAM's own planning documents from this time period revealed that observations from Paul Garrett (the public relations director for General Motors) and reports from surveys of business people indicated their sector needed to assume a more substantive public posture and express the difference it made to everyday lives of Americans (NAM, n.d.a.).

Moreover, NAM's internal documents revealed that, in 1937, the public was in a better position to hear the association's messages about the value of industry and free enterprise. A memorandum that details the role of NAM's public-information program pointed out that public opinion was shifting against the New Deal. "Doubt is replacing blind faith in panaceas which have failed to produce either the promised prosperity or, for that matter, any substantial recovery," it said (NAM, 1937, p. 1). The spread of communism and socialism in other parts of the world, it continued, allowed NAM even more opportunities to contrast those problematic systems against the benefits of American free enterprise. In doing so, it noted, NAM could encourage Americans to count their blessings and develop a harmonious resurgence in patriotism (NAM, 1937). Although the memo did not offer facts to support these assertions, it pointed out that there was an increasing demand for the association's educational information (e.g., booklets, short films). This was, it said, an indication of an "almost universal search for the facts about our democracy, our system of free enterprise and private initiative" (NAM, 1937, p. 2). The way to make clear links between the character of business and individuals' concerns—and to establish "permanent understanding and good will"—was to demonstrate that industry's existence was important to upholding democracy for all: "The public must be convinced that *free enterprise is as much an indivisible part of democracy* and the source of as many blessings and benefits as are our other freedoms of speech, press and religion" (NAM 1937, p. 3, emphasis added).

Another undated and extensive public relations planning document from the time period, called "A Suggested Public Relations Program for Smithville" (the town name acting as a generic reference to the average American mid-size city) laid out NAM's challenge. "…We have as our problem the presentation of facts concerning industry as a whole and to create a better public acceptance for what we call 'the American system of private enterprise,'" it said (NAM, n.d.a., p. 1). Americans needed to better understand that the capitalist system provided for the material well-being of all classes and did so better than any other system known to man, the document continued. Moreover, the public needed to realize that industry did more than focus on products and profits, because it realized it also had "definite responsibilities to its employees, to the public and to the development by progress and evolution of a more stable economic system" (NAM, n.d.a., p. 1). What had greatly necessitated this need to enlighten the public, it said, was that the U.S. government, beset with "false leaders … seeking selfish ends," had distributed fragmentary and misleading information about business in America (NAM, n.d.a., p. 2). To combat this disservice to the populace, NAM needed to share its point of view in a straightforward and factual way but "not in a spirit of defending, preaching or even teaching" (NAM, n.d.a., p. 2). Instead, people needed to have the sensation that they were drawing their own conclusions, said the Smithville plan. The best way to accomplish this, the document said, was to stress that what industry did (e.g., through payrolls, paying of taxes, charitable contributions, etc.) aligned with the well-being of Americans and their communities. The plan indicated that the best way to reach key audiences (including "foremen, workmen, clergymen, teachers, lawyers, doctors" and members of churches, unions and "foreign racial groups") was through short motion pictures, slide films, speakers' bureaus, workplace posters, direct mail, and newspapers (NAM, n.d.a., p. 4).

In the following years, NAM followed through on this document's assertions, bolstered by emerging trends they saw as opportunities for industry to assert its public face. In 1938, James Selvage of NAM's public relations department noted a growing resistance to labor's influence in the public arena, with more members of the Senate voting against sit-down strikes, and the House taking steps to investigate labor movements. These events, though heartening, were only a partial rebuke of "unscrupulous unionism and radicalism," he said. NAM should capitalize on them by promoting "better understanding between all the forces in a city responsible for its progress and prosperity" (Selvage, 1938, pp. 1–2). By 1940, with the intensification of World War II, NAM sensed that the association needed to make a few adjustments. Minutes from a meeting of the public relations advisory group that year noted that, since 1937, NAM had adopted some sound approaches that were effectively making logical contrasts between the rise of totalitarianism abroad and the ability of the free enterprise system to stymie possible similar dictators in the U.S. It held that free enterprise was showing that these government bureaucrats could not deliver on the promises of a planned economy through the New Deal (NAM, 1940a). In addition to pointing out free enterprise's defense of domestic economic freedom, NAM played on Americans' growing awareness of threats from militaristic nations overseas. NAM was well-positioned, said the advisory group, to point out how business could act as the key resource, in case the country needed to go on a war-time footing. Speaking of both the international peril of war and the domestic threat of a planned economy, the group wrote that business was the source of the physical weapons and the high standard of living which could prevent "isms" (e.g., collectivism, socialism, Nazism, etc.) from taking over the country. Accordingly, NAM would be intensifying the message that "What is good for industry is good for you" and exposing the fallacies of "isms" by focusing on "outright Americanism" (NAM, 1940a, p. 3). To accomplish this, the association continued its reliance on multiple outreach approaches (e.g., speakers' bureaus, mass media, and internal communication materials for employers). An undated report circa 1940 noted that NAM had made substantial inroads into getting newspapers to pick up the association's offerings: more than 200 daily newspapers carried a regular NAM economic-expert column, and 1,600 weekly newspapers subscribed to its weekly pro-business cartoon service (NAM, n.d.b., p. 2). The outreach to newspapers alone was a significant investment; in 1940, the association reported that its regular news service (e.g., distribution of pre-written, pro-business news stories), distributed to some 7,300 small-town newspapers and 593 large dailies, cost over $81,000 (NAM, n.d.c., p. 1).

The years leading up to the U.S.' entry into World War II, then, are a particularly revealing period to examine how the National Association of Manufacturers used these public relations strategies and tactics to demonstrate to the public that business had a persona that Americans could relate to and, furthermore, see as an affinitive entity that shared their own goals and values. After December 7, 1941, when America went on a full-fledged war footing, the concomitant rise of war-related messages (from the media, government, and other business sectors) would allow NAM to amplify its communication about the role industry played in preserving the American way of life. But selling such a message in the pre-war America of the late 1930s and early 40s had a different dynamic—the crisis at hand was a loss of faith in American business' ability to right the devastation of the Great Depression. In examining this particularly daunting challenge for NAM, one finds that the association attempted to convey, through multiple vehicles, three main points: (1) that it shared values common to Americans; (2) that it was a beneficent fellow actor in society; and (3) that turning to alternatives, like a planned economy or socialism, would interfere with the mutually beneficial relationship between the individual and the private company.

We share common values

NAM's messaging made appeals to prevailing American sensibilities, most notably U.S. exceptionalism's valorizing of the individual as uniquely self-starting, self-reliant, and ever-bent on an autonomous drive to improve one's condition. One in a series of circa-1938 talking points (designed for use by NAM members at local community events) pointed out that Americans created a society based on freedom, democracy, and the importance of free enterprise. The individual is predominant, informed by a sense of cooperation with others to achieve the greatest overall benefit. America, then, was a country "wrought by creative and instructed minds, thrifty and hard-working bodies, inspired and consecrated souls," NAM said, resulting in the "most prosperous, happy and developed" of all nations (NAM, n.d.d., p. 1). The average person's sense of drive, persistence, and need to accomplish helped make America what it was, said the association. Another set of concurrent talking points said that what lay behind the increase in productivity—which led to more jobs, higher wages, and increases in leisure time—was the American individual's push for progress. All Americans were interested in their future and how to "earn more money, have better homes and more of the good things in life in the years to come," leading to an increase in the standard of living that was the envy of the world (NAM, n.d.e., p. 1). Through their ingenious applications of machinery, Americans had devised a system of industry that "succeeded better than any ever devised by man …" making it possible, NAM claimed, for the country to realistically do away with the possibility of the "underprivileged" (NAM, n.d.e., p. 7).

In 1939, NAM released a 20-page pamphlet that asserted an indivisibility in how the corporation operated in the marketplace and the importance that Americans placed on freedom. Early in the document, NAM said that there was a symbiosis between the country's democratic system, the free market, and individuals' liberties. Those fundamental aspects of American freedom should be preserved, it said, because they had "made possible the development of our natural and human resources, and … resulted in the greatest degree of personal freedom" while also leading to America developing an unparalleled standard of living (NAM, 1939, p. 1). NAM articulated that individual drive reflected that everyone wanted to achieve both the daily necessities and luxuries but that we also wanted to feel culturally and spiritually satisfied. Our democratic and free market system helps Americans achieve such ends because it allows the individual to feel secure "in his liberties and for his person, in his job and for his old age, in himself and for his family" (NAM, 1939, p. 1). Furthermore, with our system, individual initiative and corporations work together to allow people to realize these aims as both pursue a course "on a plane of enlightened self-interest" (NAM, 1939, p. 2).

One of NAM's core appeals to Americans was the enterprising actor—the everyday person and the company—doing well. Howard Coonley, the association chairman, pointed out that Americans are focused more on being productive than on achieving security through someone or something else. Coonley continued, offering a view of the American person that found a sense of fuller life through a market-enabled self-direction that had little need for the New Deal:

> It is to safeguard our people from moral and spiritual decay, to preserve their standards of life, to maintain their liberty that we must labor to save a free system of economic activity—a system premised on freedom to learn, freedom to think, freedom to worship, freedom to plan and invent, freedom to acquire, freedom to invest, freedom to give. America was not forged out of the wilderness by men who were seeking security. Theirs was a quest for freedom and the only security they asked was that of opportunity to work out their own destinies in their own way.
>
> (Coonley, 1940, p. 9)

By mid-1940, NAM issued additional speaking points that asserted more firmly the link between the corporation and the citizen. The association claimed an inseparable bond between the country's representative democracy, its freedoms of expression (e.g., the press, religion, right to assemble), and its free marketplace, which it called the "Tripod of Liberty." Henning Prentiss, NAM's president, stated that American business cherished all three areas. Corporations understood that these tripod elements reflected "the spiritual principle of the sanctity of the individual soul" which, was the "foundation of our entire American system…" ("Industry ready," 1940, p. 24). Concurrently, former NAM president Colby Chester affirmed that business understood, appreciated, and sought to amplify Americans' essential, self-directed nature. Americans were just plain different, he said, and citizens needed to be reminded that

> …we can run faster, build taller buildings, eat more, jump higher than anyone else; … our women are lovelier; our men are more honest; our children smarter; our history more dazzling than that of any people on the face of the globe. America needs to be reminded that we can lick our weight in wildcats … that we build a bungalow or a school for every outhouse a dictator builds.
>
> (NAM, 1940a, pp. 27–28)

NAM continued to develop this message and, 6 months before Pearl Harbor, it released the short pamphlet "I'm Glad I'm an American." Indirectly referencing the international and domestic strife of World War II, the pamphlet began with a recitation of the tripod elements but then quickly went into how Americans were not going to follow the path of violent or revolutionary actions to express themselves. Rather, Americans knew that their institutions would respond to affect the changes demanded by public opinion. It said that Americans held "fast to what [was] good," were more constructive than destructive, and did "not covet the land or resources of other nations..." (NAM, 1941a, p. 2). The reason Americans, for the most part, were sanguine lay in its citizens' understanding that they were "better off here than elsewhere" and that they could strive for the opportunity to live their highest standard of living, where other peoples had to struggle with "arbitrary power [that controlled] the minds and work and destinies of men" (NAM, 1941a, p. 2).

Across these several years before U.S. entry into World War II, NAM worked to clearly signal to citizens that it understood the essential nature of the American individual and that, furthermore, business shared these values. In this way, the association attempted to demonstrate that a corporate entity had a seemingly human-like affinity for Americans. Beyond that, NAM offered that both the individual and the organization acted out of a shared worldview and that Americans had an exceptional drive to individually be constructive forces in the world.

Business works as a benevolent fellow actor

One of the most important things to understand about business, NAM stressed, was how it was a beneficent force in the country, a presence that helped Americans realize their desires for progress. One of the best stories of our country, it said in talking points from circa 1938, was not in a movie or theater. Instead, it was the drama of American industry, a story

> ...that has enjoyed an unbroken run of more than 162 years, one which has 11 million people in the cast, that cost $13 trillion in payrolls last year to enact, that vitally effects every one's life, and plays night and day to bring comforts and better living to its audience.
>
> (NAM, n.d.f., p. 1)

Furthermore, Americans could have confidence that all businesses, from smallest to largest, had a key role in making a better life for all citizens, it said. In fact, business enterprises could not exist to satisfy only selfish aims. For example, manufacturers employed 25% of all the workforce and had to take into account how what they did rippled across other businesses and communities. Many large manufacturers and other companies had stockholders, and those companies had to account for their shareholders' interests. Finally, society, through its demands for products and services, necessarily called upon business to get beyond any selfish temptation and act in a way that showed it realized that "the well-being of every person in this country [was] directly or indirectly connected with industrial progress" (NAM, n.d.g., p. 5). Businessmen understood that what they did effected society and had to work to bring initiatives that would help the most people, demonstrating "What's good for business is good for you. There is no begging that fact" (NAM, n.d.g., p. 6). Workers had good wages, good working hours, and the ability to save and invest in life insurance, showing that the "free land of free enterprise with the cooperation of industry and the public [had] resulted in the highest standard of living" in the world (NAM, n.d.d., p. 2). In fact, business and the free enterprise system had allowed us to mine the gifts of the terrain (e.g., aluminum, paper) just like we could individually harvest music, poetry, and drama from "the mystic souls of men with the dynamic urge of creation" (NAM, n.d.d., p. 4)

Circa 1940, NAM issued a pamphlet that laid out some figures about the beneficial effects of a hypothetical manufacturing plant in an average community with a population of 1,650. A plant of 150 employees would bring an annual payroll of $180,000, with the total amount of yearly turnover of money (i.e., exchange of monies among different service providers, retailers in the community, etc.) of more than $7 million. Additionally, based on the average American family size of four, the plant salaries would directly support 600 people in such a community. Finally, for every one plant job, more than four other jobs would be created in the community; essentially, the plant would have helped create a working population of 650 (NAM, n.d.h., p. 2). NAM asserted that this was one case study of how business and Americans relied upon each other. This dynamic, it said,

> is repeated and multiplied the country over, until, in great sum total, we have America—the greatest industrial nation in the world, the country with the highest standard of living and the best and happiest communities yet conceived by man!
>
> (NAM, n.d.h., p. 3)

Not surprisingly, a 1940 NAM speakers' bureau talk on private enterprise pointed out that, through business, more families had access to goods and services than ever before, with America leading the world in inventions over the previous 50 years. The country's health and education had also improved. Living could be even better if it were not for the New Deal's nettlesome socialistic tendencies, according to NAM. "Sometimes we even indulged in a little prophecy and painted a glowing picture of the still more abundant life that private industry, *freed from present handicaps*, could bring about in the next decade," it noted (NAM, 1940b, p. 8, emphasis added).

By the middle of 1941, the association asserted in a short pamphlet that Americans, assisted through the enabling force of business, were able to display clearly that they, and not some privileged class, owned America. There was no marked concentration of wealth in the U.S., it said, because the free enterprise system allowed for Americans to fully participate in the production of financial wealth (e.g., small business owners) and comfort wealth (e.g., owning material goods). It cited the example of a Notre Dame, Indiana, study that found that less than 50% of the total national wealth was involved in production; within that production wealth, 25% was "owned by individual farmers, another substantial fraction by individual businesses and professional men" (NAM, 1941b, pp. 2–3). It also pointed out that the same study said most Americans share in comfort wealth (e.g., autos, appliances, etc.); NAM asserted this was no surprise, as the latest U.S. Department of Commerce figures showed "that the portion of the national income going to wage and salary earners [had] been increasing for many decades" and continued to do so (NAM, 1941b, p. 5). Americans, who were increasingly owning more wealth, should know that they also owned America, said NAM. Using their own energies and initiatives, they were choosing freely within our private enterprise system, which furthered their ability to build the "wealth and income which distinguish this nation" (NAM, 1941b, p. 5).

We need to stick with free enterprise

Accompanying NAM's assertions of consonance with individual values and the beneficence it brought to Americans was an urgent appeal: the people needed to join with industry in holding fast to free enterprise. Both domestically and internationally, it said, there were actors who sought to magnify the power of the state by attempting to persuade the average American that governmental actions could bring about a better society and an increased sense of security for all. With this line of reasoning, NAM obviously was critiquing the continued popularity of the New Deal, but it was also speaking to other pressures like the collective actions of unions and the rise of socialism and communism around the globe. NAM's rhetoric, however, was mostly directed at the state. Another one of the speaker's bureau talking points from circa 1938 specifically rebuffed criticism against corporations, calling such critiques the words of "exuberant theorists and calculating agitators" that were designed to centralize "economic and legislative power in the hands of the federal government" (NAM, n.d.i., p. 1). It held that Americans needed to be on guard against government's propensity for a planned economy; it led to too much state intervention in the marketplace, including legislation that reduced incentives to invest, costly overregulation beyond necessary public safeguards, and wealth redistribution policies that imposed overly burdensome taxes on business. Such actions were based, in large part, on "utopian philosophies" that actually did damage to the American system and needed to be resisted (NAM, n.d.i., p. 2). An invasive state hurt profits and, in turn, damaged the well-being of the average American because "profits are nothing more nor less than public welfare" (NAM, n.d.i., p. 10).

Around this same time, a report from one of NAM's committees put forth clearly that the state's tendency to intervene in the market needed to be actively resisted. The association said that the federal government was pushing economic collectivism—or a planned economy—that was injurious to the economic welfare of the citizenry. Furthermore, "freedom of the individual in those fields of human interest which [were] not economic, such as religion or culture, [could] not be maintained in the face of collective control of his economic interests" (NAM, n.d.j., p. 2). Such centralized planning—an approach that relied on bureaucrats attempting to balance production and distribution against consumption demands—could not work because it simply went against the American individual's inclination toward progress and creation. The free market revealed that individuals were putting forth innovative products that the state could not envision how to develop or manage, it stated. "Social engineering has lagged behind mechanical engineering," said NAM, and private enterprise was best situated to roll out products and services and, through a responsiveness borne from the profit motive, make the proper adjustments (NAM, n.d.j., p. 3).

The association's 1939 pamphlet on the principles of American industry stated explicitly that the planned economy was a harbinger of the totalitarian state. It was an alien system that was repellent to Americans since it destroyed "personal liberty, religious freedom and individual initiative" (NAM, 1939, p. 3). Furthermore, planned economies were inflexible and could not meet the demands required of production chiefly because "no one man, no one central authority attempting to dictate the operating practice in industry [had] the knowledge required to solve these problems" (NAM, 1939, p. 3). Only the profit motive and competition could generate the knowledge and understanding necessary to drive the complex components of an industrial enterprise that benefited everyone, it maintained. Americans needed to have faith in the free enterprise system, said NAM, because the free marketplace was the "guarantor of individual opportunity" (NAM, 1939, p. 19). Corporations showed that they were the true actors for social welfare because they provided employment, goods, and services that benefited all. Then, they received profits which, in turn, allowed them to continue their efforts, lifting the standards of living of the American individual. The profit motive, not a planned economy, was the engine that drove this virtuous circle—it created "a stimulus that works for the public good," fortifying people "with hope and purpose [of] the spirit..." (NAM, 1939, pp. 19–20).

As NAM warned against collectivism in 1940, it made sure to point out that freedom was under attack. This was no surprise, it said, because such attacks happened when there was "economic difficulty and confusion, when people [were] filled with fear" (NAM, 1940b, p. 6). State officials who wanted to control events and people pursued powers and privileges in a pledge to restore order and re-install prosperity. The people listened and believed, and over time the state leadership expanded its control until the entire tripod was put in jeopardy. This was a very real threat, it warned, because when there was a hardening of centralized control, the planners would no longer allow their schemes to be questioned, resulting in the disappearance of other civic freedoms of speech, press, and assembly. When this happened, representative government would only be a hollow structure (NAM, 1940b).

Americans could avoid such calamities by holding to the rewards and promises of the free enterprise system, urged NAM. The corporation, and not the state, was the actual fellow sojourner on the journey of the American way that understood—and more than that, contributed to—everyone's welfare. In undated speaker's bureau points from circa 1940, NAM said:

> Free initiative and individual enterprise upon the foundations of honest and intelligent competition is at the very heart of the American way. Honest profit for industrious endeavor is a vital part of the American way of life. Well-conceived and well-supported industry is essential to the American way of life. The American Government is one where the people tell the Government what to do and never where the Government tells the people what to do.
>
> (NAM, n.d.k., p. 1)

What of the corporate persona?

During these strife-filled years for business, it is clear that the National Associ-ation of Manufacturers worked hard to approximate a public face for industry—that of a caring, fellow American who shared similar values, worked in mutual benefit with its fellow Americans and urged its fellow citizens to protect the common gains achieved by resisting those who would want to plan the economy. In many ways, this seems like an intuitive approach; NAM had chapters at local levels throughout the country, and its membership included smaller enterprises where it was possible for management to be known by local community members. However, elements of its approach went beyond that: the association used several large-scale media forms (e.g., daily newspapers and movie formats) to reach across the country, while it also built into its approach behind-the-scenes outreach to various other associations and networks, in such arenas as farming, education, and religion. In sum, NAM's domestic public relations cam-paign was extensive, and its multilayered approach could have allowed it to diverge from its central messages, which stressed the projection of industry as a large, beneficent, fellow corporate American. But, as this chapter shows, and as has been indicated in other scholarship (Ewen, 1996; St. John III, 2010; St. John III & Arnett, 2014; Tedlow, 1979), NAM displayed a remarkable consistency in proffering core messages that relayed who business was and what it stood for. Across these years, NAM made a clear appeal: the valiant American can best realize his or her fullest life in cooperation with the corporate presence, which is also valiantly struggling to achieve its highest successes in the face of a med-dling federal government.

One scholar, noting the association's extensive activities, asked, "Business could tell its story over and over again, but what if no one cared to listen?" (Phillips-Fein, 2009, p. 15). However, there is some evidence that NAM's cam-paign achieved effects. In 1937, a national poll revealed that about 60% of Americans had an unfavorable impression of business (NAM, 1937, p. 4). By 1939, NAM released a poll that showed that Americans had more trust in busi-ness: 60% said that the government should look to business for advice in prompting the country's economic recovery ("Curbs on industry," 1939, p. 18).

Two years later, NAM released a poll that found that almost three quarters of Americans said they feared their liberty would be in jeopardy if the government ran the marketplace, signaling that the free enterprise system was essential to their sense of personal freedom ("NAM finds," 1941, p. 15). Indeed, as Fones-Wolf pointed out, this time period (and into the 1950s) showed that business worked hard, and somewhat successfully, to project itself as a socially conscious "good neighbor" that worked effectively to "redefine the meaning of American-ism to emphasize individualistic as opposed to mutualistic ways of dealing with inequality" (1994, p. 10). More directly, NAM's appeals affirmed that the corpo-ration was a fellow individual who worked in tandem with Americans. It stressed that individuals should focus on what they could accomplish with the support of the corporate person. Systemic concerns, like inequality, social stratification, concentrations of power, and privilege were not something that the individual should allow to become points of divergence from the journey toward self-reliance, accomplishment, and progress. That individual sojourn was fulfilling, exceptionally rewarding and, indeed, core to what it meant to be an American, NAM asserted. It said, circa 1940, in its speakers' bureau discussion of the American way:

> What a way of life it is. From the challenge of an open and undeveloped continent to the present paradise of the people. Where health, happiness and conditions of working and living are the best the world knows. Even a depression in America is a luxury in any other part of the world.
>
> (NAM, n.d.k., p. 1)

By the beginning of the 1950s, America was well past the Great Depression and World War II, but corporate concerns persisted about the lingering presence of a robust domestic government and the continuing rise of communism around the world. The public relations industry was well-positioned to speak to those con-cerns, with more than 4,000 companies employing public relations programs at the onset of the 1950s (Davenport, 1951). The time was conducive for the public relations industry to acknowledge what NAM had learned about the value of the corporate persona—that is, that public relations could use this approach to demonstrate that corporations, and not the government, were the true construc-tive force in American society.

References

Allen, F. (1952). *The big change: America transforms itself, 1900–1950.* New York: Harper & Row.

Barton, B. (1925). *The man nobody knows: A discovery of the real Jesus.* Indianapolis: The Bobbs-Merrill Company.

Batchelor, B. (1938). *Profitable public relations.* New York: Harper & Brothers.

Bird, C. (1966). *The invisible scar.* New York: Pocket Books.

Cochran, T. (1957). *The American business system: A historical perspective, 1900–1955.* Cambridge: Harvard University Press.

Coonley, H. (1940). *Responsibilities of management.* Speech given at Annual Meeting of the National Retail dry Goods Association, January 16. NAM Archives, Hagley Museum and Library, Wilmington, DE.Acc. 1411, Box 110, Series 1.

"Curbs on industry found unpopular." (1939). *New York Times*, December 8, p. 18.

Davenport, R. (1951). *U.S.A.: The permanent revolution.* New York: Prentice-Hall.

Dumenil, L. (1995). *The modern temper: American culture and society in the 1920s.* New York: Hill and Wang.

Ewen, S. (1996). *PR! A social history of spin.* New York: Basic Books.

Fones-Wolf, E. (1994). *Selling free enterprise: The business assault on labor and liberalism, 1945–60.* Urbana, IL: University of Illinois Press.

"The Fortune survey." (1935). *Fortune*, July 1935, p. 67.

Galbraith, J.K. (1954). *The Great Crash: 1929.* New York: Houghton Mifflin.

Goldston, R. (1968). *The Great Depression: The United States in the thirties.* Greenwich, CT: Fawcett.

Hawkins, D. (1963). "The development of modern financial reporting practices among American manufacturing corporations." *Business History Review 37*(3), pp. 135–168.

Heald, M. (1961). "Business thought in the twenties: Social responsibility." *American Quarterly 13*(2), pp. 126–139.

"Industry ready to battle for private rights." (1940). *Chicago Daily Tribune*, April 1, p. 24.

Lee, I. (1925). *Publicity: Some of the things it is and is not.* New York: Industries Publishing Company.

Lund, R. (1933). *Industry's opportunity and duty under the recovery plan.* Speech delivered to the National Association of Manufacturers Convention, New York, December 7. NAM Archives, Acc. 1411, Box 112, Series I,

Marchand, R. (1998). *Creating the corporate soul: The rise of public relations and corporate imagery.* Berkeley: University of California Press.

NAM. (1937). "The role of the NAM public information program." [Unpublished memorandum]. NAM Archives, Acc. 1411, Box 111, Series I.

NAM. (1939, December 8). *Declaration of principles relating to the conduct of American industry.* [Pamphlet]. NAM Archives, Acc. 1411, Box 110, Series 1.

NAM. (1940a, July). "Speaker bulletin: Quotable quotes." NAM Archives, Acc. 1411, Box110, Series 1.

NAM. (1940b). "Your stake in private enterprise." [Talking points]. NAM Archives, Acc. 1411, Box 110, Series I.

NAM. (1941a). *I'm glad I'm an American.* [Pamphlet]. NAM Archives, Acc. 1411, Box 111, Series 1.

NAM. (1941b, June). *Who owns America?* [Pamphlet]. NAM Archives, Acc. 1411, Box 111, Series I.

NAM. (n.d.a.). "A suggested public relations program for Smithville." NAM Archives, Acc. 1411, Box 111, Series 1.

NAM. (n.d.b.). "What the weekly editors say of NAM service." NAM Archives, Acc. 1411, Box 112, Series 1.

NAM. (n.d.c.). "PR advisory group subcommitee report on press services and advertising." NAM Archives, Acc. 1411, Box 113, Series 1.

NAM. (n.d.d.). "Industry and the public." [Talking points]. NAM Archives, Acc. 1411, Box 110, Series 1.

NAM. (n.d.e.). "More for your money—The pattern of American progress." NAM Archives, Acc. 1411, Box 110, Series I.

NAM. (n.d.e.). "Mutual interest." [Talking points]. NAM Archives, Acc. 1411, Box 110, Series 1.

NAM. (n.d.g.). "Your stake in industry." [Talking points]. NAM Archives, Acc. 1411, Box 110, Series 1.

NAM. (n.d.h.). "Industryville: The story of your town." NAM Archives, Acc. 1411, Box 110, Series 1.

NAM. (n.d.i.). "Your city's stake in industry." [Talking points]. NAM Archives, Acc. 1411, Box 115, Series 1.

NAM. (n.d.j.). "The characteristics of the American free enterprise system." [Committee report]. NAM Archives, Acc. 1411, Box 111, Series 1.

NAM. (n.d.k.). "The American way." [Talking points]. NAM Archives, Acc. 1411, Box 110, Series 1.

"NAM finds 11 fallacies bar to recovery." (1941). *Christian Science Monitor*, January 6, p. 15.

Perkins, M. (1934). "Grab the torch, men of means, grab the torch!" *Nation*, November 28, pp. 618–619.

Phillips-Fein, K. (2009). *Invisible hands: The businessmen's crusade against the New Deal*. New York: W.W. Norton.

Ritchie, D.A. (2007). *Electing FDR: The New Deal campaign of 1932*. Lawrence, KS: University Press of Kansas.

Roosevelt, F.D. (1937). *Public papers of the presidents of the United States—1933*. New York: Random House.

Selvage, J. (1938). "Memorandum of community public information programs to combat radical tendencies and present the constructive story of industry." NAM Archives, Acc. 1411, Box 111, Series 1.

St. John III, B. (2010). *Press professionalization and propaganda: The rise of journalistic double-mindedness, 1917–1941*. Amherst, NY: Cambria Press.

St. John III, B., & Arnett, R. (2014). "The National Association of Manufacturers' commmunity relations short film 'Your Town': Parable, propaganda, and big individualism." *Journal of Public Relations Research 26*(2), pp. 103–116.

Tedlow, R. (1976). "The National Association of Manufacturers and public relations during the New Deal." *The Business History Review 50*(1), pp. 25–45.

Tedlow, R. (1979). *Keeping the corporate image: Public relations and business, 1900–1950*. Greenwich, CT: JAI Press.

"Text of President Roosevelt's address at Virginia Dare celebration on Roanoke Island." (1937). *Washington Post*, August 19, p. 21.

Walker, S.H., & Sklar, P. (1938). *Business finds it voice: Management's effort to sell the business idea to the public*. New York: Harper and Brothers.

Wall, W. (2008). *Inventing the "American way": The politics of consensus from the New Deal to the Civil Rights Movement*. Oxford: Oxford University Press.

Watkins, T.H. (1993). *The Great Depression: America in the 1930s*. Boston: Little, Brown.

Wecter, D. (1971). *The age of the Great Depression, 1929–1941*. Chicago: Quadrangle Books.

4 *PR News*

Public relations describes the corporate persona

Howard Chase noted in 1952 that "public relations should always be remembered as an operating philosophy by which worthy institutions can become part of the daily lives of the people they serve" ("From the PR," 1952a, p. 2). By the time he had spoken these words, he had completed stints as a corporate public relations executive for both General Mills and General Foods, acted as consultant to the Commerce Department and the government's Korean War effort, and served as a public relations director for the Eisenhower presidential campaign. Chase, who later expressed the concept of issues management—a proactive approach to identifying public issues and developing methods to maximize positive outcomes for public relations clients—tended to articulate the idea of people's "daily lives" within a more clinical, rational, and intellectual sphere. Finding ways to show the everyday relevance of the corporation beyond products and services called for acknowledging individuals' propensity to filter life through their own sets of knowledge, values, and dispositions. That same year, *Public Relations News* cited New York City PR consultant G. Edward Pendray's maxims on how public relations could best speak to individuals on this level. Among his observations, the publication offered this paraphrase: "People are interested first of all in people, especially themselves; second, in things; only third in ideas" ("G. Edward Pendray," 1952, p. 2).

Two years earlier, Russell Davenport of *Fortune* magazine noted, during an address at a Midwest public relations conference, that corporations were displaying a new approach, a "principle of private initiative in social matters" ("Case study—St. Louis," 1950, p. 3). The editor of a hospital trade magazine similarly noted that company executives were pushing for a "closer contact and communication" between their companies and employees and community members, part of what he called a "human communication era" ("Examples," 1950, p. 2). What these observers highlighted was a notable development in public relations in the mid-20th-century U.S.—the conceptualizing of the corporation as an entity that could appear as a human-like, good citizen. Public relations was about the projection of a client's abilities, ideals, and aims to others in a favorable way, much like an individual makes good impressions on others, said public relations scholar Rex Harlow. This is similar to what individuals learn in kindergarten, when children are taught "that it pays to be good, even if this goodness consists merely in elementary regard for the comfort and property rights of others," he said (Harlow, 1942, p. 2). Displaying common cause between business and the individual was key. With such an association, he said, corporations could help make a bridge across any "stream of suspicion" that may persist between business and the citizenry by emphasizing to the individual a "mental and even sentimental partnership" (Harlow, 1942, p. 36). Verne Burnett (1943), VP of public relations for General Foods, described a company's public relations as analogous to behaving as a constructive fellow community member. This meant

> ....getting along well with the whole community—at least the part of it we rub elbows with ... We aren't slow in paying the doctor and dentist. As we observe the laws, written and unwritten; as we go out of our way to understand, like, and help other people, we are not only happier ourselves, but also we win more real friends ... Public relations, therefore, can be called a way of life—and a very good one.
>
> (Burnett, 1943, p. 8)

At the start of the 1950s, others talked about how public relations offered an anthropomorphic portrayal of the corporation. MacDonald (1948) said that how well a company's public relations outreach works is greatly determined by how well the corporation exemplifies "certain human attributes—integrity, unselfishness, frankness and sincerity" (p. 525). Fitzgerald (1950) similarly pointed out that "direct, intimate communication" was increasingly a province of good public relations (p. 225). He referred to criticisms of the modern world (increasing mass transportation and mass communication) and how it had frayed Americans' sense of community cohesion. He maintained that public relations must be part of a "contrary movement" that speaks for harmony between the corporation and the individual in the community, advocating for the maintenance of the "small, intimate unit" (Fitzgerald, 1950, p. 225). There was immense value in a corporation being seen as a fellow good citizen and neighbor, said Lundborg (1950), so corporations should address the individual's need to belong and encourage a perceived neighborly association with a company (Nielander & Miller, 1951). The corporation's assumption of a benevolent fellow-citizen role meant that it should help promote "the soil of self-help, moistened with mutual assistance, germinated by the warmth of personal friendship..." (Nielander & Miller, 1951, p. 13).

In retrospect, that the mid-20th century saw such an articulation of the helpful corporation as a person appears to be no surprise. As seen in Chapter 3, the National Association of Manufacturers pursued this route on a widespread scale in the years directly before World War II. After that war, the climate in America saw business still gradually recovering from the stain of the Great Depression, yet concerned with the rise of communism and socialism, and outright public ignorance of how business operated and contributed to American society (Fitzgerald, 1950; Lundberg, 1950; Nielander & Miller, 1951). Just 2 years after World War II, a nationwide survey found that 70% of workers thought that government held the key to improving the economy, especially by guaranteeing employment (Fones-Wolf, 1994, p. 36). The country also witnessed significant labor unrest, with the 1950s seeing an average of 352 union-authorized strikes per year (Phillips-Fein, 2009, p. 88). The fear of the dissolution of the American free enterprise system was palpable to several in the public relations field. In 1947, one public relations firm said, "[O]ur present economic system, and the men who run it, have three years—maybe five at the outside—to resell our so-far preferred way of life…" (quoted in Fones-Wolf, 1994, p. 37). Although that was an overstatement, some 6 years later the *Public Relations Journal* warned that business needed to keep up public relations efforts that showed the benefits of business to American life because, if it backed off, "nothing better [could] be expected than a swing again to the left—for the forces of bureaucracy and socialism are forever at it—and they are masters of propaganda" ("Let business," 1953, p. 2).

Bolstering these concerns about threats to American capitalism was a groundswell of free market ideology in the U.S. after World War II and into the 1950s, particularly spurred by the writings of Ludwig von Mises and Friedrich Hayek. Von Mises, in his 1949 book *Human Action*, wrote that free enterprise should not be construed primarily as a mechanism for transactions but, instead, be seen as a space for individuals to fulfill their aspirations through market-oriented action, pursuing activities with no guiding hand, save the logic of the marketplace. Both von Mises and Hayek were latter-day articulators of some of the precepts of selected parts of Adam's Smith late-18th-century conceptions of the invisible hand of the marketplace; both authors were advocates of the marketplace as guide for cooperation and the building of social bonds. Phillips-Fein (2009) noted that, during a time of perceived escalating threats to capitalism, these mid-century scholars promoted a romanticized notion of the individual as someone who was a "creative hero" who possessed a "world-creating power" (p. 36). This view pronounced the marketplace as "the robust force that generated all of life and human production and [was] a terribly fragile entity, threatened on all sides" (Phillips-Fein, 2009, p. 37). Accordingly, these writers' thinking were consonant with business leader concerns that the populace needed to understand that their lives were demonstrably better off with the corporation in the driver's seat. In late 1946, Advertising Council director Thomas D'Arcy Brophy talked about the need for corporate America to fight back against "the loss of faith in our traditions," by selling "the rewards still open to us individually and collectively" when Americans work diligently within its free market system (Griffith, 1983, p. 398). In December 1949, Robert Wood Johnson maintained that the corporation, through what he called "welfare capitalism," was preferable to state interventions because government was "inherently incompetent" (Johnson, 1950, p. 6). He pointed out that corporations needed to remind the citizenry, who were too tempted by socialism, that Americans operate best when they work with business to find solutions in their own backyards; to delay conveying this message was dangerous because "the price of lethargy [was] slavery" to the state (Johnson, 1950, p. 6). Several years later, director of public relations for DuPont Harold Brayman voiced his bewilderment that the public saw business as being primarily focused on profit but saw social planners as being public-minded. "Business desires a full and rich abundance for all people," he said, and the public needed to realize that the corporation was the foundation of how American society developed (Brayman, 1952, p. 4). Simply put, to corporate leaders, the American citizenry was losing its sense of productive individualism through the free market—Americans' thinking displayed a muddled inclination to turn to the government long after the start of the New Deal, revealing significant ignorance about business' constructive force. General Electric's PR director, Lemuel Boulware, said of the 1950s:

> ...too many of us in and out of government and unions and business are joyously, if not hysterically, embracing one after another of the very ideas, influences and features or ingredients of ... collectivism—this socialism that can surely lead us off the deep end into the exact type of police state we so fear.
>
> (Quoted in Phillips-Fein, 2009, p. 102)

There was, however, a regular, weekly publication that spoke in opposition to this perceived slide by touting the virtues of the corporate presence in society— *Public Relations News*. What it offered at the start of the 1950s provides evidence that, in an era where business interests still felt besieged, public relations advanced more notions of the corporation as a well-meaning and essential fellow citizen.

Public Relations News

Public Relations (PR) News was established as the first weekly public relations trade publication by Glenn and Denny Griswold in 1944. Glenn Griswold, who died in 1950, had a background in journalism and in publishing with McGraw-Hill and had worked as a public relations consultant. Denny Griswold, who lived to 2001, had worked in public relations and advertising for such notables as Edward Bernays and Benjamin Sonnenberg and had editorial experience at *Forbes* and *Business Week*. By 1950, the newsletter had achieved widespread interest in the business world—a *Harvard Business Review* poll of executives found that it was the third-most read business digest or newsletter ("Semi-annual," 1949). In a 4-page, text-heavy format, *PR News* offered short updates about recent activities in the public relations field, normally sandwiched between front-page commentary about a notable trend (e.g., how the U.S. government should turn to public relations leaders to help combat communist propaganda) and a description of a case study across its back pages. *PR News* intermittently featured quotes from business leaders and distilled results from recent surveys. The publication, however, was primarily focused on describing the tactical elements of public relations and its role in leadership, writing with an eye toward its broader executive readership. At the start of the 1950s, *PR News* observed that management was primed for learning more about the significance of public relations: its own survey of organizations found that half were increasing their 1951 public relations budget (by an average of about a third), and 44% said they were increasing public relations staff ("Case study—*PR News*," 1951, pp. 3–4). Separately, a president of a major ad firm predicted that PR expenditures in the U.S. for 1951 would total $77 million ("Businesses in," 1951). It pointed out that public relations pioneer T.J. Ross had said there was an increasing "new consciousness" of public relations, and that the business world increasingly perceived "the organization of [public relations] as an active policy and function of management, permeating a whole enterprise" ("From the PR," 1951a, p. 2) Still, there was a need to better orient management to public relations' capabilities: "PR is still gravely misunderstood by a large part of management ... its cardinal importance in policy-making is far from recognized" it said ("One paramount," 1950, p. 2).

This chapter, then, examines how *PR News* offered the message that corporations needed to act in ways that showed they were fellow citizens and good neighbors. Each weekly edition from 1950 to 1952 was reviewed for references to both the free enterprise system and corporations' efforts to engage both internal and external audiences. Informed by grounded theory approaches (Glaser & Strauss, 1967; Keyton, 2015), articles that met the two conditions above were closely read for themes. From this, text within stories were broadly (or "open") coded until various themes emerged across the articles; patterns across those pieces were then linked and further reviewed for what continuities might be apparent. As similar points emerged in the newsletter, two broad thematic categories emerged: the importance of enlightening the public on the benefits that the corporation brings to society, and the benefits of corporations connecting with children.

PR News offered several articles that served as context for why these two approaches were critical. The chairman of General Mills, Harry Bullis, said that a corporation needed to go beyond profit: corporations must also "be considerate, public-spirited, charitable, and concerned with the welfare of the community and nation" ("From the PR," 1952b, p. 2). Corporations must reach out to the "policeman on the corner, the preacher in the pulpit, the teacher in the classroom," said R. Fullerton Place, public relations director for the Greater St. Louis Community Chest, and must cultivate relationships by "letting them know who you are, what you are, and how you serve the community" ("From the PR," 1952c, p. 2). This approach, echoed Robert Semple, president of the Wyandotte Chemical Corporation, called for moving past a focus on a "mythical, unidentifiable public" to acting in the interest of "publics we have at the elbow all the time" ("Major emphasis," 1952, p. 2). Along that line, *PR News* was adamant that open houses were essential for corporations to demonstrate that they were fellow citizens. It said, in 1951 alone, "Industry will spend a record $24 billion this year for new plants and equipment ... [Companies] will be faced with the immediate need for a planned program to become favorably known and understood by the community" ("Case study—new plants," 1951, p. 3). As such, it noted that the open house approach was ideal for making the corporation more relatable, as it was "the most widely used technique" in public relations through-out 1950; corporations were opening their doors to labor officials, civic club members, and taxi cab drivers, it said ("Major attention," 1951, p. 1). Caterpillar Tractor Company of Peoria, Illinois brought in barbers to their plant where its president, Louis B. Neumiller, helped open an on-site discussion with them about local community issues most pressing to them. Neumiller said it was important for the company to build this rapport because barbers "work on the inside as well as the outside" of their customers' heads ("Experience," 1950, p. 2). *PR News* noted that the American Cyanamid Company of Stamford, Con-necticut offered an exemplary approach for demonstrating its contributions to society. A research-heavy facility, it provided the public with tours of its labs, offering plenty of posters, exhibits, and demonstrations of its work. More than 4,000 attendees left with the clear understanding that American Cyanamid served "as a friend to them and all mankind," the publication said ("Community relations," 1950, p. 2).

But corporations did more than hold open houses to show that they were affinitive, human-like entities. When Southern Bell Telephone and Telegraph built a new building in Frankfort, Kentucky, the community wanted a 100-year-old ginkgo tree maintained on the site. The company's developer said it was not possible, so Bell hung large photos of the tree in its lobby and put cuttings in greenhouses so that new sprouts could be grown and transplanted. It also bought two small ginkgo trees and installed them in its new landscape ("Ever hear," 1951). Another utility, Pennsylvania Power and Light, was asked by Lehigh Art Alliance to help an artist initiative that featured portraits of industrial life. The company opened the doors of its Sunbury power plant to artists, leading to the creation of 95 finished works. Then, the company sponsored a traveling exhibi-tion of selected works across its 9,500 square-mile service area ("Industry and art," 1951). The Southern Railway Systems received complaints from com-munities along their tracks—the whistle on their new diesel engines sounded like a "cow in distress." The company changed it to a steam whistle and took out newspaper ads that said, "A little thing? To you perhaps, but not to us! For being a 'good neighbor' to the people we serve is one of the biggest, most important things the Southern Railway System can do" ("Case study—Southern," 1951, p. 4). Showing a similar sensitivity to individuals' aesthetic wishes, New York City's Presbyterian Hospital encouraged patients to select paintings from a menu, which the staff then hung in their rooms ("George Wharton," 1952). For some corporations, showing that they were almost omnipresent in the com-munity was the route to conveying they were persons who could be counted on. Sanger Brothers department stores in Dallas offered weekly talent showcases, lectures by visiting celebrities, club rooms for the PTA, Boy Scout workshops, and free concerts by the local symphony orchestra ("Sanger Brothers," 1950, p. 3). In Marinette, Wisconsin, a city of a little over 14,000, the Ansul Chemical Company offered non-profits the opportunity to use its noon-hour radio program and its movie equipment (and projectionist). It also offered free vocational guidance to high school students and a "rescue squad truck and its crew, on call day or night for emergencies" ("Ansul Chemical," 1952, p. 3).

All of these activities, said *PR News*, were signs that corporations understood they needed to be seen as affinitive and relatable characters. The reason was clear: the times pointed to public relations being called upon to "contribute to the solution of acute social and economic problems on a regional, national and international basis" ("That's the record," 1952, p. 4).

Corporations as the source of enlightenment

Although *PR News* was not prone to polemical positions regarding the power of the state in domestic and international affairs, it maintained that public relations had the responsibility to help organizations tell their fellow citizens about the importance of the free enterprise system. In its second issue in 1950, *PR News* asserted that while, in general, Americans favored their existing economic system, they were still burdened by too much "economic illiteracy" and were prone to vote for politicians and proposals who could "wreck our economy" ("President Truman's," 1950, p. 1). The following week, the publication stated that business leaders were gradually assuming the role of enlightening the public about the strengths of the country's free enterprise system, as opposed to communism and socialism, and were "tying it into self-interest at the community level" ("Outstanding development," 1950, p. 1). It quoted University of Pennsylvania president Harold Stassen urging business to take on the "most important single informational job" in America—to "develop a better understanding by the American workman of the modern capitalistic system" ("Biggest," 1950, p. 1). By the end of 1950, *PR News* proclaimed that public relations must step forward to help corporations act as "mentor and teacher" to the masses about the importance of the American marketplace because "continuing public ignorance threaten[ed] the perpetuation of business" ("Management," 1950, p. 1). Alarmed, the publication pointed to a survey of 500 small-town editors that found 78% of them believed the country was on the road to socialism ("In these," 1950, p. 2). The fact was, said Ben Moreell, president of Jones & Laughlin Steel Corporation, the country was threatened by an increased willingness among Americans to give up their personal freedoms for the sake of security. He said:

> The rejection of personal responsibility, combined with the insistent demand that government guarantee the "welfare" of everyone, can result only in a loss of liberty and a debased economic and social status for all, except that small handful who will direct our destinies.
>
> ("From the PR," 1951b, p. 2)

Similarly, it quoted James Q. du Pont calling upon business people to devote more of their energies to confronting the "creeping fire of statism," by "fighting in the battle of men's minds" ("From the PR," 1952d, p. 2). *PR News* pointed to Borden Company's Milton Fairman urging public relations people to "discharge their responsibilities as citizens" and help corporations push back against fiscal policies that were, said *PR News*, "destructive to the morale and ambitions of the professional and managerial groups in the country" ("A thrilling," 1951, p. 4). It was also impressed with the appearance of 51 business leaders at the Boston Jubilee. Speaking up for capitalism, these corporate executives released a declaration that warned that Americans were "being traded out of basic liberties by promises of false security" ("Case study—Boston," 1950, p. 4). Americans, said the document, needed to re-dedicate themselves to fundamental rights that link to the American economic system, like rights to personal dignity and initiative along with the individual's "right to provide for the future .... to advance or hold still; to be the judge of his own welfare" ("Case study—Boston," 1950, p. 4). Basic Refractories Inc. of Maple Grove, Ohio, performed a similar advocacy role—it took out full-page ads in newspapers in its region that carried a message from over 400 of its employees, who urged fellow citizens to watch out for the "wild accusations and failed promises" offered by critics of capitalism. Listening to such voices could lead to Americans being shepherded toward "political and economic slavery," it said ("Full-page," 1950, p. 2). Alcoa was even blunter in its rebuttal of free market critics, placing on the cover of its employee magazine a picture of its parking lot full of employee vehicles. It challenged communist and socialist sympathizers saying "How do all those thousands of Wall Street slaves, those victims of the ruling circles in America manage to purchase all those shiny automobiles?" ("Alcoa," 1950, p. 2).

In sum, said *PR News*, corporations needed to push back against the foes of capitalism by telling the benefits of business to American life. American receptivity to the welfare state perplexed the publishers of the newsletter because business was successfully helping the country by supplying its war efforts in Korea, while also producing the domestic materials that Americans demanded. Private enterprise's 1951 production record had been surpassed only by the war efforts in 1944 and 1945. *PR News* said, "Let's remember that, by telling the story then, industry stashed away, in the bank of goodwill, assets which are still yielding dividends today" ("Included," 1952, p. 4). That goodwill, it said, could help corporations assertively inform and mentor the public of the value of free enterprise. It quoted PR firm manager G. Edward Pendray's admonition that speaking back to American sympathy for socialism needed to be clear and compelling because one could not "neutralize or deflect a strong dynamic social movement with nothing but a mimeograph machine, any more than [one could] stop a V-2 rocket with a feather duster" ("From the PR," 1952d, p. 2). Millions of Americans did not understand that business was "a force for the betterment of civilization," said Austin Ingleheart, president of General Foods, chiefly because "U.S. businessmen have not educated the people as to the spiritual satisfaction profits have afforded the general public" ("From the PR," 1952e, p. 2). America's war in Korea had led to a high degree of "confusion and bewilderment" among its citizens about the depth of the military action, the newsletter said, and corporations needed to step up their efforts to increase public acceptance of the need for war-time sacrifices, while also informing them that they needed to work with business to guard against a Russian imperialism that threatened the American way of life ("Whatever," 1950, p. 1).

PR News showed that employees were sometimes the best vehicle to first spread the message about the benefits of private enterprise. The Virginian Electric Power Company engaged in a $100,000 employee-indoctrination program, which emphasized the benefits of the free market, all with the aim to develop a "contented organization … with a common purpose" ("Case study—Virginian," 1951, p. 3). Although the publication offered no evidence of the results of the effort, it claimed that the company had convinced its workers that: "they get a better deal under private ownership of the electric power industry than they would if it were government-owned, so now they are vigorous opponents of socialization" ("Case study—Virginian," 1951, p. 4). Another for-profit utility, Washington Water Power Company of Spokane, used a "Better Service Program" to train employees to go into communities to give speeches, perform service, and visit newcomers. The company secured long-term renewals of its franchise in several communities, and the company's subsequent surveys of their customers found marked resistance against socialization, as "only nine percent of Washington Water Power Co.'s customers voted for public power" ("Case study—Washington," 1951, p. 4). General Electric offered a primer that urged managers to connect with employees concerning their need for both material and spiritual rewards. One way to do so, said GE, was to "learn the arithmetic of our better way of life," communicate that reality to employees, and then emphasize that "we can all work together to make it still better" ("Five ways," 1952, p. 2).

A common approach used by corporations to show their credibility regarding the American economic system was to provide examples of how the corporation acted as a supportive economic engine that benefited society. When the Pennsylvania Railroad readied its 1950 taxes, its vice president went before the media with an oversized check for $1.2 million and pointed out that 25% of that sum was going to public schools ("A seemingly," 1950, p. 1). Seabrook Farms of Bridgeton, New Jersey, offered one of the more unique attempts to dramatize the corporation's beneficial role in the economy. For one 2-week pay period, it compensated their employees with silver dollars, resulting in more than 250,000 coins circulating across the region, some of them as far as department stores in Philadelphia. Seabrook took out radio and newspaper ads to publicize how this income found its way "into your pocket through the various channels of the American system of individual enterprise. Of this we are proud!" ("Case study—Seabrook Farms," 1951, p. 3). Seabrook was also gratified that one couple, who married near the end of the promotion, paid for their license with the silver dollars and placed one within their framed wedding picture. Dan River Mills of Danville, Virginia, although far less ambitious tactically, offered a similar message to local citizens. It used the annual Danville Fair to put up placards that told attendees that over 70% of its profits were invested in new equipment and "more than 39 cents of each dollar stayed right here in Danville" ("Dan River," 1951, p. 2).

Corporations also communicated that profits were circumscribed by the realities of living in a modern society, which imposed its own costs on businesses and individuals alike. General Mills pointed out to their employees that the way the company operated its business was much like the way a newsboy had to account for expenses. In its *Modern Millwheel* publication, the company showed how "The General" (a visual persona for the company), like the paperboy, had to borrow and spend money and had to put aside funds "for future development, depreciation (newspaper bikes wear out) and for stockholders" like the paper-boy's father ("General Mills," 1950, p. 2). The president of the Solar Aircraft Company sent a personal letter to all 5,000 of his employees that accompanied the annual report. The note said that high costs of doing business (including taxes) affected the corporation's bottom line, but it was a cost of living that the corporation was able to manage in America's free enterprise system, "just as the price of meat and shoes and the things that you and I buy in our daily living affect our pocketbooks" ("President Edmund," 1952, p. 3). Similarly Alcoa took out large ads in newspapers that portrayed the corporation as the backbone of a stable, orderly American society. The ads showed a picture of an employee receiving his Alcoa paycheck, juxtaposed with scenes of traffic policemen at work. Alcoa's tagline, "Like other good citizens, Alcoa pays taxes too," affirmed that corporations, just like their fellow citizens, financially supported vital public services ("Under the heading," 1952, p. 4).

Corporations connecting with children

The story of the helpful presence of the corporate persona went beyond enlightening the public about business' essential financial role. *PR News* also showed that corporations often displayed a helpful persona when they interacted with children. In this respect, the newsletter aligned its content with, for example, the findings of a survey conducted in the early 1950s by public relations firm Hill and Knowlton. The firm had contacted 4,000 schools across the U.S. and found that the vast majority wanted information from businesses—especially corporate-made films—and agreed with the statement that "schools should seek the understanding, support and cooperation of business and industry at all times" ("Schools are," 1951, p. 2). Corporate leadership began to show more awareness that reaching children was essential to solidifying a sense of common bonds and purpose between corporation and citizen, especially in light of the military confrontation against communism in Korea and the larger battle of minds inherent in the Cold War. W.W. Wachtel, President of Calvert Distillers Corporation, said if the country was to persevere against these international and domestic threats

> the role of young people must not be limited simply to service in our armed forces but should be expanded to include preparation through a thorough understanding of our economic and social system, to protect it against the propaganda of its enemies within.
>
> ("From the PR," 1951c, p. 2)

PR News pointed to a specific example of such outreach: the Kenosha (Wisconsin) Manufacturers Association provided ads to its local high school paper about the benefits of the American free enterprise system, emphasizing themes like

"Profits Mean Progress" and "Why are American Living Standards High?" ("Unusual," 1950, p. 1).

Most corporations, however, approached schools in a less ideologically freighted way by providing them curricular content. Quaker Oats sent a traveling exhibit to schools that showed aspects of the company's production and research and how its endeavors linked to curricular areas like agriculture and home economics ("Case study—Quaker Oats," 1950). Central Hudson Gas and Electric Corporation of Poughkeepsie attempted to better illustrate their presence by providing schools with literature and illustrations for the study of gas (which was used in physics and chemistry classes, for example). It complemented that effort by sponsoring half-hour radio shows that featured school programs like debates, athletics, and youth concerts. *PR News* observed: "The company's sincere practical efforts to win the friendship of its young community citizens, to give them frank, factual information about the utility and our economic system, have won for Central the respect" of citizens in their community ("Case study—Central," 1951, p. 4). In the Midwest, Gerity-Michigan Corporation, maker of chrome bathroom accessories, funded safety competitions among schools, and sponsored children's stories and quiz shows on a weekly radio program to reinforce the safety messages. Beyond being safety-minded, said *PR News*, the "entire county has become … Gerity-Michigan-minded" ("Case study—Gerity," 1951, p. 4). In Los Angeles, General Petroleum Corporation stepped forward to help schools meet a state mandate to provide safe-driving lessons; it brought to the schools "psycho-physical testing devices" and its own technicians to administer the test and provide results to both the school and the individual student ("A corporation," 1950, p. 3). U.S. Steel Corporation, indicative of its large footprint in American industry at that time, pursued a more widespread and systematic outreach to children. Working with the National Science Teachers Association, it provided content for a science bulletin, with a circulation of over 20,000, used by teachers in every state and in 12 foreign countries. *PR News* noted that the bulletins had no information that pushed the company or directly touted America's economic system. Instead, it said, "USS feels that by showing the technological strides made for human betterment by American industry, students will learn for themselves the social values of the free enterprise system" ("Case study"—U.S. Steel," 1951, p. 4). Some corporations saw that the best content they could offer centered on making the link between what they did and what future career opportunities might arise. At the high school level, the 3M Corporation, in St. Paul, Minnesota, worked closely with guidance counselors to provide information on company policies and job opportunities ("Hiring of," 1951, p. 2). In Indiana, the Evansville Manufacturers' and Employers' Association partnered with the schools to help students choose their careers. In doing so, said Servel, Inc.'s chairman of the board Louis Ruthenberg, "we are projecting ourselves into the future," with a special emphasis on "teaching our boys and girls the superiority of the American way of life" ("To acquaint," 1952, p. 2).

Other organizations saw value in interacting with children outside of school. The Cleveland (Ohio) Society for Savings, in partnership with 194 area schools, reached out to kids with the message "Thrift can be fun." It set up a separate department area (with small desks) where children, under the guidance of a math teacher, acted as tellers, auditors, bookkeepers, and guards. To give the program continued momentum, it worked with the schools to set up individual children's accounts. *PR News* reported that drivers were picking up deposits from schools, with almost 90,000 students accumulating $3 million in the society's accounts. *PR News* said the partnership with the society was helping students develop "qualities of self-reliance, responsibility, and integrity" ("Case study—Cleveland," 1952, p. 4). The publication reported that National Cash Register (NCR) of Dayton, Ohio, was now in its thirty-second year of holding Saturday meetings for children ages 2–16. Over the years, more than 4 million children had attended these gatherings at an NCR community center, partaking of activities like talent shows and watching movies. Some children grew up to be NCR executives: at the 1951 Christmas party, NCR president Stanley Allen said, "I may be looking at a future president of this company today, and I hope I am" ("Case study—National," 1952, p. 4). Another Dayton company, Frigidaire, brought high school students to tours of their plants because they were acting "on the premise that the high school youngster of today is the employee, customer, stockholder, and the citizen of tomorrow." One teacher complimented the company for providing information on its work processes and exemplifying "cordial relations" and "fair and honest dealings." The teacher noted that "if our students gained a deeper sense of social responsibility and wholesome attitudes, it was worth your endeavor" ("Case study—Frigidaire," 1952, p. 4).

Of all the accounts of outreach to children, however, *PR News* was most impressed with an example offered by Erie Railroad. Company president Paul Johnston received a letter from a 9-year-old boy (not identified by the publication) inquiring if the $11.25 he had saved was enough to buy a share of stock in Erie Railroad. Johnston, after discussing the letter with his public relations assistant, wrote back to the child, offering to provide him with enough additional money to buy the railroad's stock. Johnston also invited him to the next board meeting with the opportunity to tour the facility so that the child could inspect "some of the property of which you will be part owner." The railroad alerted the press and received extensive coverage of the boy's arrival. This led to increased positive views of the corporation and its association with people, said *PR News* and they quoted excerpts from citizen letters: "It makes people realize that big business has a heart"; "You drove home the idea that common stocks of the U.S. belong to the people"; and "It reaffirms my faith in the American people and in our way of life." *PR News* said that, instead of discarding a letter from a kid, Erie had offered a portrait of business that emphasized "the human qualities of the corporation and its employees" ("Case study—Erie," 1952, pp. 3–4).

PR News and the corporation as a fellow person

Across these issues of *PR News* came a depiction of the corporation as a human-like, relatable entity. The publication offered the view that the corporation was a partner in the American experience, an entity that attempted to better educate Americans that free enterprise allowed corporations to operationalize American values of self-reliance and initiative, so as to build and preserve conditions that led to a constructive life for all. It also put forward accounts of how corporations were personally invested in fellow citizens by seeking out opportunities to engage with children, both in the classroom with educational material and outside the classroom through serious (career counseling) and trivial (talent contests) activities. These messages were not by happenstance. The publication emphasized that it was essential to make such contacts with American families during these years of the ideological Cold War and the hot war of Korea. In response to these stressors, *PR News* asserted that public relations was a crucial vehicle through which the corporation could reach out to the populace and convey the message that the corporation was a fellow human traveling a road of common values and goals. Observing this dynamic, the dean of the Boston University School of Public Relations, Howard LeSourd, said that the aim of public relations was to "build morale, to effect stronger unity, to make personal sacrifices a mark of patriotism, and to bring forth maximum effort from every individual" ("Case study—*PR Review* editorial," 1951, p. 3). Communicating a corporate persona was a viable route to achieving such worthwhile ends, said *PR News*, but

> ...not enough use is being made of a company personality to influence public opinion even though research has proven that there is a direct correlation between the public's respect and admiration for a company personality and the company's overall PR reputation.
>
> ("A panel," 1951, p. 1)

And the personal appeal was crucial—*PR News* paraphrased the findings of a Roper poll, saying that a corporation's status as a good citizen was earned "more by the way it treats people as individuals than by its measurable contributions to community projects" ("Many industrial," 1950, p. 2). In fact, in its first year of Annual Achievement Awards, *PR News* recognized the Mutual Life Insurance Company for its "use of public relations for humanizing the corporation in the public interest" ("Importance," 1950, p. 1).

PR News' observations about the untapped potential of the corporate persona were not surprising. It was one thing to extol a symbiosis between the corporation and the individual, but what did this look like beyond education efforts and attempts to connect with children? *PR News* found there were some readily available examples visible in corporations' internal communications. In Racine, Wisconsin, Belle City Malleable Iron Company used an employee's silver wedding anniversary to display such an association. In its employee newsletter, it showed photos of this employee's life—his birth, his engagement, his wedding, and the arrival of his children—and paired such events with benchmark developments at the plant. The story ended with an emphasis on growth and expansion—an aerial view of the facility showed the company's growth; a picture of the employee's recent family reunion, similarly showed growth of his family ("Employee," 1951). In Minneapolis, wholesale food distributors Winston and Newell Co. gave employees a booklet titled "Opportunity Unlimited," which said the company was dedicated "to the happiness of our employees." *PR News* said the booklet clearly communicated how the organization appreciated their workers' drive to be efficient and compensated them well, revealing in the process the "human story of the company" ("Winston," 1951, p. 3). The newsletter was especially impressed with du Pont's effort to show the alignments between human behavior and corporate behavior. It noted how a recent edition of du Pont's corporate publication *Better Living* showed

> …how a corporation discharges its duties as a citizen in ways similar to the individual. When the individual bears arms for his nation, the corporation increases production and manufactures defense materials. An individual must pay a reasonable sum to anyone he hires. Similarly, a corporation should pay employees fair wages and provide safe, healthy working conditions. Both have responsibilities for being good neighbors in their communities.…
>
> ("A picture story," 1952, p. 3)

PR News also showed how organizations found various other ways to reach outside their facilities to make associations with individuals. As part of an employee safety campaign, Crucible Steel Company of America called employees' home phones near their Pittsburgh, Pennsylvania, plant to find who could recite its safety slogan of the week (which had been widely posted throughout the plant) and then win a $5 cash prize. Over the six-month effort, Crucible moved much closer to being seen more like a person, as "the company, once just a cold, impersonal name, [was] now a neighbor who [called] on the telephone…" said the trade newsletter ("Crucible," 1952, p. 3). When Franklin National Bank celebrated its 25th anniversary, *PR News* reviewed the bank's track record of activities designed to connect with citizens. Over the years, Franklin had offered display area for items from local merchants, provided meeting space to groups like the Boy Scouts and the Salvation Army, and set aside a children's bank—a space filled with miniature furniture where children could write out deposit slips and adjust their accounts. Noting the bank president's assertion that "a bank should be the useful friend of every citizen in the community," *PR News* said that Franklin was changing the public view of the bank as a "cold calculating money-till" toward that of a "human, approachable citizen-institution interested in serving the needs of its community" ("Case study—Franklin," 1951, p. 4). It said that Chase National Bank also pursued its own approach to showing its persona: it took out huge advertisements in major daily papers in New York City that featured a close-up of a man's face, with the caption "This is the façade of a bank." Rather than seeing a bank as cold and "all marble and steel," said *PR News*, people who saw the ad were now in a better position to realize that there was something more than "a hardness or coldness" when it came to that "institution's heart" ("A huge," 1952, p. 1). Even a very large industrial organization like General Motors was coming to a deeper realization about the need to show a relatable personality. GM president C.E. Wilson looked for improvements at the dealership level. "[O]ur products and services are intimately associated with the home, the family, and almost every phase of community life," he said, declaring that product association was only the beginning, however: the continuing challenge was to know people better. GM encouraged its dealers to be visible in civic organizations and to get involved in finding remedies for traffic problems and promoting street beautification. This showed a level of resonance with the community, he said, because "people like to be considered as something more than just buyers of cars" ("Case study—General Motors," 1952, p. 3).

PR News found that there were, indeed, examples of the corporate persona in action—it attempted to show the persona as a rational approach for demonstrating alliances with individuals. In fact, in an extended piece on how to make citizen committees function effectively, it encouraged its readers to understand that, regardless of the issue at hand, "a majority of citizens [could] be made to believe that some aspect of their lives [had] personal identification" with the corporation's objectives and goals ("Case study—public relations," 1950, p. 3). Logical appeals to the individual's self-interest were best, but some degree of "belligerence" might be needed, appealing to grass-roots values and attitudes by "telling the story in terms that [would] interest the man with a small family and an average income" ("Case study—public relations," 1950, p. 4). Careful envisioning of the convergence of interest between the corporation and the individual was necessary, so that the human-like persona could be projected. To this end, it offered from W.F. Flower, PR director for Outdoor Advertising Inc., this observation:

> The processes by which an organization is translated from a shapeless, ineffectual grouping of property and people into a dynamic force with all the characteristics of a friendly, stable personality, well-adjusted to and participating fully in community life is, if not mysterious and complicated, at least a full time job requiring intensive planning, constant search for new techniques and careful attention to details.
>
> ("From the PR," 1951d, p. 2)

What of the corporate persona?

Considering that NAM had pioneered large-scale corporate persona efforts only 10 years earlier, the notion of a corporate personality by 1950 was likely a bit abstract and elusive to *PR News*' readership. Still, the publication provided tactical ways to operationalize a fairly sophisticated approach: cast the corporation as a relatable, constructive presence which could enlighten the populace (both in the company's workforce and among the wider citizenry) about the benefits of the American economic system, and act as a friendly, mentor-like figure to children. What both approaches had in common was a paternalism that attempted to signal to Americans that better times were in store if only individuals heeded the bounds (e.g., values and goals) they shared with corporation. It was an assertion that had paradoxical elements: the overt message to the citizenry was to trust companies which, barely 10 years ago, were reviled by many Americans; the subtle, more latent message was a call for citizens to return to their sense of individualism and self-reliance, a disposition that corporations said they shared with everyday Americans.

However, rather than dwell on extensive psychological discussions regarding the presence of the corporate persona—the "news brief" format of the publication was not conducive to long, analytical passages—the publication focused on evidence supportive of the corporate persona's usefulness. *PR News* was often adamant that a corporation's perceived humanness was best first nurtured among its employees, and it pointed to the success of Ansul Chemical Company of Marinette, Wisconsin. Its efforts to engage its 400 employees on company issues, offering company stock and paying for employee self-improvement courses, was exemplary, *PR News* said. Ansul had drawn out the "creative powers of the individual worker" and guided them "into constructive channels," with the company avoiding absenteeism and never having a strike ("Case study—Ansul," 1951, p. 4). *PR News* also singled out the wider community engagement efforts of Caterpillar Tractor Company. The company had reached out across an area within a 250-mile radius from its Peoria plant and brought in more than 10,000 visitors to its facility, provided over 700 film showings, and sent out more than 200 employees to provide community talks ("Caterpillar," 1951). *PR News* claimed that Ansul's and Caterpillar's efforts were helping Americans to better understand the vital role that business played in society. A poll by the Psychological Corporation asked respondents to rate what kind of people were most needed in Washington. Business people led—selected by 50% of respondents, *PR News* reported ("Government's pleas," 1951, p. 1).

Offering the corporate persona as a way to convince individuals that their goals and interests were shared by corporations also had benefits for the profession. This emphasis on building a synergy both with key audiences and the wider populace, especially in times of stress for business interests, helped show the pragmatic value of public relations, said *PR News*. It noted that one wealthy businessman said, "I've resisted the PR parade; now I guess I'd better start stepping" ("Past week," 1952, p. 1). Not surprisingly, said the newsletter, in 1951 alone more than 40 public relations senior personnel were appointed as vice presidents, and 20 were elected to boards of directors. The newsletter reported:

> For the first time in a many-year struggle, PR executives felt that management was sincerely interested, sincerely sold, sincerely dedicated to the principles of good PR....[as it] is no longer falsely assumed to be an esoteric, mumbo-jumbo art, practiced by a few chosen miracle men touched with divinity...
>
> ("For public," 1952, p. 1)

This seemed to be the overriding message from *PR News*: that conveying the corporation as a friendly, helpful guide which helped all Americans achieve a better life was not a mystical, "warm and fuzzy" approach. Instead, it was a tactic that zeroed in on finding commonalities between the American individual's drive for achievement and security and the corporation's desire to maximize its own penchant for maintaining power. Corporations observed that the American ethos for accomplishment was much like its own, but the lingering post-Depression and post-World War II desire for security among citizens allowed room for the continued promotion of government welfare programs and, increasingly, discussions of state planning of the economy. Both were anathema to business interests; the corporate persona, as *PR News* showed, offered corporations a way for businesses to show Americans that they needed to rise above such promises offered by state interests, which sought to regiment American individuality and enterprise. In contrast, *PR News* offered readers countless examples of how the corporation could act as larger-than-life, friendly mentor to the average American. In 1950, it offered a particularly simple, yet effective example of the human touch of the corporation: Fourth National Bank of Wichita offered lectures to hundreds of women about how to manage the anxieties and stresses of financial management. The response was so positive, said *PR News*, that all of the women who enrolled "now [considered] the Fourth National her *guide and counselor* on all financial matters" ("Fourth National," 1950, p. 3, emphasis added). With this statement, the publication offered an excellent summary of the role of the emerging corporate persona: it addressed the concerns, hopes, and aspirations of the individual and acted as a mentor that helped guide one's journey toward a shared common end—the good life.

The corporate persona, as illustrated by *PR News*, had a clear, defined purpose—to re-direct the attention of Americans away from help from the state and toward re-embracing the good relationship citizens had with business. Its accounts emphasized that people turned to the state out of frustration—a reliance, said Howard Chase, that was the "greatest enemy of freedom … it [undermined] the will to work and the will to be free" ("Public relations," 1952, p. 1). Accordingly, as *PR News* had observed: "No public relations program is adequate unless it moves the public to think, and to do" ("Every," 1950, p. 1). *Public Relations News*, across these years, detailed such a progenitor of such action. The corporate persona encouraged audiences to think of business as a fellow traveler and to stay on the road—the free enterprise journey—that allowed both individual and corporation to arrive at a mutually beneficial end.

References

Brayman, H. (1952). "The real basis of our American way." *Public Relations Journal*, January, pp. 3–4, 16.

Burnett, V. (1943). *You and your public: A guidebook to the new career—public relations.* New York: Harper & Brothers.

Fitzgerald, S. (1950). *Communicating ideas to the public: A practical application of public relations techniques to everyday problems in human communication.* New York: Funk & Wagnalls.

Fones-Wolf, E. (1994). *Selling free enterprise: The business assault on labor and liberalism, 1945–60.* Urbana, IL: University of Illinois Press.

"From the PR platform." (1951a). *Public Relations News,* April 23, p. 2.

"From the PR platform." (1951b). December 24, p. 2.

"From the PR platform." (1951c). April 23, p. 2.

"From the PR platform." (1951d). July 16, p. 2.

"From the PR platform." (1952a). October 6, p. 2.

"From the PR platform." (1952b). January 7, p. 2.

"From the PR platform." (1952c). April 21, p. 2.

"From the PR platform." (1952d). February 4, p. 2.

"From the PR platform." (1952e). May 26, p. 2.

Glaser, B.G., & Strauss, A.L. (1967). *The discovery of grounded theory: Strategies for qualitative research.* New York: Aldine.

Griffith, R. (1983). "The selling of America: The Advertising Council and American politics, 1942–1960." *Business History Review 57*(3), pp. 388–412.

Harlow, R. (1942). *Public relations in war and peace.* New York: Harper and Brothers.

Johnson, R. (1950). "We believe." *Public Relations Journal,* January, p. 6.

Keyton, J. (2015). *Communication research: Asking questions, finding answers* (4th ed.). New York: McGraw-Hill.

"Let business tell its story—NOW" (1953). *Public Relations Journal,* March, p. 2.

Lundborg, L. (1950). *Public relations in the local community.* New York: Harper and Brothers.

MacDonald, J. (1948). "Open house." In G. Griswold, & D. Griswold (Eds.), *Your public relations: The standard public relations handbook,* pp. 524–542. New York: Funk & Wagnalls.

Mises, L.V. (1949). *Human action.* New Haven, CT: Yale University Press.

Nielander, W.A., & Miller, R.W. (1951). *Public relations.* New York: The Ronald Press Company.

Phillips-Fein, K. (2009). *Invisible hands: The businessmen's crusade against the New Deal.* New York: W.W. Norton.

Public Relations News. (1949). "Semi-annual review issue." July 18, p. 4.

Public Relations News. (1950). "A corporation has the opportunity to win good will." January 2, p. 2

Public Relations News. (1950). "President Truman's State of the Union." January 9, p. 1.

Public Relations News. (1950). "Outstanding development in public relations." January 16, p. 1.

Public Relations News. (1950). "A seemingly minor incident." February 20, p. 1.

Public Relations News. (1950). "Case study—Quaker Oats." February 27, pp. 3–4.

Public Relations News. (1950). "In these days." February 27. p. 2.

Public Relations News. (1950). "Many industrial PR lessons." March 13, p. 2.

Public Relations News. (1950). "Sanger Brothers department store enjoys high esteem." March 20, p. 3.

Public Relations News. (1950). "Fourth National Bank." March 27, p. 3.

Public Relations News. (1950). "Case study—public relations." April 17, pp. 3–4.

Public Relations News. (1950). "Importance of public relations." May 8, p. 1.

Public Relations News. (1950). "One paramount problem of PR." May 8, p. 1.

Public Relations News. (1950). "Biggest and most urgent PR job." May 15, p. 1.

Public Relations News. (1950). "Community relations greatly improved." June 5, p. 2.

Public Relations News. (1950). "Unusual school-industry project." June 26, p. 1.

Public Relations News. (1950). "Case study—Boston Jubilee." July 3, pp. 3–4.

Public Relations News. (1950). "Experience of Caterpillar Tractor Company." July 10, p. 2.

Public Relations News. (1950). "Full-page ads." July 10, p. 2.

Public Relations News. (1950). "General Mills." October 9, p. 2.

Public Relations News. (1950). "Alcoa Record." October 16, p. 2.

Public Relations News. (1950). "Every public relations executive." October 16, p. 1.

Public Relations News. (1950). "Case study—St. Louis public relations conference." October 23, pp. 3–4.

Public Relations News. (1950). "Examples continue to come to light." November 13, p. 2.

Public Relations News. (1950). "Management is beginning to develop an awareness." November 13, p. 1.

Public Relations News. (1950). "Whatever your personal interpretation." December 18, p. 1.

Public Relations News. (1951). "Case study—Virginia Electric and Power Company." January 1, pp. 3–4.

Public Relations News. (1951). "Case study—Seabrook Farms." January 8, pp. 3–4.

Public Relations News. (1951). "Government's pleas for business executives." January 8, p. 1.

Public Relations News. (1951). "Case study—*PR Review* editorial advisory board." January 15, pp. 3–4.

Public Relations News. (1951). "Employee at Belle City Malleable Iron Company celebrates silver wedding anniversary." January 15, p. 3.

Public Relations News. (1951). "Major attention to be given to planned community relations." January 29, p. 1.

Public Relations News. (1951). "Case study—*PR News* survey." February 5, pp. 3–4.

Public Relations News. (1951). "Case study—Washington Water Power Company." February 12, pp. 3–4.

Public Relations News. (1951). "Dan River Mills, Inc. chose annual fair to make mid-year report." March 5, p. 2.

Public Relations News. (1951). "Case study—Central Hudson Gas & Electric Corporation." March 12, pp. 3–4.

Public Relations News. (1951). "Ever hear of a ginkgo tree?" March 12, p. 2.

Public Relations News. (1951). "Hiring of its 10,000th employee." April 9. p. 2.

Public Relations News. (1951). "Case study—U.S. Steel Corporation." April 23, pp. 3–4.

Public Relations News. (1951). "Industry and art are discovering each other." April 23, p. 2.

Public Relations News. (1951). "Caterpillar Tractor Company gives an accounting." May 14, p. 2.

Public Relations News. (1951). "Case study—new plants." May 21, pp. 3–4.

Public Relations News. (1951). "Case study—Ansul Chemical Company." June 18, pp. 3–4.

Public Relations News. (1951). "Winston and Newell Company." July 9, p. 3

Public Relations News. (1951). "Case study—Southern Railway System." July 16, pp. 3–4.

Public Relations News. (1951). "Case study—Franklin National Bank." July 23, pp. 3–4.

Public Relations News. (1951). "Case study—Gerity-Michigan Corporation." August 20, pp. 3–4.

Public Relations News. (1951). "Schools are eager for more information about business." September 17, p. 2.

Public Relations News. (1951). "Businesses in the U.S. will spend $77 million with PR firms." September 17, p. 3.

Public Relations News. (1951). "A panel of four distinguished public opinion research-ers." December 3, p. 1.

Public Relations News. (1951). "A thrilling demonstration of statemanship in PR." December 3, p. 4.

Public Relations News. (1952). "George Wharton, administrative assistant for public interest." January 7, p. 3.

Public Relations News. (1952). "Five ways to a happy new year in employee relations." January 14, p. 2.

Public Relations News. (1952). "For public relations, 1951 was a crucial test." January 21, pp. 1–4.

Public Relations News. (1952). "Included in the record for 1951." January 21, p. 4.

Public Relations News. (1952). "That's the record of PR for 1951." January 21, p. 4.

Public Relations News. (1952). "Case study—Erie Railroad." February 18, pp. 3–4.

Public Relations News. (1952). "Case study—Cleveland Society for Savings." March 10, pp. 3–4.

Public Relations News. (1952). "A huge, seven-column close up." March 17, p. 3.

Public Relations News. (1952). "Past week marked by fresh evidence." March 17, p. 1.

Public Relations News. (1952). "Crucible Steel Company." April 7, p. 3.

Public Relations News. (1952). "Case study—General Motors." April 14, pp. 3–4.

Public Relations News. (1952). "Case study—National Cash Register." April 28, pp. 3–4.

Public Relations News. (1952). "To acquaint 6,800 high school students." May 5, p. 2.

Public Relations News. (1952). "Public relations prominently featured." May 12, p. 1.

Public Relations News. (1952). "A picture story." June 16, p. 3.

Public Relations News. (1952). "G. Edward Pendray." June 23, p. 1.

Public Relations News. (1952). "Case study—Frigidaire." June 30, pp. 3–4.

Public Relations News. (1952). "President Edmund Price sends 5,000 employees personal letter." August 4, p. 3.

Public Relations News. (1952). "Ansul Chemical Company." September 8. p. 3.

Public Relations News. (1952). "Under the heading 'New Jersey area shares in progress'." September 8, p. 4.

Public Relations News. (1952). "Major emphasis given to PR at American Chemical Society annual fall meeting." October 6, p. 2.

5 The railroad and you

The watchful Norfolk and Western helps chart the destination

The railroads in the United States, note scholars (Cutlip, 1994; Olasky, 1987), were likely the earliest users in the U.S. of modern public relations. Ivy Lee, considered to be at the forefront in advancing the practice of public relations, helped propel his year-old public relations firm, Parker & Lee, by taking on the Pennsylvania Railroads as a client in 1906 (Cutlip, 1994). But the railroads already had a long history of communicating that they were a helpful, constructive force for society. Beginning with the construction of the Baltimore-to-Ohio track in 1830—the first public line—railroad publicity trumpeted that the railways were a force that helped promote and build a free market and increased nationwide prosperity. Lindley (1999) noted that 19th-century U.S. railroad publicity in newspapers, pamphlets, and fliers lauded the lines as the great civilizer of the young nation. The railroads, he said, touted themselves as the answer to social and economic maladies and were the "last best hope to hold the young United States together" (Lindley, 1999, p. 62). Moreover, throughout the latter half of the 19th century, as westward migration persisted, the railroads developed an interest in moving the crowd. That is, the railroads needed the support of westward migrants (including foreign immigrants) to build pioneer communities near their tracks, so that the railroads would have a steady supply of commerce and human resources. Their publicity efforts were massive—railroad-initiated advertisements, pamphlets, news stories, and guidebooks flooded towns and villages both domestically and internationally—and would-be explorers were sold on the notion of westward migration in concert with the constructive force of the railroads. The industry's efforts were so successful that, by the 1890s, almost all of the 155 million railroad-adjacent acres that the U.S. government had deeded to the railroads had been sold to migrants and investors (Cutlip, 1995, p. 163). Scholar J. Valerie Fifer (1988) said that the railroads had done more than promote Western development, they had "stimulated the growth of a new spirit of American nationalism" (p. 2).

By the mid-20th century, U.S. railroads had an established track record of emphasizing the importance of American progress through a sense of pioneering self-reliance and enterprise. However, the railroads, like many business entities featured in Chapter 4, were concerned about a post-World War II slump in once-dominant values like individualism and liberty. The industry viewed these aspects of Americanism as under siege by such developments as the increase in the size of the American government and its involvement in the marketplace, the rise of the labor movement, the international ascendancy of communism and socialism and, by June 1950, the beginning of the Korean War.

This chapter shows that, in response, Norfolk and Western Railway (now Norfolk and Southern) attempted to cast itself as a fellow individual who advocated for the American way of life through the preservation of the free market system. Specifically, the company used its *Norfolk and Western Magazine* to make the case that a portion of the populace, both in the citizenry and in officialdom, was displaying a tendency to embrace socialism. The magazine asserted, both in its own columns and through offering supportive testimony from others' speeches and writings, that there was no place for socialism in American society because it served to undermine the industrious and individualistic values shared by corporations and individuals. Accordingly, this chapter examines how this railroad used the publication to attempt, through the conveyance of the corporate persona, to portray itself as a "larger-than-life" individual who advocated against socialism in the cause of beliefs it shared with average Americans. In doing so, Norfolk and Western sought to amplify points of convergence between itself and the readers of the magazine (primarily employees) so as to solidify acceptance of its viewpoints and mobilize readers to act on those areas of agreement.

Norfolk and Western's challenges

The Norfolk and Western Railway originated in 1881 and by the 1950s had been through several downturns, but it had thrived more recently due to its involvement in moving equipment, men, and supplies during World War II. The railway, however, faced significant challenges as the 1950s approached. The company was incensed with the government increasingly subsidizing competition—airlines, trucking operations, domestic waterway companies, and even the Post Office—with huge amounts of tax dollars. The *Norfolk and Western Magazine* said that government subsidies to these alternative transportation networks, from 1921 to 1947 alone, totaled $54 billion (May 1950, p. 256). While the government was supporting these other transportation services, the railway's operating revenues had decreased by 60% since 1948 (August 1949, p. 479). Passenger ticket sales were down by 6% in the first half of 1949 alone (July 1949, p. 406). The publication repeatedly talked about two challenges that hurt the company's viability: an interventionist government—both in the transportation marketplace and in the wider economy—that eroded its ability to be a viable contributor to the country, and an increasing societal disposition to embrace socialism instead of traditional individualistic values of resourcefulness and initiative. These two overarching concerns were apparent across publication articles that critiqued dependency on the state and advocated, instead, for reliance on the self in the free market. Accordingly, the company spoke out against what it saw as trends in American society that threatened its sustainability and undermined the free market understanding of the American way of life.

This chapter examines how the *Norfolk and Western Magazine*, from 1949 to 1952, demonstrated the company's attempts to manage these stressors through offering articles that emphasized the company's role as a fellow advocate in the preservation of the American free enterprise system. This monthly magazine, which began in 1922, was a central communication vehicle for the railroad, normally carrying about two dozen news and feature articles per issue, along with recurring columns that provided information about local employee happenings, retiree news, and material for children. Each edition's original articles and reprinted pieces (e.g., speeches, columns from other publications, etc.) were scanned and noted for references to the presence of both the government and the free market as related to the individual and the corporation. From this, a pool of full-length pieces, often one to two pages long, was carefully read and re-read, with themes identified using the grounded theory approach detailed in Chapter 4. With this method, this chapter found in the *Norfolk and Western Magazine* these three areas of emphasis: both the individual and the corporation were under attack by socialism; both the corporation and the individual profited from the American free enterprise system; and the highest calling for both the individual and the corporation was to work together to defend the free enterprise system.

On the watch against attack by socialism

The *Norfolk and Western Magazine* consistently alerted its readers to the country's growing tendency to accept socialism in lieu of capitalism. These alarms normally appeared either within the first-person column "A Train of Thought," in news stories that featured testimonials against socialism (normally given at Norfolk and Western events), or in articles that were reprinted in whole or part.

In the first issue of 1949, "A Train of Thought" featured a warning that the country was ignoring its history of individual effort succeeding through private enterprise. Instead, author "Cap'n Jim" said, "There are alarming numbers of our own people drifting little by little toward the belief that they would fare as well or better under government ownership as under our traditional private ownership of business" (January 1949, p. 29). Jim asserted that Americans with socialist sympathies needed only look at countries that had followed that path: they had seen their liberties superseded by "government ownership or control of private enterprise.... That in itself should be enough to tell us in plain language that their way is not our way" (January 1949, p. 29).

Subsequent editions of "A Train of Thought" returned to this concern about the advance of socialism in the U.S. In January 1950, in a statement resonating with the idea of a New Year's resolution and alarmed by socialism, Cap'n Jim asked if all Americans were "Amer I CAN enough" to be self-reliant go-getters who would avoid the controlling hand of government, or "[D]o we sometimes toy with the idea that the government is looking after our security and that we really have nothing to worry about?" (January 1950, p. 31). In subsequent months, Jim became more explicit about the dangers of home-bred socialism, telling readers that the upper echelons of government were deviously trying to undermine the American way of life and the free enterprise system. These people were smart, he said, because they said that they upheld democracy but actually sought "to destroy our freedom—and our power ... [and to] disguise their sabotage by making it seem attractive" (August 1950, p. 499). We must realize, he said, that their intents were "to squander what we have" and dominate American lives either by "a gradual and deceptive process," but also, if need be, by force (March 1951, p. 159).

The magazine also featured extensive warnings from businessmen who spoke at Norfolk and Western employee meetings about the rise of socialism in the U.S. The May 1949 issue featured remarks from Clement Johnson, president of Roanoke Public Warehouse, who warned Americans to be wary of appeals to give up their American way of life, as that would entail sacrificing freedom for security. They knew this, Johnson said, because they needed merely observe a pattern that had befallen other socialist countries: "They beguile with promises, then paralyze with tax burdens, stifle individual thinking, and suppress the right of protest. Then comes the inevitable collapse" he said (May 1949, p. 276). Furthermore, he continued, Americans' attitudes were contributing to conditions that furthered the rise of socialism. Americans claimed they were responsible people, he said, but they elected people who wanted to give them things. He bemoaned that

> [f]ew of us seem to want to keep government out of our personal affairs and responsibilities. Many of us seem to favor various types of government-guaranteed and compulsory security. We say that we want personal freedom, but we demand government housing, government price controls, government-guaranteed jobs and wages.
>
> (May 1949, p. 277)

The May 1949 issue also provided cautionary remarks from E.G. Otey, president of the First National Bank of Bluefield, Virginia. He observed that, in the U.S., "...we have listened to the seductive philosophy of the 'cradle-to-the-grave' advocates of paternalistic government," but Americans needed to reassert that the government was the servant of the people (May 1949, p. 279). Then, the following spring, the magazine opened up several more pages to alerts about the rise of socialism. Douglas Freeman, editor of the *Richmond News Leader* and the author of a 1935 Pulitzer Prize-winning book on Robert E. Lee, spoke on how the road to socialism was deceptive because it was not a war against the audience but rather a "war against your children!" (May 1950, p. 244). Profligate government spending in a pursuit of rolling out socialistic programs was "...Eating up the patrimony of America," he said (May 1950, p. 244). Also cautioning readers were comments by Daniel Richberg, who was a Washington, DC, lawyer and a lecturer on constitutional law at the University of Virginia. He warned that the country had seen the rise of socialistic reformers in the 1920s and was going through another similar phase. These socialism advocates, he said, did not understand that placing the government in more control of daily life allowed the state to exert compulsory powers that would impinge on the "individual liberties which are the most valuable heritage of the American people" (May 1950, p. 245). To that end of exerting more control, he said the government was "making great headway in socializing ... many industries without government ownership," and he pointed to state efforts to direct food production by subsidizing eggs, wheat, and corn (May 1950. p. 247). This attempt to advance socialism counted on Americans believing the illusion that they would still have the liberty of the private marketplace, when actually they were being led to government dependency, he said. Social security was a similar scheme for government control, he suggested, where the state attempted to assure Americans that it would provide support for their old age while taxing away money which workers could be putting aside for their own security. He warned the audience to be aware of "impatient, political-minded individuals [who] are always calling upon government to relieve them of the pains and problems of self-discipline," asking for government measures to compel all into programs of cooperation (May 1950, p. 248). In the April 1952 issue, a Norfolk and Western manager cautioned about similar efforts by the government to manipulate the marketplace, particularly at the state level. I.E. Ward, Jr., an industrial and agricultural manager for the railroad, described how states were reaching out to business operations who might want to place their facilities along the rail lines. Some states subsidized municipal bonds so that their cities, in an effort to entice business relocations to their area, could construct the buildings for these companies, he said. "We do not believe this plan to be just or proper, but it is another evidence of the creeping socialism which is taking place in our country today" (April 1952, p. 241).

The publication featured two reprinted pieces that amplified concerns about the onset of socialism. In the summer of 1949, it ran a piece with no byline, originally written by the Standard Steel Spring Company that, while excoriating communism, explicitly linked that term to socialism. It pointed out that Marx originated communist ideology out of fear that capitalism abused the working man and would leave him "in a state of pitiful destitution unless all people of the world could be organized on a uniform socialistic basis" (August 1949, p. 473). Marx, said the article, had the "big idea ... to attack capitalistic countries, bore from within, promote collectivist measures through governmental agencies, and defeat the opponent by turning his own strength against him" (August, 1949, p. 473). The piece warned readers that one needed only look at the government for signs of being attacked from within—large government spending and almost 2,000 federal offices provided the evidence of the spread of state planners who wanted to control Americans' lives and destinies. Three summers later, the *Norfolk and Western Magazine* reprinted a piece from the *Saturday Evening Post* titled "The America We Lost," authored by Mario A. Pei, a professor of Romance philology at Columbia University, New York. Pei, an immigrant to the U.S., began his piece by describing the overactive government in his native Italy, claiming it was an intrusive state that was typical of several post-World War II countries in Europe. He did not miss such a meddling government, he said, but unfortunately, in the last 20 years the U.S. had witnessed the "Europeanization of America," marked by the rise of the "government octopus, along with the vanishing of the American spirit of freedom and opportunity" (Pei, 1952, p. 428). Americans, he said, were falling prey to a "breathless search for security that is doomed to defeat in advance of a world where nothing, not even life itself, is secure" (Pei, July 1952, p. 428).

Norfolk and Western was unequivocal in its advisory to its employees—and to American society—that the U.S. was under attack by those who would attempt to sell the citizenry the premise that the government, through its exertions, would help improve daily life. The company was adamant that accepting the seemingly helpful hand of the state would come at the cost of violating what it meant to be an American. That is, accepting a bigger government presence would undermine Americans' earnest, self-starting values. Instead, Americans needed to be better aware of the benefits they derived from the country's free enterprise system.

On the watch to preserve a profitable life through free enterprise

Across these years, the *Norfolk and Western Magazine* attempted to contextualize the significance of the threat of socialism by reminding readers what was at stake if Americans abandoned capitalism. Accordingly, it laid out for its readers how Americans profited from the free enterprise system. To do this, it continued to rely on news stories that featured remarks from speakers at Norfolk and Western events, and it also reprinted material from pro-capitalist sources.

Several of the speakers who alerted the audience about the rise of socialism also made sure to point out the benefits of free enterprise. Johnson emphasized that Americans needed to realize that, unlike socialism, free enterprise encouraged pockets of innovation that benefited all (May 1949, p. 276). Otey asserted that, with free enterprise, Americans experienced both "practically unlimited" opportunities to achieve "great success" and a wealth of "comforts and conveniences of life" that in the past 50 years had eclipsed what humans had been able to develop in the previous 5,000 years (May 1949, p. 278). The Pulitzer Prize-winning Freeman told his audience that the free enterprise system also was the great enabler of the individualistic American. It was the vehicle through which they could show initiative and better their station in life. "We weren't going to guarantee him a profit; we weren't going to save him against a loss," he said, "but we were going to give him a chance to rise with this great continent that our fathers had conquered" (May 1950, p. 241).

Attorney Richberg amplified the contrast between the opportunity of capitalism versus the constraints of socialism:

> We have a thousand proofs that when men rely on voluntary agreement as the basis for human cooperation they advance their common welfare and their individual security; but when they rely on organized force they eventually destroy more than they create and they increase their individual insecurity.
>
> (May 1950, p. 247)

The publication added to these voices several others who spoke on the beneficence of the free market as opposed to the dysfunctions of socialism. At a meeting of 2,500 former employees of the Norfolk and Western, Forest Williams, chairman of the board of the Williams Shoe Manufacturing Company, pointed out that England's socialist system led to people being rationed only a few ounces of bacon and butter per week. The country's low standard of living was attributable to the public's "belief that government [was] a productive organism," causing them to believe that the state would take care of them (June 1950, p. 315). Under socialism, "very few want to work or produce," he said, which resulted in a "bare existence and ultimately a police state" (June, 1950, p. 315). Meanwhile, under our free enterprise system, Americans worked "almost maternally to make life easier and more comfortable for [themselves], [their] wives, and children and for the generations yet unborn" (June 1950, p. 334).

In the spring of 1951, T. Coleman Andrews, the owner of an accounting firm, explained that a key difference between socialism and free enterprise was that free enterprise had the spirit of calling all together in a joint effort to build a better existence where all workers, and not the government, were the center of that life-enhancing project. Industry and workers were delivering services and goods at cheaper prices, what he called "wondering working" offerings, because all could share in profits and savings. While there were those in the U.S. who said it was sinful to make a profit and thought that "the government ought to control and manage all the means of production and distribution," Americans should realize that they were already profiting from free enterprise, he said (May 1951, p. 282) If a person made $5,000 a year and then saved $1,000, then that $1,000 was a profit, he said. "There is no essential difference between your savings and a corporation's profits," he said, and those savings and profits allowed Americans to live a better life and help others. Americans had "never known want," and, moreover, were able to "succor most of the rest of the world," while also positioning their children and grandchildren to avoid the ignominy of being leveled to "a common place of life" through socialism (May 1951, p. 284).

In the winter of 1952, Prince Thornton, inspector for the Appalachian Electric Power Co., spoke of socialism as a cancer. "A little socialism is just as welcome and just as needed in the life of a democratic nation as a little cancer is needed in your body or mine," he said. "Eventually that little cancer, that little socialism, will bring about our destruction" (November 1952, p. 680). Instead, he told the audience, they already had much at stake in the capitalist, free market system. Capitalism simply meant owning something, he said, and "if you own an automobile, if you own your home, if you own a horse, a cow, you are a capitalist" (November 1952, p. 680). He pointed to the conveniences that come from capitalism: America had only 6% of the world's land mass, yet had almost half of the world's radios, 85% of all automobiles, and more than 90% of the world's bathtubs. The U.S. had almost half of the world's wealth, he said. Yet communists and socialists tried to sell Americans on materialism;

"but how can they possibly hope to deliver something that we've got them skinned hands down on?" he said (November 1952, p. 680). He closed with this reminder:

> In America, we're on top. Of course, in a depression, it goes down, but when it hits bottom it is still above the rest of the world in its best times. Now you can trade or swap if you want, but you had better look at the horse you are trading for before you get hold of him… There's not another spot in the world that can give you and me the freedom and advantages that we have here in America.
>
> (November 1952, p. 680)

The magazine reprinted pieces designed to remind readers how they benefited from the free market in the U.S. In the January 1949 edition, it reproduced a chart from the Freeport (Illinois) Chamber of Commerce titled, "The Magic of America." The graphic showed that, with the free market system, the U.S. had 20 telephones per 100 people. Meanwhile, socialist England, had only 8 per 100, and communist Russia has only three quarters of a phone per 100 people (January 1949, p. 54). Later that year, the magazine's reprint of the Standard Spring Steel article pointed out that Americans were profiting from free enterprise's trailblazing embrace of machines. For example, in 1850 only 33% of the U.S. population was employed, but in late 1948 that figure was about 41%—with machines doing about 94% of the labor, reported the magazine. "…The machines that men feared have been responsible for the biggest labor force, working the shortest hours, at the highest wages in world history," it said. Free enterprise's encouragement of capital investments—on the magnitude of "twice to ten times that [per] worker in other countries"—was what made this possible in the U.S. (August 1949, p. 473). Another graphic from the J. Walter Thompson agency, called "The Fruits of Their Own Labor," emphasized to readers that the American experience features individuals who can "do better for themselves" than rely on the government (March 1950, p. 184). It showed illustrations of workers in agriculture, labor, and white-collar jobs. These images were accompanied by a reminder that

> With full freedom of choice and acceptance of individual responsibility, we in America have been able to attain the highest standard of living and family security in the world, far higher than any country has been able to establish for its people through state provision.
>
> (March 1950, p. 184)

In stressing the beneficence of the free market, the magazine emphasized what was at stake if Americans embraced socialism. The company wanted Americans to understand that socialism's attack on American free enterprise threatened to destroy a system "under which we have prospered, reared and educated our children and passed on to them the opportunity to make good with successful lives," said Cap'n Jim (March 1951, p. 159). In proffering this view, Norfolk and Western attempted to convey itself as a fellow person well-positioned to advise its countrymen on what they could do about this threat to their shared, profitable way of life.

Preserving our way of life is the highest calling

Across these issues, the *Norfolk and Western Magazine* established that social-ism was attacking the U.S. free enterprise system, a way of life that Americans profited from. In the publication, the company pointed out that Americans had built this system that was reflective of their initiative, self-responsibility, and drive to create. The railway's message to its readers was an assertion of common values and shared ways of understanding the American way of life that needed to be defended. Such a declaration of advocacy was typically offered by the Cit-izenship Committee of the Norfolk and Western's better-service conference, who said that protecting free enterprise "is absolutely necessary if we expect to retain the right of free speech, the right of individual initiative, and the right to worship God according to our own dictates" (May 1949, p. 291). This asserted commonality between the company and the average American called for both the corporation and its fellow citizens to jointly shield the country from mis-guided individuals who had a naïve belief that government had an active role in the marketplace. Standing up against those who would spread socialism, it stated, was an essential calling for all Americans. The magazine spoke to this mission through the "A Train of Thought" column and comments from speakers at Norfolk and Western events.

Cap'n Jim's commentary in his columns regularly urged readers to speak out about the importance of preserving free enterprise. In January 1949, he said that if Americans would remember that the country was founded by those who escaped despots, they would

> be more than ever zealous to keep it the place it has always been … the one place on earth where a man can rise to any heights by his own efforts … where he is free to think and express himself in his own way, the American way.
>
> (January 1949, p. 29)

Then, several months later, Cap'n Jim said that America was on a dangerous road toward socialism, falling prey to a something-for-nothing appeal that would lead to "more government control over our lives and [taking] more taxes from our pocketbooks" (November, 1950, p. 631). He urged readers to push back against socialism by not taking government handouts and insisting that the state become more efficient. "It will take determination and hard work, but that is what made this country in the first place," he said (November, 1950, p. 631). Later that winter, Jim relayed how he attempted to convince a discouraged fellow employee that it was important to reach out to congressional representa-tives about reining in the state. Jim warned his fellow worker that he had a "rare and precious privilege" to stand up for the American way of life, and that "the less vigilant we are, the greater will be the danger ... of a dictatorship" (February 1951, p. 97). The following month, Cap'n Jim asserted that Americans could lose their democracy and free enterprise system through "laziness and indifference" (March 1951, p. 159). Americans needed to speak up for the free enterprise system so that they could continue to "engage in any business we feel best fitted for and to prosper in that business to the maximum extent of our abilities..." (March 1951, p. 159).

Several speakers, who earlier in this chapter touched upon the themes of the rise of socialism and how it threatened the good life brought by capitalism, said that it was imperative for Americans to take action. Otey observed that Americans should push back against socialistic thinking by advocating free enterprise; in doing so, they were "correcting faults, eliminating abuses and ... grasping and enjoying to the fullest the benefits of a life in a country and atmosphere that is free" (May 1949, p. 279). Johnson encouraged his audience to think of free enterprise as a valuable commodity to spread to all. Those intent on government control feared this kind of "export" because "private enterprise is the automatic, natural action of individuals in their own self-interest ... it is self-healing, it embodies the survival of the fittest, and is, therefore, enduring" (May 1949, p. 276). Richberg added that embracing free enterprise more fully called for rejecting "the briberies and the appeals to our fears made by socializing politicians who promise us the pitiful security which is enjoyed by Indians as wards of the government" (May 1950, p. 249). Williams criticized the tendency of the government to tempt Americans away from free enterprise with a promise of security that demanded no effort on the recipient's part. He urged his audience to resist socialism by doing an inventory of their doctrines to make sure they understood that Americanism emphasized their security came only "from hard work, cooperative effort, respect for your fellow man, [and] honor and integrity" (June 1950, p. 335). Andrews underscored that Americans could best thwart socialism through increased self-reliance. He shared a discussion he had with his son about the vision that drove the evolution of the United States: a desire to reach "the very heights of industrial greatness, of intellectual attainment, of advances in religious thought, [and] in the arts and in the sciences" (May 1951, p. 283). All of that, however, was predicated on protecting the free enterprise system which gave all "a right to fail," while they "follow[ed] their own devices, free to choose their own course, free do to as they pleased, but subject, of course, always to the obligation of self-reliance" (May 1951, p. 283).

Other speakers at Norfolk and Western events urged Americans to see that defending free enterprise was a high and valuable calling. The Reverend C.C. Bell's invocation urged that Americans not put their liberty in jeopardy "in the bogs of the isms of today," emphasizing that God would help Americans save themselves from the "heresies of today that would ultimately enslave us and regiment us and cause us to lose our freedom" (May 1950, p. 240). Norfolk and Western vice president George Dunglinson told employees that there was no more worthwhile task ahead than to resist the road to socialism and its intention to replace free enterprise with governmental power and, in the process, make everyone "servants of the State rather than its masters" (May 1950, p. 251). Norfolk and Western general superintendent C.P. Blair said that Americans had a duty to stand up for their free market system because they had special privileges that no one had anywhere else in the world. Yes, this included freedoms of speech and worship but also the freedom "to choose our own vocation or avocation; in other words to be almost anything we want to be and do almost anything we want to do within bounds of a very broad, reasonable and understanding society" (March 1951, p. 144). Another Norfolk and Western manager, assistant superintendent R.E. McGuire, said the challenge of protecting free enterprise rested within the efforts of the average American and not from "the acts of rulers, congresses or parliaments" (January 1952, p. 23). The very American qualities of "humility, perseverance and resilience" were essential to resisting socialism. (January 1952, p. 23).

Across these articles, the third major message from the *Norfolk and Western Magazine* centered on enlightening Americans that they, in concert with the corporation, had an essential duty to protect free enterprise. Fred McWane, assistant to the president of the Lynchburg Foundry Company, exemplified this approach when he encouraged Americans to become diligent activists in the cause of protecting their free market liberties in the face of expanding socialism and communism. He said, however, that Americans appeared to be risking their freedoms because they had neglected to join the fray. They needed to pursue such an effort and realize its full potential for success when done in partnership with the corporation. He said:

> Democracy has not failed. It is we who failed. It still is a growing, living thing that needs our best efforts at all times. We must reaffirm the determination of our fathers to be free men. We have the need today for united action; united against the destruction of our ideals. We all have a pact, you and I.
>
> (November, 1950, p. 624)

What of the corporate persona?

Norfolk and Western's efforts to establish itself as a fellow American who fought to preserve the country's free enterprise system were notable for how they carried forward and intensified corporate persona, free-market advocacy language used by the National Association of Manufacturers prior to World War II (see Chapter 3). Determining direct effects of Norfolk and Western's persona conveyance, however, is problematic, primarily because the magazine offered no data that reflected its readers' viewpoints on the free enterprise system. It is also difficult to extrapolate how its efforts may have effected broader public opinion. For example, a 1951 opinion poll of high school seniors revealed that only about one third believed that profits were central to the American economic system (Fones-Wolf, 1994, p. 193). However, scholars have also found other surveys that revealed, from the 1950s through the 1960s, a move away from interest in socialist/collectivist tendencies toward re-embracing an ethos of individualism and anti-statism (Fones-Wolf, 1994; Lipset, 1986, 1996). Furthermore, evidence persists that the American individualistic bent also leads to favorable views of free enterprise, even in the aftermath of the Great Recession of 2008–2009. Two years into the effects of that recession, a Gallup poll revealed that 86% of respondents had a positive view toward free enterprise (Newport, 2010) and, by 2012, Gallup found that number had risen to 89% (Newport, 2012). Also in 2012, Pew Research found that anti-statism persisted, with a little over a third of Americans agreeing that government regulation of business was helpful to Americans ("A majority," 2012). More recently, a poll of Americans by the Legatum Institute revealed that, by a 3:1 margin, Americans believe that the free enterprise system is better equipped to help people move out of poverty than is the state (Montgomerie, 2015).

It is apparent that the U.S. has an enduring free market orientation, rooted in the country's mid-20th-century reassertions of notions of self-advancement through capitalism. As the Norfolk and Western's attempts at corporate persona conveyance were strongly consonant with prevailing American sensibilities about the importance of individualism, self-reliance, and initiative, a more useful understanding of the railroad's efforts can be seen through Foucault's understanding of self-governance. As initially discussed in Chapter 1 and then seen at work in Chapter 3's examination of the National Association of Manufacturers, modern American society encouraged the individual to pursue life decisions through embarking on a self-governed navigation that, in the industrial world, aligns with marketplace imperatives. Foucault's articulation of self-governance essentially describes a drive to act upon oneself so that a person maximizes his or her productivity and, in the process, avoids interventions from the state (Foucault, 1977, 1997). He identified five preparation stages involved in orienting oneself for an effective journey toward self-governance: (1) establishing a general sense of direction; (2) charting a plan toward a particular aim or objective; (3) identifying that objective as being a "place of safety" or a "home-port"; (4) realizing that the journey will have dangers; and (5) developing "a knowledge, a technique, an art" so as to be able to successfully complete the journey (Foucault, 2006, p. 248). These stages align well with the themes in the *Norfolk and Western Magazine*. Using the same stages, one can see that the publication established: (1) self-fulfillment through free enterprise as Americans' sense of direction; (2) resistance to government handouts and being self-reliant as the plan toward that objective; (3) free enterprise as the arrival point that is the "place of safety"; (4) socialism as the danger on the journey toward self-fulfillment through free enterprise; and (5) coupling one's self-reliance with the helping hand of the Norfolk and Western corporate persona as the way to avoid socialism and successfully set out on the journey toward self-fulfillment through the free market. As such, Foucault's five-stage preparation for self-government provides a helpful window into how Norfolk and Western attempted to align its prerogatives with its audience's worldviews. Moreover, it also provides a valuable platform for increased consciousness about how corporations may adopt a corporate persona that is designed to leverage enduring American values in a way that can advance the corporation's interests in times of stress or crisis. A larger concern, then, is the exertion of power through the reality-shaping potential of an affinitive (or "just like you") corporate persona approach. This can be seen, for example, in the contemporary American milieu of discussions that involve macro-level socio-economic concerns (see Chapter 10 for more). Moreover, the power of the corporation (and not necessarily the state) greatly frames micro-level decisions about, for example, viable career options, the range of choices for health care and child care, and feasible alternatives to expensive energy sources for the car and home.

In such an environment, the corporate persona has more space within which to articulate choices for the individual by displaying that the concerns of corporations fit within the "flow" of American daily life. Much like NAM's earlier efforts during the New Deal, Norfolk and Western called for reasserting the harmony between the corporation and the individual during a time of increased unionism, softening economic performance, and a Fair Deal administration that was perceived by business as too active in the marketplace. The company was worried that citizens, rather than seeing how their interests aligned with corporations, would increase their reliance on the state. This could lead to a scenario detailed in the 1944 book *How We Live*:

> ...One of the most difficult problems is to prevent government-taking-and-giving from becoming a heavy burden on the productive worker, and it is all the more difficult because the taking is frequently caused by political pressure groups demanding gifts from the public purse. This demand forces government into a hard choice: If it does not increase government taking, it cannot increase government giving as demanded by pressure groups; if it does increase government taking it is only a matter of time until the people, including the individuals within the pressure groups, rise up in violent protest against the taxes.
>
> (Clark & Rimanoczy, 1944, p. 23)

This possibility of such confiscation of wealth, and resulting societal chaos, spurred Norfolk and Western to offer a rosier picture of a future shaped by individual reliance on business. Corporate personas (like the individual) are on a journey to successfully master the marketplace orientation of the country, and they have the wisdom, experience, and congruent values to offer advice to fellow Americans on how to best improve their lot. In this vein, Cap'n Jim wrote in his "A Train of Thought" column that the power of the corporation was beneficial to American life. The U.S. was producing more in areas like steel, copper, and aluminum, he said, and the country had 10 million more people employed than when Pearl Harbor happened. He asserted:

> In short, American production and transportation are working better today than they ever did, and they will always work if we put our reliance in

ourselves, keep steadfast our faith in the free enterprise way of life, and maintain peace within our own ranks.

(August 1950, p. 499)

The collective "we" apparent in such statements from Norfolk and Western demonstrates the optimal kind of collectivism that the corporate persona exemplifies—rather than any reliance on an intrusive and impersonal state, self-reliance through the corporate persona is best because that entity understands what it means for fellow family members to strive to better their lot in life. As surveys of Americans continue to indicate a strong support for the free enterprise system, Norfolk and Western's efforts show that scholars and citizens would do well to observe where corporations, through the corporate persona, attempt to construct allegiances between the private interests of companies and the values of the citizenry, especially in times of stress for free enterprise.

References

"A majority says that government regulation of business does more harm than good." (2012). *Pew Research Center*, March 7. Retrieved from www.pewresearch.org/daily-number/a-majority-says-that-government-regulation-of-business-does-more-harm-than-good/.

Allen, D.S. (2001). "The First Amendment and the doctrine of corporate personhood: Collapsing the press-corporation distinction." *Journalism 2*(3), pp. 255–278.

Arnold, T. (1937). *The folklore of capitalism.* Yale, CT: Yale University Press.

Clark, F.G., & Rimanoczy, R.S. (1944). *How we live: A simple dissection of the economic body.* New York: D. Van Nostrand Co., Inc.

Crable, R.E., & Vibbert, S.L. (1983). "Mobil's epideictic advocacy: 'Observations' of Prometheus-bound." *Communications Monographs 50*, pp. 380–394.

Cutlip, S. (1994). *Public relations: The unseen power.* Hillsdale, NJ: Lawrence Erlbaum.

Cutlip, S. (1995). *Public relations history: From the 17th century to the 20th century.* Hillsdale, New Jersey: Lawrence Erlbaum Associates.

Ewen, S. (1996). *PR! A social history of spin.* New York: Basic Books.

Fifer, J.V. (1988). *American progress: The growth of the transport, tourist and information industries in the nineteenth-century West.* Chester, CT: Globe Pequot Press.

Fones-Wolf, E. (1994). *Selling free enterprise: The business assault on labor and liberalism, 1945–60.* Urbana, IL: University of Illinois Press.

Foucault, M. (1977). *Discipline and punish: The birth of the prison.* New York: Pantheon.

Foucault, M. (1997). *Ethics: subjectivity and truth* (Vol. 1). New York: The New Press.

Foucault, M. (2006). *The hermeneutics of the subject: Lectures at the College De France, 1981–82* (F. Gros Ed., & G. Burchell Trans.). New York: Picador.

Gans, D., & Shapiro, I. (2014). *Religious liberties for corporations? Hobby Lobby, the Affordable Care Act and the Constitution.* New York: Palgrave Macmillan.

Krannich, J.M. (2005). "The corporate 'person': A new analytical approach to a flawed method of constitutional interpreation." *Loyola University Chicago Law Journal 37*, pp. 61–109.

Lipset, S. (1986). "North American labor movements: A comparative perspective." In S. Lipset (Ed.), *Unions in transition: Entering the second century*, pp. 421–452. San Francisco: Institute for Contemporary Studies.

Lipset, S. (1996). *American exceptionalism: A double-edged sword.* New York: W.W. Norton.

Lindley, D. (1999). *Ambrose Bierce takes on the railroad.* Westport, CT: Praeger.

Livesey, S.M. (2002). "Global warming wars: Rhetoric and discourse analytic approaches to ExxonMobil's corporate public discourse." *The Journal of Business Communication* *39*(1), pp. 117–148.

Marchand, R. (1998). *Creating the corporate soul: The rise of public relations and corporate imagery.* Berkeley: University of California Press.

Montgomerie, T. (2015). "What the world thinks of capitalism." November 3. Retrieved from https://social.shorthand.com/montie/3C6iES9yjf/what-the-world-thinks-of-capitalism.

Newport, F. (2010). "Socialism viewed positively by 86 percent of Americans." Gallup, February 4. Retrieved from www.gallup.com/poll/125645/socialism-viewed-positively-americans.aspx.

Newport, F. (2012). "Democrats, Republicans diverge on capitalism, federal gov't." Gallup, November 29. Retrieved from www.gallup.com/poll/158978/democrats-republicans-diverge-capitalism-federal-gov.aspx.

Nielander, W.A., & Miller, R.W. (1951). *Public relations.* New York: The Ronald Press Company.

Norfolk and Western Magazine. (1949). "A train of thought." January, p. 29.

Norfolk and Western Magazine. (1949). "The magic of America." January, p. 54

Norfolk and Western Magazine. (1949). "The story of a conference." May 27, pp. 272–291.

Norfolk and Western Magazine. (1949). "To the members of the Norfolk & Western Family." July, p. 406.

Norfolk and Western Magazine. (1949). "Isn't a hundred years long enough to prove a point?" August, p. 473

Norfolk and Western Magazine. (1949). "Yes, we can do something." August, p. 479.

Norfolk and Western Magazine. (1950). "A train of thought." January, p. 31.

Norfolk and Western Magazine. (1950). "The fruits of their own labor." March, p. 184.

Norfolk and Western Magazine. (1950). "The story of the annual better service conference." May, pp. 234–260.

Norfolk and Western Magazine. (1950). "A big day in Roanoke." June, pp. 315, 334–335.

Norfolk and Western Magazine. (1950). "A train of thought." August, p. 499.

Norfolk and Western Magazine. (1950). "The price of freedom." November, p. 624.

Norfolk and Western Magazine. (1950). "A train of thought." November, p. 631.

Norfolk and Western Magazine. (1951). "A train of thought." February, p. 97.

Norfolk and Western Magazine. (1951). "An American duty." March, p. 144.

Norfolk and Western Magazine. (1951). "A train of thought." March, p. 159.

Norfolk and Western Magazine. (1951). "Your better service conference." May, pp. 281–293.

Norfolk and Western Magazine. (1952). "The test of a man." January, p. 23.

Norfolk and Western Magazine. (1952). "Ward tells Pulaski Club how better service attracts industries." April, p. 241

Norfolk and Western Magazine. (1952). "Socialism as dangerous as cancer." November, p. 680.

Olasky, M. (1987). *Corporate public relations: A new historical perspective.* Hillsdale, NJ: Lawrence Erlbaum.

Pei, M.A. (1952). "The America we lost." *Norfolk and Western Magazine*, July, pp. 428–429.

Pollman, E. (2011). "Reconceiving corporate personhood." *Utah Law Review 4*, pp. 1629–1674.

Schmertz, H. (1986). *Good-bye to the low profile*. Boston: Little, Brown and Company.

St. John III, B. (2014). "Conveying the sense-making corporate persona: The Mobil Oil 'Observations' columns, 1975–1980." *Public Relations Review 40*(4), pp. 692–699.

St. John III, B., & Arnett, R. (2014). "The National Association of Manufacturers' commmunity relations short film 'Your Town': Parable, propaganda, and big individualism." *Journal of Public Relations Research 26*(2), pp. 103–116.

Stoker, K., & Stoker, M. (2012). "The paradox of public interest: How serving individual superior interests fulfill public relations' obligation to the public interest." *Journal of Mass Media Ethics 27*, pp. 31–45.

Tedlow, R. (1979). *Keeping the corporate image: Public relations and business, 1900–1950*. Greenwich, CT: JAI Press.

Wimmer, R.D., & Dominick, J.R. (2010). *Mass media research: An introduction* (9th ed.). Belmont, CA: Thomson/Wadsworth.

6 The oil company and you

The corporate persona as encourager of self-governance

By the early 1950s, as previous chapters have shown, companies had begun to assert a human-like kinship between corporations and the individual. The National Association of Manufacturers, perceiving the pre-World War II domestic threats of unionism, the lingering Depression, and a robust New Deal, articulated an affiliation between the corporation and the individual on notions of democracy, liberty, and free enterprise. By that time, *PR News*, the only weekly trade publication devoted to public relations, amplified such links by pointing to how corporations, during the combined stresses of the threats of communism and an active Fair Deal program, offered a more personal face in communities (e.g., by reaching out to communities to educate them on free enterprise and developing more approaches to connect with children). Similarly, the Norfolk and Western Railway, through its house publication, spoke to its employees and stakeholders as a beneficent, corporate fellow human. It defended free enterprise during a time of increasing economic strains for the railroads—a vulnerability it saw as exacerbated by Americans' increased willingness to indulge socialistic concepts and the Fair Deal's increasing marketplace interventions. As Chapter 5 showed, the company conveyed that the best way for Americans to face the difficulties of the time (e.g., the Korean War, the threat of foreign ideologies, and the dangers of a potentially controlling government) was to turn to self-reliance within the free market, guided by the wisdom of the human-like corporation. This is a Foucauldian message of self-governance—that one can maximize one's sense of accomplishment and fulfillment in proportion to which one's actions comport with the demands of the marketplace. As discussed in Chapters 1, 3, and 5, the self-management appeal of the corporate persona asserts an already-existing affinity between individual and corporation, redirecting audiences toward actions that exemplify shared corporate/individual worldviews and goals.

This chapter shows how another corporate entity, Standard Oil of California (SOCA), used its *Standard Oiler* publication in the early 1950s to affirm the value of self-government to its readers. SOCA began operating in 1907 and, after the breakup of the Standard Oil Trust in 1911, retained the Standard Oil name. In the late 1920s, it was part of an oil industry that oversupplied the market and, with the turmoil of the Great Depression, turned to the incoming

New Deal and its National Recovery Administration for industrial planning (e.g., codes) to help steady its financial footing (Schlesinger, 1958). The industry saw it as a fractious relationship, especially when the New Deal's justice department began anti-trust proceedings against hundreds of oil companies in the late 1930s (Yergin, 2008). Not surprisingly, by the 1950s, the oil industry and SOCA felt long-besieged by the activist tendencies of the federal government as continued by the Fair Deal. In response, SOCA pointed out that the essence of American life was greatly rooted in the constructive force of the marketplace, an understanding that appeared to be in peril because of the continued prominent role of the federal government during the Fair Deal era. Significantly, by 1950, SOCA was in the government's crosshairs as the U.S. Department of Justice pursued an anti-trust suit against the company and six other West Coast oil firms, alleging that these companies fixed prices and controlled oil production (SOCA, 1952). More broadly, SOCA was concerned about federal government intrusions such as the persistence of Fair Deal social welfare programs and state interventions into the marketplace, either as a regulator or a participant. In early 1950, it reprinted a commencement speech from Northwestern University president Franklyn B. Snyder that encapsulated SOCA's view. Snyder warned against the rise of "social planners" within the federal government who were propagating a "wasteful and inefficient federal government [that] is reaching out like an octopus to wrap itself around more and ever more phases of your lives and mine." He said, "I hope the college men and women of this country still have the hardihood of their pioneer ancestors" and he hoped they would show that they resisted government paternalism (Snyder, 1950, pp. 9, 21).

SOCA's public relations messages in the *Standard Oiler* paralleled and amplified Snyder's concern by proffering articles that questioned the expansive role of the state, valorized the private marketplace, and thereby encouraged self-government. SOCA's messages, rather than offering a direct appeal to identify with the corporation, addressed existing societal values that prized self-direction, encouraging readers to channel their energies toward maximizing their lives through the free market. With this approach, SOCA affirmed an already-existing allegiance with the individual to revivify among its employees, their families, and their stockholders a desire for self-governance, instead of turning to the state for assistance in navigating life.

To determine how the *Standard Oiler* attempted to signify the importance of self-government during a time when the company perceived threats from continued state expansion (e.g., a federal anti-trust suit, concerns about increased state-initiated social planning), a textual analysis was conducted (Wimmer & Dominick, 2010) of every issue of the publication across the years 1950–1952. Begun by Lee Peck in November 1938, this monthly publication originally circulated to employees in the western part of the United States. However, by the early 1950s, it had reached a circulation of 40,000 and was also widely circulated to employees and stockholders worldwide. The publication normally carried 9 or 10 larger articles, several continuing features like stories on

recipients of company awards, and lists of who recently retired ("Your magazine," 1953, p. 3). Similar to the approach used in Chapter 5, each edition's original articles and reprinted pieces (e.g., speeches, columns from other
publications, etc.) were scanned and noted for references to the presence of the
government as relates to the reader and to the presence of the free market as
relates to the reader. Informed by grounded theory approaches first discussed in
Chapter 4, stories that met the two conditions above were closely read for how
various themes relevant to the government emerged throughout each piece. From
this, a pool of full-length pieces, often one to two pages long, was then re-read.
As similar points appeared in the newsletter across the years examined, broad
thematic categories emerged. From this approach, this chapter details that the
Standard Oiler stated three rationales for the importance of self-management:
the inefficiencies of the federal government; the tendency for the federal government to dominate individuals' lives; and the marketplace being the ideal arena
for realizing individual aspirations.

The inefficiencies of the federal government

Heading into 1950, the *Standard Oiler* published a series of pieces from Robert
L. Johnson, chairman of the Citizens Committee for the Hoover Commission, a
panel that had been established by Congress in 1947 to put forward legislative
proposals to modernize the federal government. The full-page columns that ran
in the fall of 1949 and into early 1950 offered a view of the government as an
inept businessman, owning "$29 billion worth of goods, including a million
automobiles" but failing to put in place effective accounting and inventory practices, leading to "enough [federal] records and documents—mostly worthless—
to fill six Pentagon Buildings" (Johnson 1949a, p. 9). Moreover, said Johnson,
there was plenty of evidence of poor management of employees: managers, in an
attempt to build empires, overstaffed their areas at a cost of $76 million in sal-
aries. Still, low pay and lack of advancement in the civil service led to dwindling
morale and to 25% of that workforce quitting each year. These kinds of wasteful
practices affected everyone's quality of life, he noted: "You, and all the rest of
us, must pay, in increased taxes, for such government waste and inefficiency"
(Johnson, 1949b, p. 14). As 1950 dawned, Johnson said that the commission, in
the course of producing a 19-volume report for Congress, developed an urgent
warning for Americans: Uncle Sam is the world's worst businessman. He said
that each American should get involved (especially with state committees tied to
the Hoover Commission) to make sure they all had a better government that
would reduce citizens' taxes and allow them to lead a "more normal life"
(Johnson, 1950, p. 5).

As the United States became engaged in the Korean War, the *Standard Oiler*
maintained that the ineffective practices of the federal government put the nation
at further peril while facing communist aggressions. Citing more information
from the Hoover Commission, it said that the nation's government spent about
10% of the federal budget on "unnecessary materials and services," even wasting

money by having two different federal agencies "bidding against each other for irrigation, reclamation, and other public works projects" ("War," 1951, p. 10). The following year, the publication asserted that such inefficiencies were compounded by a bureaucratic structure that continued to reward empire building. For example, when a federal agency hires a person, it determines that employee's wages based on how many people are subordinate to that individual. Rather than providing incentives that promote efficiency and productivity, the state's pay structures reward those who build more departments under their purview. This is a recipe for ineffectiveness, said the *Standard Oiler*, and "the result is that we have a lot of [government employees] working for us whose usefulness is hard to explain" ("It's tough," 1952, p. 12). It found it particularly troubling that, since 1941, the federal civilian workforce had increased by 85%. Referring to the struggle against communism, both domestically and in the Korean War, it said that such a hiring binge, coupled with inefficient incentives, led to "wasteful government practices [that could] help our enemies more than ... divisions of men in their own ranks" ("It's tough," 1952, p. 13).

The publication was particularly alarmed about the government's propensity for wasteful spending. The state's interventions into the marketplace lead to egregious expenditures that, in turn, resulted in a huge federal debt and a 50% decrease in the value of the dollar ("It's only," 1952, p. 12). First, it said, the government needed to cut out excessive and wasteful spending within its $52-billion public-works program. Second, as the state was a poor manager of its funds, it also needed to "get out of the private money-lending business"; the Farm Home Administration's excessively large loans to farmers were a prime example of the government's inefficient management of money ("It's only," 1952, p. 12). What the government failed to understand, it said, was its need to "to limit expenditures with the same intelligence and prudence that we plan and limit our own expenditures" ("It's only," 1952, p. 12).

SOCA's message was clear: one could not count on the federal government as a platform through which to improve one's life. The government was inept, and its wasteful tendencies actually caused it to not only mismanage its own workers but also damage all people through its inefficient use of individuals' tax dollars. Behind these observations was SOCA's implied appeal: the free market is the sensible arbiter of financial soundness, and one's effort to achieve a satisfactory (and financially viable) life rests on one pursuing such self-advancement in concert with the market.

Government's tendency to dominate

The *Standard Oiler* wanted readers to understand another significant dysfunction of the state—the government exhibited a strong tendency to want to take over too many sectors of a working person's life. The newsletter reported SOCA president T.S. Petersen's 1950 speech to the Los Angeles Rotary Club, where he asserted that there were many social planners within the state who wanted to particularly focus on large enterprises like SOCA and drive them out of business, thus allowing "government to step into the breach and take over ... establishing a single, great monopoly for all enterprise" ("Steel," 1950, p. 24). This is not necessarily because these planners were communists, he said, but because they had a need to exert power and establish control over people's lives.

Building on these observations was Snyder's earlier-referenced commencement address, which established a significant self-government message that the *Standard Oiler* repeatedly alluded to: individuals needed to be wary of the federal government asserting too much of a presence in their daily lives (e.g., through socialism), as the state would move toward dominating each individual's affairs. Snyder warned that social planners wanted to remove a sense of struggle in life by offering various government programs that purported to offer lifetime security. He urged the graduates to consider ancient Rome, a civilization that collapsed because the government sold the formerly industrious people on the notion of giving up their hard-won freedoms for security, and the populace "succumbed to the insidious poison of the idea that 'the government will do it'" (Snyder, 1950, p. 9). He finished the speech by encouraging them to "think and live like free men," to resist "any bureaucrat who tries to plan our lives for us," and thereby assert, "We want no state socialism" (Snyder, 1950, p. 22).

The publication continued with its warnings about socialism in the summer of 1952. It detailed how socialism had gradually spread around the world, purporting to "uplift the masses ... by bringing the means of production and distribution under government ownership" and "bring about a fairer distribution of wealth and avoid the exploitation of the downtrodden" ("Who wants," 1952, p. 24). However, said the newsletter, such a concentration of power in the government allowed it to dispense favors to certain parties to get their acquiescence, impose onerous taxes that destroy private initiative, and use its unlimited resources to compete with private businesses. Since the oil industry was essential to the daily life of the country, it said, the socialists' push to exert control put Standard Oil employees in a potentially vulnerable position. "There is a special duty upon us ... to be alert to the game and know the answers," as such social planners would hold out the promise of "cradle-to-grave security, full employment [and] a variety of free services" ("Who wants," 1952, p. 24). It finished the piece by reminding employees:

> The plain fact is that the American system of private ownership pays off in both freedom and prosperity, and Socialism, as a way of life, never has. Our system, using the productive virtues of opportunity and competition, has given all its people more of the good things of life—including freedom— than Socialism has ever dared to promise, let alone produce.
>
> ("Who wants," 1952, p. 24)

One of the publication's more graphic arguments against the looming domination of the state appeared in the summer of 1952, with the piece "The Perfect

Security State." The article, accompanied by a full-page picture of a monkey in a cage, asked in bold type, "Is this security?" The piece then pointed out that living in a cage may, indeed, be a picture of security because the monkey has housing, food, and all medical bills taken care of, without having to hold down a job. Building on this metaphor, the *Standard Oiler* stated that being alert to the risk of such imprisonment was essential because, across the ages, governments had proven that they would try to get people to give up their liberties in perilous times. A particularly insidious attempt to get people to give up freedom, said the publication, was when the state tried to buy such surrender with the taxpayers' own money. The state proclaimed that it gave the people financial help, courtesy of the government's money. "Of course, no politician has *anything* to give, except that which he first takes from *you*," said SOCA ("The perfect," 1952, p. 18; italics in original). As more citizens came to believe they could not do without such support, collectivists worked toward their vision of Utopia; they did not intend on making serfs of the citizenry, "but the mechanics of administering every detail of the people's lives [made] it inevitable that absolute obedience be enforced" ("The perfect," 1952, p. 18).

With this second theme, SOCA warned that, in addition to exposing oneself to harmful inefficiencies, reliance on the federal government could put one in danger of loss of self. Company president Petersen, in a 1950 address to a banking conference, said that socialistic reformers within government normally wanted to put the means of production in the government's hands. Pointing to the ramifications of this very development within the Soviet Union, he said that the state then controlled "the way to make a living," resulting in the government also controlling "the lives and *the thoughts* of the people" ("What's bad," 1950, p. 24; emphasis added). With these warnings about state dominance, SOCA implied that, when one turns to the state, instead of self-governing in accordance with the market, one risks the possibility that the state will confiscate one's livelihood, constraining what one can focus on for self-betterment, contributing to one's loss of self.

Realizing aspirations through the market

The *Standard Oiler* complemented its warnings about the inefficiencies of an intrusive, meddling government by urging its readers to consider more carefully how America's free enterprise system was the optimal route toward citizens' freedom to achieve a productive and more satisfying life. T.S. Petersen, in a 1950 speech to the Los Angeles Rotary Club, claimed social planners did not realize that the marketplace was the true arena for allowing Americans the opportunities to display their penchant for achievement and progress. These social planners might think their insights into using government to improve lives were profound, but, he said, "[I]f they are that good, why aren't they already in these businesses, offering their talent on the open market where authentic ability commands the highest respect and the highest price in the world?" ("Steel," 1950, p. 24). Petersen's answer was apparent in a separate 1950 speech: big business and free markets were emblematic of the full flowering of what it meant to be an American, he said. The founders welded the concept of free enterprise into the Constitution, he claimed, thereby allowing corporations to be the foundation for "the furthest development of the courage, wit, and energy of free men" ("What's bad," 1950, p. 23). Granted, there were self-seeking interests within government who wanted to roll back business, he said, but the everyday citizen knew that such an effort would reduce the opportunities to better oneself and would resist such efforts by the state. The average American knew what "citizenship [meant] in point of wealth, opportunity and freedom [and did] not want to move backward [but] ... toward more wealth, more opportunity, more freedom" ("What's bad," 1950, p. 24).

The free market system, said the *Standard Oiler*, helped Americans exercise their impetus toward freedom, particularly by rewarding citizens for displaying a self-directed, hardy productivity that contributed to the development of the country's wealth. Despite social planners' lauding of socialism, "the American system of private ownership [paid] off in both freedom and prosperity" because, in contrast to socialism, it hinged upon the individual acting upon "the productive virtues of opportunity and competition [and] freedom" ("Who wants," 1952, p. 24). Americans need to be reminded that self-reliance was crucial toward achieving freedom through the marketplace, said the publication. As a central part of America's heritage, self-reliance revealed the "backbone, daring enterprise or moral courage" that allowed the country to continue to "fight for ... ideals of dignity [and] self-respect," freely traversing a road toward "improved natural greatness" ("The perfect," 1952, p. 19).

The publication further asserted that, while democracy is certainly important, the country's political processes, by themselves, do not establish America's prosperity. In fact, the American embrace of freedom as realized in the marketplace was at the cornerstone of the country's well-being, it said. Like any country, the United States must develop the best ways to harvest its natural resources, and that was achieved through individual initiative and not necessarily the form of state governance. American democracy, like the common good, was bolstered because the American free enterprise system allowed the individual to "express himself, fulfill himself and enrich himself [of] all that [lay] within his power—so long as he [did] not encroach upon the freedom of others" ("What do," 1952, p. 13). Free enterprise was more essential than democracy for the uplifting of self, said the *Standard Oiler*, because the U.S. marketplace allowed every citizen the possibility to unleash the ambitions or ingenuity within.

With these assertions, SOCA maintained that the state must be seen as eclipsed and that individuals should understand that the truest realization of freedom was to express oneself in ways that allowed one to advance in the marketplace. The self-reliant, self-governing American was a prime exemplar of American freedom, it said, and SOCA declared that it shared with Americans the desire to uphold that freedom in the face of social planners' advocacy for an overbearing, activist state.

What of the corporate persona?

By 1950, Standard Oil of California faced a series of events that challenged its ability to present itself as a constructive force in shaping what it meant to be an American. The intrusive presence of the federal government alarmed SOCA—it was concerned that the Truman administration's Fair Deal attempted to foster more government growth and citizen reliance on many state social-safety-net programs. It was also distressed that socialism had taken root within the government and that social planners would find various ways to convince the public that essential services, like oil, were goods that should be taken over by the government. Additionally, the state had already revealed its propensity for inserting itself into various industries like real estate, electric power, transportation, and farming—showing little inclination to leave those arenas, even when its approaches were, to SOCA, costly and ruinous to the markets involved. The government, the company said, exhibited a penchant for "confiscation, competition and compulsion" ("Government," 1952, p. 24). SOCA saw this as a particularly alarming dynamic during a time when foreign statist powers like Russia and China challenged Western concepts of free market pre-eminence, emblematic in the hostilities of the Korean War. Finally, SOCA was embroiled in a government anti-trust suit that came from interventionist tendencies in government, it said, a punitive legal action that came from "the winds of [a] political doctrine, blowing from a new quarter, which jeopardize our existence" (SOCA, 1951, p. 42).

Determined to counteract a series of events that could shake employee and stockholder alignment with the company's concerns, SOCA's messages set out to re-affirm that the company was a bedrock for upholding what Americans held dear: the freedom to chart one's life in a direction of continual progress. SOCA was adamant that the times, marked by a government that was inclined to fritter away the effectiveness and self-empowerment of the free market, called for it to speak out in defense of Americans' traditional disposition toward liberty. It encouraged readers to visualize that free enterprise, and the corporation, worked in concert with Americans to liberate workers from those who would constrain them. The *Standard Oiler* pointed out that, at the birth of the country, only about half of the colonists supported the revolt against the British at Valley Forge. Yet, those people were heroic men and, despite the rise of statist impulses at home and abroad, it exhorted, "we can take heart in that our cause is just, and will prevail" ("What do," 1952, p. 13). SOCA's president Petersen, sounding an alert against "hot-house economists ... fly-by-night philosophers [and] ... power-hungry demagogues," asserted that business was "the main source of the American dream—the greatest force for good the world has known" ("What's bad," 1950, p. 24). Americans needed to be vigilant about letting free enterprise and corporations be destroyed, because, if both went into decline, it would be "the one thing our grandchildren could not forgive us" ("What's bad," 1950, p. 24). Using the Korean War as a frame, he highlighted how statist inclinations within the U.S. government were working to dismantle businesses, like the oil industry, that had the scale, resources, and expertise to help fight the battle. Petersen noted that "it's a glaring inconsistency," and that

> the American people should insist that it be knocked off, and fast. *We* in the oil industry have a job on our hands—a job that is basic in a conflict that may at any time develop into the roughest, toughest life-and-death struggle our country has ever fought—and one such job at a time is about all *we* can handle.
>
> ("Industrial," 1950, p. 11, emphasis added)

The first-person "we" in Petersen's message is one of the company and its workers and shareholders self-governing to get the mission accomplished in the face of an inefficient, intrusive, and hectoring federal government. This tone of re-affirmation, visible across the *Standard Oiler* of the early 1950s, worked at a subtle level. Rather than attempting to sell readers on corporate worldviews concerning, for example, specific social welfare policies or the intricacies of the anti-trust case, the approach that SOCA used was more nuanced. It emphasized what it saw as a subtext for what it meant to be a productive American: free market self-governance permitted individuals to propel themselves toward an optimal self-construction, allowing people to demonstrate that they had provided something of lasting value. That is, the self-directed individual did more than, for example, play an important role in refining, processing, and delivering oil— that individual's productivity revealed that the true nexus of constructive action within the U.S. was in the aligned actions and values of both the corporation and the citizen.

Similar to Norfolk and Western Railway's efforts described in Chapter 5, it is difficult to determine what effects SOCA's corporate persona conveyance had on audiences at that time. The *Standard Oiler* published survey results that came from over 2,500 in-person interviews of the public; it found that there was a 35% decrease in those who saw SOCA as "short-sighted and selfish" and an unspecified increase in those who saw the company as "progressive and public spirited" ("Opinion," 1951, p. 15). A similar poll 2 years later found that a little over 50% felt SOCA was a good company ("Public," 1953). In the summer of 1952, the magazine published employee survey results that indicated 86% of employees felt that the government should not be involved in running any business, except for the Post Office ("Government in," 1952, p. 24). Other than those examples, the magazine offered no research involving its audiences that could shed light on the reach and effectiveness of its pro-free-market messages. However, efforts to convey a helpful (if not, cajoling) corporate persona fit in well with an overall attempt in the mid-century U.S. by the oil industry to effect a more engaged personality in American society, casting forth the image of the corporation as a source of strength and wisdom for fellow Americans in the face of an overweening state. At the beginning of the 1940s, speaking of the dangers of an activist federal government that offered social security and sought more intervention in the market, Socony-Vacuum president John Brown said that if the country yielded "to the doubtful security of large-scale economic planning by a central-ized bureau, we shall probably sacrifice both safety and liberty and the well-being which have resulted from the operation of free enterprise" (Brown, 1939, p. 8). SOCA's sister oil company, Standard Oil of New Jersey (SONJ), had pre-dicted as early as 1942, when it set up its first public relations department: "[I]n another ten years … the thing that will stand out most notably will be the growing realization in the company and industry of social responsibilities" (SONJ, 1952, p. 3). That prognostication held true as the oil industry, in the 1950s, promoted business as a benevolent friendly giant that was a better guide to human fulfillment than any well-meaning state apparatus. Standard Vacuum, a joint venture of SONJ and Mobil Oil, pointed out in a planning document the company's public relations efforts were designed to project that it was "open, friendly and communicative," while contributing to the "economic strength of the country and the well-being of the people" (Standard Vacuum, 1950, p. A-3). President of General Petroleum Company Robert L. Minckler, in a speech that railed against government attempts to disintegrate the holdings of larger oil com-panies, said that oil company bigness was due to the industry successfully serving the public and bettering their lives. In fact, the country's "astronomic" use of oil (along with other forms of energy) allowed the United States to estab-lish itself as "the strongest, the most productive nation in the world," displaying a standard of living not achieved "at any time in the world history at any place in the world" (Minckler, 1950, p. 5). Similarly, Socony-Vacuum executive Albert Nickerson, in a 1953 speech before college educators, emphasized the bounty that came from avoiding government reliance. State interference in the market-place revealed a "dead hand of government," he said; this led to the removal of profits, which in turn hurt productivity, efficiency, and cost control. Inevitably, he said, "…the standard of living is lowered, the clock of human progress is turned back, [and] freedom is diminished" (Nickerson, 1953, p. 13). By 1956, speaking for what became known as Socony Mobil, chairman of the board B. Brewster Jennings said that the large corporate entity showed leadership in society (for example, promoting pensions before the creation of social security, taking the initiative in safety and conservation measures, etc.), offering "social benefits [that rested] on factors inherent in their bigness" (Jennings, 1956, p. 8). A large company, he said, acted as the "pilot of a great ocean liner" who took "the long view" toward a richer life (Jennings, 1956, p. 8). In sum, SOCA's efforts to cast the corporation as a wise benefactor to society crystallized in other oil-company public relations across the decade. By 1960, Mobil Oil, in a docu-ment on how to do PR, urged its managers to read newspapers and magazines to look for opportunities to demonstrate how the corporation was a good neighbor:

> When you read a story of people who have suffered ill luck, ask yourself: How can we help? If there is something you can reasonably do, do it. If some community project seems to be faltering, again the question: Can we help? And if you can, do it.
>
> (Mobil, 1960, p. 8)

The underlying message—that society needed the guiding hand of the corporate person in order for all to truly advance—was similar to NAM's pre-World War II appeals and the accounts in the 1950s offered up by both *PR News* and the *Norfolk and Western Magazine*. And, as seen in this book's Introduction, Herbert Schmertz's efforts at Mobil Oil in the 1970s and 80s continued to carry forward oil industry attempts to portray itself as a helpful, beneficent force. At a fundamental level, these public relations messages were designed to encourage Americans to turn away from government as an aide and rely on self-advancement through the marketplace. It was important to corporations, as Irwin Ross (1959) noted, that they sell Americans on capitalism and the organizations that embody that system. Still, trying to convince someone to visualize the American free market system is a rather daunting task. Rather than focusing exclusively on making the marketplace comprehensible to the average person, SOCA, much like Norfolk and Western, worked to amplify a sense of a personal connection between the corporation and the individual's adherence to values of Americanism, like independence and self-reliance. Accordingly, its efforts to disparage the state (both for its inefficiencies and its tendency to dominate) and its upholding the marketplace as the optimizer of American freedom reveal an organization that was not so much concerned with a courtship of identification but, rather, a *courtship of re-affirmation* of shared values and interests between the corporation and the individual, a distinction with a difference pointed out in Chapter 1.

Self-governance plays a vital role in solidifying such an appeal because it furthers this sense of consonance between individual and the organization. That is, when SOCA proclaimed that the best of American life came through optimizing oneself through the free market, it was articulating that it worked in tandem with citizens toward building a mutually shared vision of a prosperous society. With such an approach, the idea of separate public and private interests became blurred. Instead, SOCA offered that both public interest and private interest were conjoined. It used the *Standard Oiler* to portray this mutuality of interest between the corporation and individual as self-evident and sensible. It was a commonality that was readily apparent, the company claimed, through the accumulation of individuals practicing techniques of self-governance that benefited themselves, the corporation that provided the work venue, and the larger society. That is, the more that Americans distanced themselves from any act compelled by the state and, instead, pursued market-oriented self-governance, the more they were, in aggregate, placing themselves in position to act in the interest of improving society. Such a perspective stressed that the corporation and the individual were fellow sojourners, who, when they worked together in partnership, offered society "the mass production of benevolence" (Ross, 1959, p. 170).

However, in recent years, events have pointed to how an excessive focus on self-governance makes problematic assertions that the corporation and individuals act as a co-joined constructive force for society. When individuals identify their sense of self and well-being with marketplace concerns, there is the increased risk of disconnecting the self from addressing wider systemic concerns that do not immediately appear to align with self-advancement. For example, the United States is now entering a fifth decade of a trend toward significant wage inequality. From 1975 to 2012, a majority of the gain of household income in the United States was in the upper 5% of all wage earners—those households, by 2012, held 22% of all income wealth in the country, up from 16% in 1975 (U.S. Metro Economies, 2014). In the U.S., the income of the richest 10% is 14 times higher than the lowest 10%, a gap that is significantly higher than the international average ("An overview," 2011). These disparities are, in large part, a product of flat, real hourly compensation in the U.S. since the mid-1970s (Mishel, Bivens, Gould, & Shierholz, 2012) that is accompanied by American corporations storing $2.1 trillion in profits overseas (Drawbaugh & Temple-West, 2014). Such a persistent trend of social stratification and wage inequality calls into question U.S. self-governance messages that stress that individuals, through maximizing their efforts in the marketplace, will realize a fuller sense of prosperity.

Indeed, self-governance's strong orientation toward individual formation guided by marketplace imperatives tends to obscure how corporate power centers nest within the associations they make between private and public interest. As Livesey (2002) pointed out, efforts to ameliorate or obscure inherent differences between what benefits the common interest and the private entity often rest on how well public relations can take the "competing social interests of the citizenry" and force those concerns "into the private sphere of the market" (p. 135). In the case of SOCA, Livesey's observation is particularly apt, as the *Standard Oiler*'s messages were not focused on the broader milieu of contesting viewpoints in the public sphere. Instead, the publication appealed to entrenched American values that focus on self-propulsion through individual effort.

The findings here point to a need for further examination of how public relations attempts to influence society in more intricate ways than may be apparent. For example, broad terms like "the public interest" and the "marketplace of ideas" may tend to elide how public relations works at a very visceral and personal level. That is, what needs greater acknowledgment is that public relations may have particular resonance in a culture because it works to confirm an individual's inclination—performing a courtship of re-affirmation—rather than attempts to attract that person to a particular precept, principle, or action.

This ability of public relations to inform and intensify already-existing structures of self-direction contributes to a more nuanced understanding of how the profession attempts to assert the interests of private entities within the public sphere and imbed those self-same interests within the private lives of individuals. Simply put, the use of the corporate persona allows the corporation to demonstrate its claim that it lives in concert with the desires and aspirations of its fellow citizens. General Petroleum, one of SOCA's contemporaries, explicitly discussed such an appeal. Marion Dice, the company's assistant to the president, told its foreman's association that the company needed to assert that it was like a human:

> How does a company get itself liked entirely aside from selling good products? Well, the rules are pretty much the same as for individuals. We must align ourselves with things that people like and want and cherish—we must

try to help them when they want help—and above all, we must make a sincere showing that we are interested in people and their community activities in ways other than just trading products for dollars. This means that *companies should act like people* ... and make [our] leadership a constructive force in community life.

(Dice, 1955, p. 4, emphasis added)

Undoubtedly, power centers have much to gain by establishing a sense that the corporation and individuals are entwined when it comes to valuing the marketplace as the locus of self-advancement. Indeed, as SOCA demonstrated, affecting the voice of an authoritative constructive mentor—what Stuart Ewen (1996) had called the stance of a "friendly giant"—increasingly became seen as a tactic that could be used to build affiliation between corporations and the public in stressful times. This was a realization that, from time to time, became more visible in the public milieu, especially in light of the heightened profile that Herbert Schmertz, as touched upon in the Introduction, pursued for Mobil Oil in the 1970s and 80s. Since those days, the contemporary corporate persona can be seen, and even tracked, in some various and disparate venues (reality television, the fracking industry, and within social media), as the next three chapters of this book show.

References

"An overview of growing income inequalities in OECD countries: Main findings." (2011). *The Organization for Economic Co-operation and Development*. Retrieved from www.oecd.org/els/soc/49499779.pdf.

Brown, J.A. (1939). "Causes and catchwords." Founder's speech at Girard College, Philadelphia, May 20. Briscoe Archives, Box 2.207/E89.

Dice, M. (1955). "Our place in the community." *Doings in General*. [Newsletter]. November. Briscoe Archives, Box 2.207/E89.

Drawbaugh, K., & Temple-West, P. (2014). "Untaxed U.S. corporate profits held overseas top $2.1 trillion: Study." *Reuters*, April 8. Retrieved from www.reuters.com/article/2014/04/09/us-usa-tax-offshore-idUSBREA3729V20140409.

Ewen, S. (1996). *PR! A social history of spin.* New York: Basic Books.

Finckler, R.L. (1950). "Oil and the public." Speech given at the Rocky Mountain Spring Meeting of the American Petroleum Institute, Casper, WY, April 13. Briscoe Archives, Box 2.207/E89.

Heath, R. (2006). "A rhetorical theory approach to issues management." In C. Botan, & V. Hazelton (Eds.), *Public relations theory II*, pp. 55–87. Mahwah, NJ: Lawrence Erlbaum Associates.

Jennings, B.B. (1956). "A richer life in a poorer world." Remarks presented to the Rotary Club of Los Angeles, September 14. Briscoe Archives, Box 2.207/E89.

Johnson, R. (1949a). "The world's worst businessman." *Standard Oiler*, October, p. 9.

Johnson, R. (1949b). "A career in government." *Standard Oiler*, December, p. 14.

Johnson, R. (1950). "It's your federal government." *Standard Oiler*, January, p. 5.

Livesey, S.M. (2002). "Global warming wars: Rhetoric and discourse analytic approaches to ExxonMobil's corporate public discourse." *The Journal of Business Communication* 39(1), pp. 117–148.

Minckler, R.L. (1950,). "Oil and the public." Address before the American Petroleum Institute, Casper, WY, April 13. Briscoe Archives, Box 2.207/E89.

Mishel, L., Bivens, J., Gould, E., & Shierholz, H. (2012). *The state of working America*. Ithaca, NY: Cornell University Press.

Mobil. (1960). *Working at public relations.* [Guidebook]. Socony Public Relations Department. Briscoe Archives, Box 2.207/E119.

Motion, J., & Leitch, S. (2007). "A toolbox for public relations: The oeuvre of Michel Foucault." *Public Relations Review 33*, pp. 263–268.

Nickerson, A.L. (1953). "Business and human values." Address before the College English Association Institute, Corning, NY, October 16. Briscoe Archives, Box 2.207/E114.

Ross, I. (1959). *The image merchants: The fabulous world of public relations.* Garden City, NY: Doubleday & Co., Inc.

Schlesinger Jr., A.M. (1958). *The coming of the New Deal.* Boston: Houghton Mifflin.

Snyder, F. (1950). "The years that lie ahead." *Standard Oiler*, February, pp. 9, 21.

Standard Oiler. (1950). "Steel, oil and wheels." March, p. 24.

Standard Oiler. (1950). "What's bad about bigness?" April, pp. 23–24.

Standard Oiler. (1950). "Industrial strength and national security." November, p. 11.

Standard Oiler. (1951). "War and the Hoover Report." March, pp. 10–11.

Standard Oiler. (1951). "Opinion poll." December, pp. 14–16.

Standard Oiler. (1952). "It's tough enough." March, pp. 12–13.

Standard Oiler. (1952). "It's only money." April, pp. 12–13.

Standard Oiler. (1952). "Who wants socialism?" June, p. 24.

Standard Oiler. (1952). "The perfect security state." July, pp. 18–19.

Standard Oiler. (1952). "Government in business." August, p. 24.

Standard Oiler. (1952). "What do you mean—democracy?" August, pp. 12–13.

Standard Oiler. (1953). "Your magazine has a birthday." November, p. 3.

Standard Oiler. (1953). "Public opinion." December, pp. 20–22.

Standard Oil of New Jersey (SONJ). (1952). *Notes on the North American public relations conference of SONJ and affiliates.* Briscoe Archives, Box 2.207/E83.

Standard Vacumn Oil Company. (1950). *Stanvac public relations handbook.* Briscoe Archives, Box 2.207/G120.

"U.S. metro economies: Income and wage gaps across the U.S." (2014). The United States Conference of Mayors and The Council on Metro Economies and the New American City, August. Retrieved from www.usmayors.org/metroeconomies/2014/08/report.pdf.

Wimmer, R.D., & Dominick, J.R. (2010). *Mass media research: An introduction* (9th ed.). Belmont, CA: Thomson/Wadsworth.

Yergin, D. (2008). *The prize: The epic quest for oil, money and power.* New York: Free Press.

7   Reality television and you

The corporate persona observes and rewards on *Undercover Boss*

As Chapters 5 and 6 showed, by the mid-1950s, major industrial operations like the railroads and oil companies offered to their stakeholders, through an affinitive, human-like persona, assertions that Americans needed to hold on to common values shared by both the individual and the corporation. Organizations like Norfolk and Western Railways and Standard Oil of Southern California said that Americans needed to re-affirm, in concert with corporations, that the American free enterprise system was the most constructive way to advance through the marketplace toward a productive, prosperous life. These claims, much like NAM's assertions in the ramp-up to World War II and *PR News'* reporting in the early 1950s, were not pleasantries. They were propounded by industries concerned about the advance of government intrusion into the marketplace and fears that the populace would be persuaded to listen to advocates of socialism.

But what of the contemporary appearance of the corporate persona? The challenges American corporations have faced since the mid-20th century have shifted. Socialism, although notably visible in forms within the governance of several European countries, is no longer seen as a significant threat by American business. One of the reasons for corporate America's lessened anxiety about socialism is the American public's solidified disaffection for it—a spring 2016 poll found that only 35% of Americans had a favorable view of socialism, with 60% voicing approval of capitalism (Newport, 2016). American viewpoints, in the main, show consonance with mid-20th-century corporate persona messages that a secure and constructive life comes through hard work within America's free enterprise system. *The Atlantic* magazine and the Aspen Institute (McCoy, 2015) reported that, among the general population, 50% of Americans believed they were living the American Dream (e.g., having financial security and stability), as did 72% of elites (those who were college-educated, making a minimum of $75,000, were engaged in politics, and savvy about technology). High proportions of the general population (65%) and elites (71%) believed the American Dream is attainable through hard work and is, in fact, more important than one's birth circumstance or luck. Bernie Sanders' near-successful run for the 2016 Democratic nomination notwithstanding, a majority of Americans voice their continued allegiance to individualism and self-reliance that can be optimized through capitalism.

In the face of such widespread acceptance of the notion of a better life through hard work within the marketplace, why would the corporate persona likely persist today? One essential reason for its viability to corporations are the dysfunctions within the American economic system. From 2003 to 2012, over 90% of profits among Fortune 500 companies were channeled to investors and not into growing business enterprise. Since 1968, only one 3-year cycle (1998–2000) revealed real-wage increases of at least 2% or more (Lazonick, 2014). While workers have experienced wage stagnation, many long-established jobs in areas like manufacturing have disappeared in the U.S., correlated to the increasing attractiveness of lower wages in other nations. While the Urban Institute cites conflicting studies on the risks and benefits of globalization to the American workforce (Lerman & Schmidt, 1999), the disruptions from increasing globalization accompanied a significant downward trend line in the U.S.'s annual productivity gains. During the 1950s–1970s, annual average productivity in America was 2.6%; by the period 2010–2015, that had dropped to 0.4% (Samuelson, 2016, p. A15). Additionally, while the U.S. economy achieved a gross domestic product (GDP) average annual growth of 3.22% from 1947 to 2016, the majority of GDP reports since 2008 revealed yearly GDP barely at or below that growth rate ("National data," 2016; "United States," 2016). Beyond this stagnation of economic growth and a parallel flattening in incomes, wealth inequality has grown to levels not seen in decades. Thomas Piketty (2014) points out that much of American wealth inequality came from a resurgence of inherited wealth since the 1980s. That is, those who had assets over the last 30 years increased their savings, cash-flowed their lifestyles, and then passed on their untouched assets to the next generation. In times of low GDP growth and stagnant wages, this leads to the elderly building up most of the wealth in the country, as younger generations cannot "level the playing field with their elders" (Piketty, 2014, p. 400).

With these kinds of economic realities, it is not surprising that a 2016 Gallup poll found that the average trust Americans had for 14 key institutions was 32%, significantly lower than an average trust score of 43% in 2004. Only 18% of respondents indicated significant trust in business; only Congress had a lower number—9% (Norman, 2016). In weekly surveys since 2009, Rasmussen Reports has consistently found that approximately a 2:1 majority of Americans believe the country is on the wrong track ("Right direction," 2016), which is a percentage mirrored by *The Atlantic* magazine and the Aspen Institute's poll on the American Dream. The latter also found that 75% of the general population said the American Dream is suffering (McCoy, 2015).

These statistics point to an unsettling of faith in the American workplace as a venue for self-fulfillment and a concurrent crisis of confidence in the free market system that, as this book has shown, has been conducive to corporations projecting reassurance through the corporate persona. Indeed, some trends appear favorable for the assertion of corporate beneficence. Columnist Jennifer Rubin (2016) pointed out that life expectancy in the United States has increased, the poverty rate has decreased, and violent crime has been on an extended downward trend. Still, the story for many Americans is that of living paycheck-to-paycheck, with almost half reporting, in a nationwide survey, that they did not have ready funds to deal with an emergency expense of $400 ("Report on," 2015). Barbara Ehrenreich, reflecting on her semi-ethnographic, undercover journey as a minimum-wage worker in the U.S., voiced the harsh reality of what it meant to be an ostensibly self-reliant worker attempting to build a constructive life in the low-wage stratum of the American workplace. She wrote, in the book *Nickel and Dimed*:

> The shocking thing is that the majority of American workers, about 60 percent, earn less than $14 an hour. Many of them get by … teaming up with another wage earner, a spouse or a grown child. Some draw government help in the form of food stamps, housing vouchers, the earned income tax credit, or—for those coming off welfare in relatively generous states—subsidized child care. But others—single mothers for example—have nothing but their own wages to live on, no matter how many mouths there are to feed.
>
> (Ehrenreich, 2001, p. 213)

Ehrenreich's book was a best-seller in 2001, receiving accolades from, among others, *Newsweek* and the *New York Times*, and has held a certain cultural relevance, its 10th anniversary featured on NPR's "Marketplace," in the *New Yorker* magazine, and on "Democracy Now!" In a special column for CNN, Ehrenreich reflected that, 10 years after her undercover experiment, more than 75% of jobs created in 2010 were in the $9–15 range. "We don't just need more jobs," she said. "We need more jobs that treat employees like humans and pay what you could actually live on" (Ehrenreich, 2011, para 12). Interestingly, one year before *Nickel and Dimed*'s 10th anniversary, a new reality TV show appeared— *Undercover Boss*—that purportedly offered its own version of ethnography. In this case, rather than a journalist, the corporation sent an executive to surreptitiously examine what life looked like in the low-wage sphere.

Undercover Boss and reality TV

Realty television, which ascended in the United States in the early 2000s, is a format that ostensibly shows viewers slices of unscripted, everyday life. The formats, although diverse, customarily include some form of competition—whether in shows that are more like games, such as *Survivor*, *Storage Wars*, and *American Idol*, or ones that appear to be more about life happenings such as *Wife Swap*, *Jersey Shore*, and *The Real Housewives of Atlanta*. Within these broader categories are hidden camera shows, talent searches, dating shows, makeover programs, historical re-creations, home remodeling shows, law enforcement programs, and celebrity-focused docu-soaps. Not surprisingly, with the ascent of such diverse programming, scholars have found it difficult to come to one central definition of reality television. Reality TV, said Wood and Skeggs (2012), takes social hierarchies and commodifies them "into forms of spectacle" that can allow for attracting and retaining audiences (p. 8). Other scholars identify reality television more by attributes: (1) it purports to be unscripted and authentic; (2) it customarily focuses on individuals' narratives; (3) those narratives are about constructing a way to deal with their respective environments; and (4) it makes a claim that the discourse it spotlights is real (Beck, Hellmueller, & Aeschbacher, 2012; Murray & Ouellette, 2008; Nabi, 2007). Some have tracked reality TV for its effects, noting how it can lead to self-reflexive dispositions (Sender, 2015) that can contribute to deeper perspectives about such items as self-improvement and altruism (Tsay-Vogel & Krakowiak, 2016). Skeggs and Wood (2012), however, see that self-performance, rather than representations of reality, is the hallmark of reality television. That is, they maintain that the format is particularly notable for demonstrating how "new understandings of value and ideology are coming into effect" (Skeggs & Wood, 2012, p. 233). They refer to this as "the idea of personhood" or the "legal, social and moral states generated through encounters with others" (Skeggs & Wood, 2012, p. 4). In observations that resonate with findings in this book about the self-governing messages of the corporate persona, other scholars add that encounters on reality television are customarily presented as opportunities for individuals to self-actualize and demonstrate who they are, within the demands and constraints of the neoliberal structures and values of the United States (Kavka, 2012; Ouellette & Hay, 2008; Skeggs & Wood, 2012). These comments are, in large part, inspired by Foucault's work, which stressed the importance of examining how the rise of neoliberalism emphasizes that self-governance is a way to avoid harmful interventions from the state (Foucault, 1997). With self-governance, as clarified in earlier chapters here, individuals are encouraged to see themselves as the locus of power: individuals "act upon themselves," following their inclinations to be productive and pursue their goals without top-down intervention from the state (Paras, 2006, p. 13).

Since the early 2000s, there have been several reality shows that promoted self-advancement while also making the boss a central character. For example, *Cake Boss* showed the behind-the-scenes dynamics of a family-owned bakery in New Jersey. Other programs, like *The Rebel Billionaire*, *Shark Tank*, and *The Apprentice*, used competition formats where show participants attempted to receive approval and reward from the boss who evaluated their efforts. There have been some docu-soap programs that centered on the importance of the boss (e.g., *Does Someone Have to Go?*, *Secret Millionaire*), but *Undercover Boss* is distinctive in that the corporate entity, represented through the top executive, walks among employees as a seeming peer, yet, by show's end, asserts the patterns that inform frontline workers on how to improve their self-governance.

The February 7, 2010, arrival of *Undercover Boss* on CBS, immediately after the Super Bowl, featured top executives (normally CEOs, but sometimes owners, chairpersons, and other lower-level executives) disguised as ordinary workers, taking on tasks at their companies' multiple work sites. On that night, more than 38 million viewers (the largest number up to that time for a series debut after the Super Bowl) tuned in and saw the president of Waste Management Incorporated pick up trash and clean portable toilets under the ruse that he was being filmed for a program that featured workers competing for entry-level jobs. This "contestant for a job" approach became common across the series, with the top executive often in disguise, getting thrown into frontline work that he or she had no familiarity with, assisted by an employee acting as a mentor. The tasks, though sometimes physically demanding (or sometimes merely disgusting), allowed the executive to traverse the workplace and meet a variety of workers. In the course of this journey, the top executive typically noted what worked well and what might need to be changed, with an especial eye toward employees who were good role models and who appeared to be prevailing against personal challenges. Sometimes the boss came across troublesome employees and had to make decisions on how to plan for a course correction—either in real-time, but normally during the "reveal" portion at the end of the program, where the undercover executive would eschew his or her disguise and meet with his "mentor" employees one-on-one. During this reveal, the boss would deliver a reward (e.g., cash, promotions, vacations) for the workers who had shown persistence and self-reliance and provide needed re-direction for the dysfunctional employees. Critics have noted that *Undercover Boss* aligns with the age-old trope of the powerful persona (gods, kings, princes) who descends into the world of the common person, taking on that lifestyle so as to learn large lessons about humility and empathy (Carter, 2010; Stanley, 2010a). Hiltbrand (2010) noted that the aim of the program was to show viewers the importance of a "compassionate corporate master" who, in rewarding the saints and correcting the sinners in the workplace, acted out of a desire for workers' best interests (p. H1). These critiques, however, are centered on how *Undercover Boss* would overtly cast the top executive. This chapter, informed by Foucauldian observations about self-governance, is more concerned with exploring how the program transmits a larger message about constructive navigation within the neoliberal American society. Furthermore, the show's focus on top executives allows for examining the corporate persona in action, as the senior executives are seen as representative of the character of the organization and the values of their enterprise. Accordingly, *Undercover Boss* provides a distinctive window into how the senior executives can embody the corporate persona and thereby demonstrate the guiding hand of the corporation that supports the effective, self-governed American.

Undercover Boss and the world of fast food

As discussed in previous chapters, the corporate persona emphasizes self-governance as a way for individuals to better their lives. This chapter, through an analysis of interactions between senior executives and workers on *Undercover Boss*, moves into exploring a key aspect of self-governing in the capitalist system: the need for the individual to be persistent in overcoming personal challenges so as to be productive (Foucault, 1977; McGushin 2011). One of the key areas for exploring the corporation's encouragement of self-governance is within the fast-food industry. Scholars have noted that this is a particularly fraught area of relationships between management and frontline workers because profit margins are low, employee turnover is high, cost control is a way of life, and, accordingly, worker pay is low (Leana, Mittal, & Stiehl, 2012; Newman, 2007; Royle, 2010). Many workers earn the minimum wage of $7.25 per hour which, adjusted for inflation, equals the 1966 standard of $1.25 per hour (DeSilver, 2013).

By December 2014, the issue of working conditions for fast-food employees—especially low wages—received more attention as workers held strikes in 190 American cities (Berman, 2014). They advocated for a $15-per-hour minimum wage, along with paid sick days and affordable child care (Berman, 2014). Some states, since 2014, responded by raising the minimum wage, most notably New York, California, and, in the 2016 elections, Arizona, Colorado, Maine, and Washington followed suit. The fast-food worker advocacy group, Fight for $15, held protests in 340 cities around the county in late November 2016 ("Thousands protest," 2016).

With the fast-food arena revealing contentious relationships between workers and their employing corporations, this chapter examines episodes that, across the first four seasons of *Undercover Boss* (2010–2013), featured nine fast-food restaurants to see how their disguised executives interacted with employees and, in the process, highlighted and then rewarded worker self-governance. Following a textual analysis and grounded theory approach used earlier in this book, this chapter finds that the program offers, at a minimum, three ways for viewers to see the value of self-governance. First, the program often showed employees not only physically displaying that they were following work routines but, more importantly, at times voicing *how the individual should approach those routines to be optimally productive.* Second, the program often offered "cutaway" shots from the on-scene action so that the executive could talk directly to the camera to indicate who the good role models were and point out those who were not self-governing effectively. Finally, *Undercover Boss*'s format called for an end-of-show reveal of the executive—a one-on-one with the featured employees—that further allowed the program to signify how the corporation supported the individual in his or her self-governing efforts. This end segment allowed the corporation, embodied through the senior executive, to give out rewards to employees who exemplified persistence in self-management and, conversely, offer course corrections to those who were poor role models. Across the first four seasons of *Undercover Boss*, nine fast-food corporations appeared, their executives observing and rewarding employees for their productivity and, moreover, for exhibiting workplace orientations that were in concert with the values, aims, and goals of the organization.

Season 1—White Castle

In Season 1, White Castle owner and board member David Rife first goes undercover at a new store in Hamilton, Ohio, where he notices there are far too many employees who appear confused about what they should be doing. For a first appearance of a fast-food restaurant, the episode is particularly notable because, from this beginning and then throughout his visits, with one exception (Joe in

Kentucky, below), Rife does not encounter employees who voice a self-governing orientation. Instead, as the program progresses, it depicts his strong interest in who are role models in the workplace. At Hamilton, he meets Donna, a loyal, 23-year-employee who had a heart attack in 2003 due to a poor diet and is now overweight and having difficulty managing stress. Her husband is on disability and relies heavily on her income. The fact that Donna has persisted through these difficulties to be her household's reliable provider concerns Rife because he was once heavy. "If I found out that Donna had a heart attack two months from now, I'd have a lot of guilt," Rife says.

In Kentucky, Rife works on the overnight shift with Joe, who displays his mastery of working the drive-through window. In self-governing observations, he emphasizes to Rife that interactions with customers should be informal but polite. Joe says that every transaction should be finished with phrases like "Have a nice day" or "Have a great evening." Rife is impressed with how Joe makes the work look effortless and, during a break, Joe shares with Rife that he has a visually impaired son. When Rife says to him that he would think that Joe would be depressed about the help his son needs, Joe says, "I depend on this job to take care of my family. That's why I work so hard at it." In a cutaway, Rife says that Joe has an exemplary attitude, one that "pulls you up to his level."

Later, in Chicago, he meets 17-year-old Jose, who shares with Rife his ambition to be a chef and run his own restaurant. Jose has even developed his own salsa, which Rife tastes and finds impressive. During their shift together, Jose states that his parents are not supportive of his career ambition, to which Rife replies, "You're very driven. You're very focused. That's very rare in somebody your age." Then, when Rife goes to a frozen-product site in Kentucky, he finds a less positive picture. Vicki, a production line worker, tells him that things used to run smoothly, with better product quality. Now, she says, the supervisors spend a lot of time in the breakroom and "people who are picking up the slack are getting more aggravated every day." Rife notices that when a production line backs up, the assistant supervisor, Brenda, does not jump in to help.

During the last segment reveal, Rife tells Donna that he was struck by her persistence in the face of her health concerns and will put in place a wellness program across the company that she can benefit from. The rewards for Jose and Joe are more direct. Rife indicates to Jose that the company believes in him and will give him a $5,000 college scholarship. Rife says that Joe has inspired him to create a leadership program for White Castle and wants him to write the curriculum. Joe will also receive $5,000 to help him take care of his son. For Brenda and Vicki, course correction is in order: he instructs them to work better together and that he will come back to see how things are progressing at the frozen-product site.

Season 2—Subway, Johnny Rockets, and Baja Fresh

Season 2's first portrayal of a fast-food operation features Subway. Chief development officer Don Fertman finds, in Orlando, Florida, in his first interaction with an employee, that it is difficult to learn what components are needed in various sandwiches. The first employee he interacts with, Jessi, is intent on "breaking him." She times him to see if he can make sandwiches in two minutes; he takes too long and she pulls him off the sandwich assembly area, saying "a five-minute sandwich is a lost customer." In a one-on-one discussion with her, Fertman finds that Jessi lives with her dad and is planning on going to college. Her mother skipped out on her family years ago and that resonates with Fertman, because his mother had done the same thing.

Next, in Alabama, he works with store manager Sherri. She offers self-governing pointers. When customers first arrive Fertman should say, "Hi, how can I help you today?" When another customer comes in line while Fertman is putting together an order, Sherri tells him to say "I will be right with you" because when "they can see you're doing something they'll not be upset." Fertman, however, wants to talk with customers as he is filling their orders; Sherri warns Fertman about offering too much chatter because it slows down the line, saying "We're going to have a conversation and we're going to get our hands to move." In a one-on-one conversation between Fertman and Sherri, he finds out that she is a 19-year employee who once thought about being a general manager, but she is concerned that a promotion would take her away from dealing with customers, which is her passion. Fertman finds her to be an exemplary role model because "Subway is ingrained in her" and, even if she does not know all of her customers, "she makes them feel like she knows them."

Next, in a new store in Orlando's Science Center, Fertman pairs with 20-year-old store manager Efrain and finds out he is the youngest store manager in that area. Efrain shares that, when he started out, he was a minimum-wage sandwich maker who took the bus to work. A role model for advancing at work, he was recently named manager of the month among a pool of 293 Subway stores in central Florida. He says he wants to adopt a child and also foster children because his adoptive mother gave him a second chance at life. Then, in New York State, in a store that is within a church, Fertman does deliveries with Duane, the store manager. Duane (who is also a minister at a different church) tells Fertman that he has four adopted children; he works so much, however, that he only has Saturday nights for time with his family. Fertman also meets Darius, the head pastor of the church who says that the Subway and Duane's leadership of the store are vital for providing skilled-labor opportunities to the local community.

In the reveal, Fertman voices his admiration of Efrain's ambitiousness and asks him to join Subway's innovation committee. He also gives him $5,000 to donate to a foster organization of his choosing and an additional $1,000 to spend on his mother. Sherri, whom he calls the "Subway Lady," will be the star in a training video about handling customers; she gets $5,000 for her participation. Fertman tells Jessi that Subway will pay for the rest of her college education; she also receives a paid vacation to take her father anywhere in the world. Fertman tells Duane that he displays a connectedness to his community, he has inspired Subway to start a program that will help communities build job skills, and he will be a paid advisor for the effort. He also receives a total of $20,000 for an education fund for his four children.

Later in Season 2, the president and CEO of Johnny Rockets, John Fuller, finds several examples of workers who offer self-governing observations. At a store in New York City, lead cook (and would-be rapper) Ajay shows Fuller every rule that must be followed—wearing latex gloves, mixing tuna materials the proper way, monitoring carefully the time allowed for each burger on the grill. Ajay tells Fuller that there is a "technique to everything I do" and "we don't do things willy-nilly here … We're not animals … We don't just run around and just do things without purpose." Fuller, in a cutaway, says that Ajay "takes it very seriously… It's kind of a thrill to watch this guy in action."

At a casino-based branch in Atlantic City, Tony, a "food runner," shows Fuller how to quickly move back and forth from serving and cleaning tables, telling him that such hustle allows him to make more in tips. Fuller notes that this kind of self-governing is rigorous; "I was starting to break out in a sweat," he says. Then, during a break, Tony shares with Fuller that, years ago, his daughter had been murdered and he took it upon himself to bring justice to the perpetrator. He served 3 years for that assault and, upon release, was homeless for 3 months until Johnny Rockets hired him. Tony says the job has helped change his life, and later Fuller says to the camera, "I'm just thrilled that we … [were] able to employ him and put some money in his pocket so that he doesn't have to live under the boardwalk. It feels good that we can make a difference."

Fuller also focuses on an employee whom he perceives as an important role model. Janice, a server at a casino-based Johnny Rockets in Connecticut, tells Fuller that it is important to "take care of [customers] like they are your family, your daughters, your mom, your dad." Janice literally gets on her knees to take an order, laughing at a simple joke from a customer; she uses words like "honey" and "sweetie" with customers. Then, as Fuller clumsily attempts to take a customer's order, she stands smiling at his side, leading him through everything that needs to be asked. Finally, Janice encourages all employees to energetically dance on the floor (which, says Fuller, is part of the Johnny Rockets' "brand experience"). Janice points out that the corporate dances "stink" and leads him in ones she developed. Then, during a break, she tells Fuller that she has custody of four daughters and is the primary wage earner. Janice says, "I survive with this, but I have [no money] put aside." Later, Fuller reflects, "She strikes me as someone who is very selfless and would do anything for her kids."

As the program ends, Fuller dispenses rewards. He tells Ajay that Johnny Rockets wants to recognize his rap ambitions by flying him to the American Music Awards. Tony will receive $5,000 to help pay his rent, and Fuller will send him and his family to an amusement park. Johnny Rockets will also donate $5,000 to the National Center for Missing and Exploited Children in honor of Tony's deceased daughter. For Janice, the company will send her and her family on a vacation and will set up a $2,000 college fund for each of her kids. Fuller also indicates she will be paid to roll out her dances in stores nationwide.

In the third appearance of a fast-food restaurant that season, Baja Fresh sends CEO David Kim undercover, who discovers some impressive role models. In Nevada, he goes to a high-revenue store to shadow Jose, its general manager. Jose gets upset with Kim possibly contaminating the food by touching his own face (which calls for Kim to put on new gloves). But Kim notes that Jose keeps his calm and "[is] very gracious to me." Jose says that he gets involved in the food preparation and clean up as he does not, as a manager, want to "sit around and tell [the employees] what to do." In a one-on-one conversation with Jose, Kim finds out that Jose came to the country unable to speak English and worked his way up from cook, continually focusing on striving for more, taking management courses at night at his local college, and aiming to own a business. Kim notes that "Jose sacrifices for his family so that they and the next generation can have a better life. That's America! That's what makes this country so great."

Then, in California, Kim meets Anthony, a 20-year-old cashier. In a one-on-one conversation, Kim finds that Anthony had to move away from his mother and his siblings in San Diego to find a job so that he could help support her. "So, for now, I guess I just have to work harder, for them, because I know they're counting on me," Anthony says. Kim remarks that this certainly must be a burden, but Anthony says that it is also a blessing because, "it is one of my stepping stones to becoming a better person."

At a previously poorly performing store in Arizona, Kim shadows store manager Rami, whom he finds "energetic and engaged," with an outgoing personality that has helped turn around the store. In a conversation with the CEO, Rami indicates that he has only been manager for 3 months but, if he had to, he would "read training manuals all day just to make sure I'm doing everything correct." Then, at a store in Idaho, Kim is paired with operations manager Carrie, who takes him on a delivery, something not normally done by Baja Fresh. Carrie tells him that she wants the company to do these kinds of things (including adding more affordable, smaller portion menu items) and to avoid couponing because, to her, it tells customers the food is not worth its stated price. As their conversation continues, she tells him that she and her husband work different shifts while they care for a 2-year-old.

In the reveal portion of the program, Kim tells Carrie he is impressed with her "gold mine of great ideas" and wants her to travel, expenses paid, to help the company implement them. She also gets $7,500 for her daughter's college education. Rami will receive $5,000 toward his college courses and another $5,000 for a golf trip with his father. Anthony will receive $15,000 so that he and his family can be together. Speaking directly to the camera, Anthony says that he has been wrong thinking that his life has been so hard and that he would never experience a blessing. His rewards show, he says, that "God's working wonders. This blessing is like a miracle for me." Jose gets his very own Baja Fresh franchise, with the company waiving $50,000 in fees. When Jose calls his sister to tell her the news about this gift, she asks "Who does that?" He replies, "People with good hearts; people who want to make other people's dreams come true."

Season 3—Checkers and Popeyes

In Season 3, *Undercover Boss* features Checkers, a drive-through fast-food operation based in Florida. The company's CEO, Rick Silva, first works with Todd, a cook at a store who shares with Silva that he has always wanted to be a chef but cannot go to school because he has to help his mother pay her bills. "I'm her rock right now," Todd says. "I don't think of it as me being in a tough bind, or tortured by anything; I'm doing what I can and I'm doing it to the best of my needs." He says he received no training from Checkers, that he taught himself, and then shows Silva how to keep multiple grills going and how to "speed it up, because it's all about time right now." However, at this same store, Silva also observes a poor role model. Stevens, the store supervisor, repeatedly yells at Todd and other employees. Stevens tells a female employee, "So if you go on overtime, I can take you outside and beat you up, right?" Then, when Silva gets confirmation that Stevens talks that way to employees consistently, he confronts the supervisor, a significant deviation from the normal flow of the show. Silva reveals to Stevens his position as the company's CEO and informs him that he is improperly managing his people and providing a poor product. The executive says to him, "You don't belong in that restaurant. Right here, right now, we're going to shut the restaurant down."

Silva also encounters employee self-governance in Alabama, where sandwich maker Johanna explains that she begins to make the sandwich the minute she hears the order over her intercom. That way, she says, when the customer pulls up "I want his food to be tagged ... and out the window." Johanna then shows Silva all the sequences to sandwich making, using a poster template. In a subsequent, one-on-one conversation, Johanna tells him that, after 7 years at Checkers, she makes only $8 per hour; she says that she lives paycheck-to-paycheck and has difficulties with reliable transportation.

In a store in Florida, Silva asks Joyce, a general manager, how she displays so much energy. She says she is grateful for her job because her father, mother, and brother all died within a recent 6-month span, after which she lost her previous job. When she was unemployed, she used Checkers' free food coupons to feed her and her young daughter. "That's why I'm so loyal to Checkers," she says. Silva says to her, "I would never, ever in my wildest dreams have imagined that you had this much that you have overcome." She answers that she is struggling on a tight budget and is in severe debt.

By show's end, Silva offers to pay all of Todd's expenses to go to culinary school and promises him $15,000 for his family. He also points out to Todd that the verbally abusive Stephens is being retrained. To address Johanna's struggles, he pledges $20,000 for her to buy a car and will promote her to a manager-in-training, with a 25% salary increase. For Joyce, Silva says the company will give her $10,000 to help with debt and $10,000 to spend as she likes.

Later in Season 3, Popeyes chief talent officer, Lynn Zappone, first goes undercover in food preparation at a store in New Orleans. She shadows Aaron, who says he wants to ascend the corporate ladder but also refers to upper-level management as "corporate clowns." He voices resentment about curt, tie-wearing managers who come in reeking of Dolce & Gabbana cologne and know nothing about what it is like to work at the store. Aaron says that management should spend more time with employees and let them know that management is supportive. Zappone also witnesses Aaron yelling back to other employees, in front of customers, to stop badgering him about promptly filling orders, something that Zappone, in a cutaway shot, says is inappropriate.

At a different store in New Orleans, Gina, a shift manager, trainer, and 27-year-employee, not only imparts the five steps of service but even tells Zappone to make sure to not stand with her hands on her hips as management does not like that. Additionally, you have to be sincere about greeting the customer, she says laughing, or "I'm going to take one of those chicken bones and whip you with [it]." She also instructs her, as she leads her to cleaning the bathroom, "If you have time to lean, you have time to clean." In a one-on-one conversation, Gina reveals that, when she was displaced by Katrina, Popeyes fired her for not getting back to work, despite her 20 years of experience. Zappone says, to the camera, that what she has heard is heartbreaking.

At a third location in New Orleans, Zappone meets Josh, who shows her how to pack customers' orders; Zappone is impressed with how Josh and the other employees work efficiently and pleasantly under pressure. Josh exhibits a warmth that "feels real genuine," she says in a cutaway. When they take a break, however, Zappone is dismayed when he asks if she would go with him to Taco Bell because the menu at Popeyes is too expensive (they receive no employee discounts). She finds out Josh does not have a car and walks an hour to get home. He was once homeless due to his family not accepting his homosexuality. He indicates he is working hard so that he can get a car and then go to school to study hospitality management. Then, at an outlet in Mississippi, she works with Doug, a maintenance man, who does things he does not have to do, like clean the dumpster and purchase his own kid-friendly soap for the lobby—it leads to his store getting high department of health ratings. He does it because he feels ownership of the store. "It belongs to Popeyes, but it's mine," Doug says. Zappone states, to the camera, "This guy is an angel...where can I get more of him?" Doug has persevered: he had lost everything from Katrina and lived with a pastor in Alabama, who provided him support for two years. She finds his commitment to the brand impressive and says, in a cutaway, that he has a "personal purpose to serve others" and that those are the kind of people Popeyes wants.

During the reveal, Zappone tells Aaron that she was not happy with the way he represented the brand but that underneath his sarcasm about management "is a really smart guy who knows what is right." He will get a mentor who will help him be a better trainer. For Doug, Popeyes will make a donation of $10,000 to his pastor's mission. She tells Josh that Popeyes will re-instate the employee discount program; he will also receive $20,000 toward his education and $10,000 for a car and living expenses. For Gina, Popeyes will pay for a family reunion and set up an employee relief fund—she will receive $10,000 from that fund to help get her life back on track, says Zappone.

Season 4—Moe's, Boston Market, and Fatburger

In the fourth season of *Undercover Boss*, Moe's president Paul Damico is immediately impressed with several examples of employee self-governance. In Charleston, South Carolina, store manager Angelisa guides him on the cash register, informing him that the standard is to fill an order three minutes after it is taken; you must multitask and be happy, she says. As Damico struggles and causes the line to back up, she reminds him that, nevertheless, "You really want to greet your customer before you start pushing buttons" and to smile when he talks. Then, Damico travels with Janet, the catering director in Columbia, South Carolina. They go to a sheriff's office and, afterward, Damico says that she was extremely organized: "Every piece of that catering was meticulously delivered," he says, "from the marketing to the branding to the spoon location; it was pretty awesome to see." Later, in Tennessee, Damico works with Damon, who shows him how to cut up tomatoes with a hand machine. As they prepare guacamole, Damon says that no matter how long an employee has been there, they should always have prep (preparation) sheets in front of them, so that all the steps will be followed. Damico reflects that Damon kept him to the sequences on the prep sheet and that is "the sign of a great teacher."

While Damico is encouraged by these self-governing employees, he also encounters a young manager whose highly visible behavior does not meet his standards. Tito, a 19-year-old shift manager, tells Damico he will show him only one time how to roll a burrito and, if he does not understand, he should go find another crew member. Damico later observes that this first interaction was "a bit shocking to me, because that is not how you train within Moe's." As the day progresses, Tito loudly chastises Damico for being slow and not yelling "Welcome to Moe's" when customers come in. Damico witnesses Tito acting belligerent, calling one female employee a "ding dong," and then yelling out "I'm King Ding-a-ling around this bitch."

At other stores, Damico finds examples of better role modeling. For example, at the Charleston, South Carolina, store with Angelisa, she tells him, "I don't want to come to work and just ask people if they want rice, chicken and beans on their burrito—I want to come to work and ask them how their children are doing." She shares that she is a single mom with two young kids and aspires to a bachelor's degree. She also has a new idea for Moe's—a dessert burrito line. Paul observes that "she puts her heart and soul into this job" and that he cannot imagine what it is like to work 50 hours per week and "try to make time for two young kids." Damico is similarly impressed by his time with Damon in Tennessee. Damon explains that his 10-year-old daughter Mackenzie accompanies him to Moe's when he does not have a sitter. When Damon takes Paul out to the lobby to meet Mackenzie, Damon mentions that he had only about two hours sleep before work that day but that Mackenzie keeps him going. Paul says, "There's no question [Mackenzie's] learning about work ethic right now … And I see him trying to give her the absolute best."

By this episode's end, Damico is effusive while dispensing gifts. He tells Angelisa that she is a "one in a million manager." He will send her to Moe's headquarters to share her dessert ideas. Moreover she will receive $15,000 toward getting a bachelor's degree and $40,000 total college fund money for her two children. Damico says to Janet that she is executive-worthy material and he wants her to help design a special Moe's catering symposium—giving her $15,000 and paying for her flight and hotel stay. Paul then tells Damon that Moe's will give him $15,000 to get a reliable car. He will also give him $20,000 to use for "quality day care, so that when you come to Moe's ... you're not worried about Mackenzie" and another $20,000 to start her college fund. However, Damico has one course correction: he informs Tito that his treatment of employees is unacceptable; Moe's will send him to its corporate headquarters for proper training.

The next appearance of a fast-food organization involves Sara Bittorf, the chief brand officer of Boston Market, going undercover at several locations. Bittorf first arrives at one of the company's stores in Georgia to work as a shift supervisor shadowing Ronnie. He tells Bittorf, with a sarcastic tone, that they have to use scripts with customers, because "we have to [put] customers on a pedestal" while trying to "force" customers to buy menu items. He indicates that he despises customers and that employees are to simply act like robots and follow the company's "ridiculous standards." Bittorf, upset, breaks her cover, sends him home, and convinces his store manager to fire him.

Then, Bittorf goes to Tampa, Florida, to work as an assistant general manager, shadowing Sash. She works carefully with Bittorf at the carving station, pointing out that, if one finesses the knife and meat correctly, it is like cutting butter. In a one-on-one conversation, Sash says that her staff is like her family, and she wishes she could take better care of them (like giving them breaks and one meal per day). Sash also works a second job, with an eye toward getting a degree to become a nurse. Bittorf, in a cutaway, says that Sash is passionate about her job and that the company needs to work to keep that kind of employee.

In Fort Lauderdale, Florida, Bittorf works the drive-through with AJ, who points out signs and a beeping timer that reinforce the goal of getting each order done in 60 seconds. He emphasizes the need to always smile and make customers feel welcome. He notes, in an aside to the camera, that the job is stressful but that you "always have to keep your cool ... because you don't want [customers] going to corporate on you." AJ shares with Bittorf that he was out of work for 2 years before coming to Boston Market; he had served jail time as a juvenile and now wants to repay Boston Market for his job by working hard. "Whatever they need me to do, I would do it, because they didn't have to give me that chance," he says, thinking aloud that he might be a shift manager one day. Then, in North Carolina, Bittorf shadows April, an assistant general manager of one the company's top stores for sales. She takes Bittorf around the store emphasizing that it is her job to make everything presentable; she moves, in Bittorf's words, like an "Energizer bunny." In a one-on-one conversation, April, a single mom, says she dreams of advancing in the organization; she goes to school full-time on her days off. However, April believes that the only way to advance in Boston Market is to get a degree, then quit, then try to come back into a higher-level management position.

In the episode-ending reveal, Bittorf tells Sash that she will receive $20,000 so that she can quit her second job and be "happy, engaged and committed" at Boston Market while pursuing her nursing degree. AJ will receive a promotion to shift supervisor and $20,000 to use toward achieving his dreams. AJ says his reward is a blessing, revealing that "God works in mysterious ways. You never know what can happen; you just have to have hope, faith and belief.... I've just been shown that ... everything and anything's possible." April will receive a fully paid relocation to a general manager job, $10,000 toward her son's education, $20,000 toward her own student loans, and $5,000 toward a vacation.

Later in Season 4, Fatburger CEO Andy Wiederhorn notes a striking example of employee self-governance in California, where store manager Val shows him every distinct step used in building a burger. Wiederhorn asks if there is a chart to follow, and she indicates that he simply has to learn it. As he makes mistakes, she calmly talks him through the process. Then, in Nevada, shift leader Lisa trains him on the register. She tells him to greet customers in an animated way: "They walk in and they see you. So you have to be like, 'Hi, how are you? Welcome to Fatburger.' You've got to be super happy and super excited." Finally, at a processing plant in California, Wiederhorn meets Ramon, a bakery supervisor, who shows him how to quickly find and discard any imperfect buns from a conveyor belt and then line up the good buns for automated packaging.

Beyond such employee self-governance, Wiederhorn is impressed with how these employees have persisted despite obstacles. Val, as store manager, wants her employees to feel recognized. Even though Fatburger does not offer structured recognition programs, she gives free meals out to exemplary employees and tries to give others some weekends off. She wants them "to know that I have their back," she says. Then, while working in Nevada with staff leader Lisa, Wiederhorn finds out that she is a single mom of three kids. She recently separated from her husband, who then died from drug abuse, after which she lost her house and her car; she and her three kids now sleep in her sister's living room. She does not have medical insurance and faces $250,000 in medical bills. Nevertheless, she asserts, "I'm here to raise those kids and give them a good life." Wiederhorn praises her for having a great attitude, saying "It's great that you got your head around it" and "Look at the ownership you take of your job here.... You're a stellar example of how [a restaurant] should be run." Wiederhorn is also impressed with the example set by Ramon, who has been at the bakery for 25 years and does not plan to leave because it is the "right place to work." He has four children to raise on his own because his wife was deported due to immigration paperwork problems. Wiederhorn says that, despite this legal problem, Ramon is "committed to his family and he's committed to his job ... to come to work with such a positive attitude—it's a great testament to what a man he is."

By show's end, Wiederhorn offers numerous rewards. He asks Val to accept a $10,000 pay increase by assuming a training position at corporate headquarters.

Fatburger will also give her $15,000 cash to spend as she would like. Next, Wiederhorn offers $15,000 to Lisa to pay for her rent, another $15,000 to help her resolve her debt, and $10,000 to buy a car. Finally, the CEO tells Ramon he will receive $50,000 so that he can hire a lawyer to deal with his wife's immigration problems.

What of the corporate persona on *Undercover Boss*?

This chapter finds that *Undercover Boss* offers, through the senior executives who interact with their company's employees, representations of the corporate persona as a constructive, beneficent entity who shares the values of average Americans. More specifically, these episodes collectively offer the narrative that hard-working, underpaid, and often distressed fast-food workers toil mightily in the face of adversities and, by virtue of the monitoring (and approving) corporate persona, receive reinforcement and eventual largesse. The final reveals, in which the top executives dole out rewards, affords employees the opportunity to explicitly reflect on how the wise counsel of the corporation (which had, of course, originally encouraged employee self-governance) has allowed workers to take steps toward authentic self-actualization. When Johnny Rocket's top executive Fuller provides gifts to Ajay, the cook says to Fuller, "Not many people do good things for me. Hard work definitely pays off. You work hard all your life, you'll definitely get your shot one day." During the Fatburger episode's reveal and rewards, Lisa tells CEO Wiederhorn, "I don't feel like I deserve all this; I just do my job." Wiederhorn replies "You do deserve it ... because you're so passionate about everything you touch." These moments serve to highlight the connection the corporation's message of self-governance has with the American ethos of individual betterment through one's own work ethic, a value that repeatedly appears in surveys of the American public. For example, a recent McClatchy-Maris poll revealed that, while most Americans (85%) believed that well-connected, moneyed people got ahead through an uneven playing field, they also articulated that they had to rely on their own work ethic more than previous generations if they were to improve their lives (Lightman, 2014).

Moreover, portrayals of the virtue of self-governance among fast-food workers—in a time where these workers are protesting a stagnant federal minimum wage—allows the corporate persona to assert that, instead of relying on the state, improving one's lot through hard-working self-governance is actually best for every American. Indeed, the plight of the low-wage earner, who faces difficulties in obtaining health care, child care, and adequate transportation, is a situation ripe for a corporate amplification of self-governance messages. That is, the corporate persona does not attempt to address large and seemingly overwhelming systemic concerns (e.g., a lack of affordable education, a predominance of low-skill service jobs, and the subsidization of low wages through state safety-net programs like food stamps and Medicaid). Such macro items are not the focus of the persona's appeal; addressing them would undercut the reach of the persona by revealing that the corporation does not suffer the ill effects of these systemic problems but, instead, may often benefit from them. Instead, the corporate persona leverages the mythos of American individualism by appealing to wage-earner beliefs that hard work is the key to mastering the exigencies of the human situation. In total, these *Undercover Boss* episodes elide the notion of any externally imposed action to better the lot of employees (like a state-mandated increase in the minimum wage or improved public transportation). Instead, the program conveys that that the corporate persona is a sympathetic fellow traveler who, upon seeing the plights and hurdles of the average American, will take action to help those who are industrious, "self-regulating consumer-citizens" (Lewis, 2011, p. 82).

In the case of *Undercover Boss*, that dynamic is revealed through the senior executive's message to the wage earner: to shape yourself in a valuable way, govern yourself so as to meet market needs. The senior executive, as an embodiment of the corporate persona, projects the corporation as an articulator and amplifier of common American values (e.g., self-reliance, self-advancement, etc.) and a source of encouragement for acting on those values. In directing attention toward the practice of self, the corporate persona encourages individuals to focus their attention on the minute patterns of their lives and away from any concerns about injustices that may spring from special privileges for organizations. As Winslow (2010) pointed out, this is an approach that hinges on citizens not questioning how trauma may, indeed, be associated with the rise of self-governance as propagated by modern capitalism. Instead, as *Undercover Boss* reveals, to thrive in austere times is to pursue "more association, and more acquiescence to the institutions at the foundation of modern industrial life" (Winslow, 2010, p. 285). Indeed, the program's portrayal of the guiding, beneficent senior executive works at a very visceral level because the TV medium "gives me a chance to feel things ... trains me by forming my imagination ... [helps] me form concrete images of what I love and desire, what I hate, who I want to be and how I need to act" (McGushin, 2011, p. 132).

It is this line of analysis—what Foucault has referred to as the shaping of self—that is particularly relevant for examining the distinctive messaging of *Undercover Boss*, a program that attempts to show the corporation, through the machinations of the senior executive, assisting the lives of their companies' low-wage earners. But, as the next two chapters show, there is reason to investigate how the corporate persona may be evident in other areas of modern life.

References

Beck, D., Hellmueller, L.C., & Aeschbacher, N. (2012). "Factual entertainment and reality TV." *Communication Research Trend 31*(2), pp. 4–27.

Berman, J. (2014). "Fast food protestors take to the streets on 2-year anniversary of campaign." *Huffington Post*, December 4. Retrieved from www.huffingtonpost.com/2014/12/04/fast-food-protests_n_6268838.html.

Carter, B. (2010). "Where's the boss? In disguise, and at the top of the television ratings." *New York Times*, March 20, p. C1.

DeSilver, D. (2013,). "Five facts about the minimum wage." Pew Research, December 4. Retrieved from www.pewresearch.org/fact-tank/2013/12/04/5-facts-about-the-minimum-wage/.

Ehrenreich, B. (2001). *Nickel and dimed: On (not) getting by in America.* New York: Henry Holt & Company.

Ehrenreich, B. (2011). "We need not just jobs, but jobs that pay." *CNN*, August 23. Retrieved from www.cnn.com/2011/OPINION/08/16/ehrenreich.jobs.unions/.

Foucault, M. (1977). *Discipline and punish: The birth of the prison.* London: Allen Lane.

Foucault, M. (1997). *Ethics: Subjectivity and truth* (Vol. 1). New York: The New Press.

Hiltbrand, D. (2010). "Corporate chiefs playing lowly Indians: Spying CEOs, all altruistic and ham-handed, make for some merry reality." *The Philadelphia Inquirer*, February 28, p. H1.

Kavka, M. (2012). *Reality TV.* Edinburgh, United Kingdom: Edinburgh University Press.

Lazonick, W. (2014). "Profits without prosperity." *Harvard Business Review*, September. Retrieved from https://hbr.org/2014/09/profits-without-prosperity.

Leana, C., Mittal, V., & Stiehl, E. (2012). "Organizational behavior and the working poor." *Organizational Science 23*(3), pp. 888–906.

Lerman, R., & Schmidt, S. (1999). "An overview of economic, social, and demographic trends affecting the U.S. labor market." *The Urban Institute.* Retrieved from www.forschungsnetzwerk.at/downloadpub/1999_lerman_trends.pdf.

Lewis, T. (2011). "Globalizing lifestyles? Makeover television in Singapore." In M. Kraidy, & K. Sender (Eds.), *The politics of reality television*, pp. 78–92. New York: Routledge.

Lightman, D. (2014). "McClatchy-Marist poll: American Dream seen as out of reach." *McClatchydc.com*, February 13. Retrieved from www.mcclatchydc.com/2014/02/13/218026/mcclatchy-marist-poll-american.html.

McCoy, S. (2015). "The American Dream is suffering, but Americans satisfied: 15 Charts." *The Atlantic*, July 1. Retrieved from www.theatlantic.com/politics/archive/2015/07/american-dream-suffering/397475/.

McGushin, E. (2011). "Foucault's theory and practice of subjectivity." In D. Taylor (Ed.), *Michel Foucault: Key concepts*, pp. 127–142. Durham, NC: Acumen.

Murray, S., & Ouellette, L. (2008). "Introduction." In S. Murray, & L. Ouellette (Eds.), *Reality TV: Remaking television culture*, pp. 1–20. New York: NYU Press.

Nabi, R.L. (2007). "Determining dimensions of reality: A concept mapping of the reality TV landscape." *Journal of Broadcasting and Electronic Media 51*(2), pp. 371–390.

"National data: GDP and personal income." (2016). *Bureau of Economic Analysis.* Retrieved from http://bea.gov/iTable/iTable.cfm?ReqID=9&step=1#reqid=9&step=3&isuri=1&904=2008&903=1&906=q&905=2016&910=x&911=0.

Newman, J. (2007). *My secret life on the McJob: Lessons from behind the counter guaranteed to supersize any management style.* New York: McGraw-Hill.

Newport, F. (2016). "Americans' views of socialism, capitalism are little changed." *Gallup*, May 6. Retrieved from www.gallup.com/poll/191354/americans-views-socialism-capitalism-little-changed.aspx.

Norman, J. (2016). "Americans' confidence in institutions stays low." *Gallup*, June 13. Retrieved from www.gallup.com/poll/192581/americans-confidence-institutions-stays-low.aspx.

Ouellette, L., & Hay, J. (2008). *Better living through reality TV.* Malden, MA: Blackwell Publishing.

Paras, E. (2006). *Foucault 2.0: Beyond power and knowledge.* New York: Other Press.

Piketty, T. (2014). *Capital in the twenty-first century* (A. Goldhammer, Trans.). Cambridge, MA: Belknap Press of Harvard University Press.

"Report on the economic well-being of U.S. households in 2014." (2015). Board of Governors of the Federal Reserve System.

"Right direction or wrong track: 33% say U.S. is heading in right direction, matching 2016 high." (2016). *Rasmussen Reports,* November 21. Retrieved from www.rasmussenreports. com/public_content/politics/top_stories/right_direction_wrong_track_nov21.

Royle, T. (2010). "Low-road Americanization and the global 'McJob': A longitudinal analysis of work, pay and unionization in the international fast-food industry." *Labor History 51*(2), pp. 249–270.

Rubin, J. (2016). "Giving thanks." *Washington Post,* November 22. Retrieved from www. washingtonpost.com/blogs/right-turn/wp/2016/11/22/giving-thanks/?utm_ term=.3a7f6badc1a1.

Samuelson, R. (2016). "Greenspan's grim forecast for growth." *Washington Post,* November 21, p. A15.

Sender, K. (2015). "Re-considering reflexivity: Audience research and reality television." *Communication Review 18*(1), pp. 37–52.

Skeggs, B., & Wood, H. (2012). *Reacting to reality television: Performance, audience and value.* New York: Routledge.

Stanley, A. (2010). "The boss in meek's clothing." *New York Times,* April 11, p. WK1.

"Thousands protest, hundreds arrested: 'We. Won't. Back. Down.'" (2016). *Fight for $15.* Retrieved from http://fightfor15.org/thousands-protest-hundreds-arrested-wont-back/.

Tsay-Vogel, M., & Krakowiak, K.M. (2016). "Inspirational reality TV: The prosocial effects of lifestyle transforming reality programs on elevation and altruism." *Journal of Broadcasting & Electronic Media 60*(4), pp. 567–586.

"United States GDP growth rate." (2016). *Trading Economics.* Retrieved from www. tradingeconomics.com/united-states/gdp-growth.

Winslow, L. (2010). "Comforting the comforable: Extreme Makeover Home Edition's ideological conquest." *Critical Studies in Media Communication 27*(3), pp. 267–290.

Wood, H., & Skeggs, B. (2012). "Introduction: Real class." In H. Wood, & B. Skeggs (Eds.), *Reality television and class,* pp. 1–29. London: Palgrave Macmillan.

8 Beyond fracking

The corporate persona as a relatable, credible entity

As this book continues with a more contemporary analysis of the corporate persona, marketing constructs and practices concerning the corporate identity loom large. For at least the last two decades, many corporations have been grappling with the idea that, while needing to continually assert the pre-eminence of their brand presence, they also need to demonstrate to stakeholders and wider publics that they are meeting broader obligations to the societies that they operate within. As pointed out in Chapter 2, corporate social responsibility (CSR) is receiving increasing interest within academe and the marketplace as both an orientation and a series of policies and practices that can allow the corporation to achieve brand prominence and societal stewardship. In essence, the CSR philosophy stresses that the corporation takes a "giving back" stance toward its fellow citizens, allowing the corporation to project a human-like persona. This viewpoint is visible in an extensive volume on CSR in America that states, "At the core of the corporate responsibility concept is the idea that *people and institutions alike have rights and responsibilities* by virtue of their existence in a society" (Carroll, Lipartito, Post, & Werhane, 2012, p. 23, emphasis added). As L'Etang (2006) pointed out, CSR often presents the corporation "as a moral person who can do good in society to the benefit of all" (p. 421).

An attempt to project a relatable, credible corporate entity can be fraught with execution problems, however, for a company like Chesapeake Energy (CE), the second-largest producer of natural gas in the U.S. (Chesapeake Energy, 2015a, p. 1), with operations in Pennsylvania, New York, Oklahoma, Texas, and Wyoming. CE's efforts in these states have come under criticism. For example, by 2011, CE owned almost half of 200 miles of pipeline that gathered gas from fracking operations in the Marcellus Shale region that is primarily located within New York, Pennsylvania, Ohio, and West Virginia (Chesapeake Midstream, 2011, p. 1). Their presence has led to protests against fracking in New York and Pennsylvania—a process where massive amounts of water, in conjunction with chemicals like hydrochloric acid, methanol, and sodium chloride, are injected far underground so as to loosen up rocks and free gas. Critics have maintained the procedure is wasteful, promotes continuing dependence on fossil fuels that aggravate climate change, and leads to groundwater contamination ("Anti-fracking groups," 2013; Maykuth, 2011). Other observers point to concerns with the release of methane due to fracking and the increased burning of natural gas: both are factors in the raising of carbon dioxide levels that trap heat and result in adverse changes to the earth's climate (Brantley & Meyerdorff, 2013; IPCC, 2013). Protests in New York led to that state banning large fracking operations that use more than 300,000 gallons of water; such operations, said the state, pose "significant public health impacts that cannot be adequately mitigated" (Campbell, 2015, para. 5). Fracking has also been linked to a rapid increase of earthquakes in Oklahoma (Fitzpatrick & Petersen, 2016) with the disposal of wastewater linked to that state's third-largest earthquake (a magnitude of 5.1) in February 2016 (USGS, 2016) and more than 1,000 earthquakes of a 3.0 magnitude in that state in 2015 alone (Phillips, 2016, para. 3).

Fracking companies have taken note of these developments and have put in place public relations efforts to blunt criticism of the industry. Observers note that pro-fracking messages in the U.S. strongly emphasize economic opportunities (Margonelli, 2013; Metze & Dodge 2016; Rich, 2016). In particular, Matz and Renfew (2015) analyzed thematic messages used by the fracking industry in the Marcellus Shale and found that natural gas businesses used appeals that resonate with enduring American values which prize both progress and the free market. One specific fracking company in the Marcellus region, Range Resources, emphasized to communities that they were part of an industry that brought extensive benefits to the economic well-being of all—bringing new jobs to the region and helping the country turn away from energy sources like coal and oil that emit more heat-trapping carbon, which damages the climate (St. John III & Pearson, 2017). These messages from Range emphasized another benevolent aspect of fracking: it was a "bridge fuel" that could help the country transition from higher-carbon-emitting energy sources like coal to renewables like solar and wind (Masters, 2013; Metze & Dodge, 2016).

It is apparent that the industry perceives threats to its continued existence and has embarked on many strategic appeals to citizens to bolster its position in society. In light of the controversy over fracking and Chesapeake Energy's large-scale operations across the country, CE similarly made a concerted effort to project its character as one which is a constructive force that works with a "powerful purpose," displaying a commitment to "environmental stewardship in the communities" they operate in (Chesapeake Energy, 2015b, p. 1). Accordingly, this chapter tracks how effective its community newsletters were in offering a portrait of a corporation that embodied the sense of societal obligation that is a fundamental aspect of CSR. In particular, this chapter tracks how respondents, exposed to variations in visuals (particularly, the presence of photographs) within CE's newsletter *Community Ties*, viewed the publication's story credibility, perceived the credibility of CE itself, evaluated its relatability (e.g., how well it engaged with the community), and perceived its corporate persona.

One specific approach within CSR relates to this study: company–consumer (C–C) identification, as described in Chapter 2, is a particularly notable marketing-oriented approach that attempts to build a brand affiliation between a company and its audiences through the company's products or services.

However, as observed in Chapter 2, while useful for analyzing these more trans-actional elements between a company and various groups, C–C identification, as currently understood, tends to neglect how companies can go beyond the brand to try to stoke identification with audiences who are *not* necessarily consumers. This chapter, therefore, addresses that gap through exploring how Chesapeake Energy attempted to build such relationships in newsletters directed to audiences that, while located in close proximity to CE's drilling operations, are not neces-sarily consumers of CE products. Specifically, this chapter provides measure-ments on how readers of its *Community Ties* newsletters, who do not have direct experience with CE (e.g., in purchasing products or services), responded to attempts by Chesapeake to use the newsletter to portray itself as a relatable persona who tells credible stories of obligation to its fellow citizens. In doing so, this chapter pursues a more quantitative approach to determine how the interplay of images and text in a corporate newsletter may signal that a corporate persona is being conveyed to its readers.

Perceived credibility and visuals in corporate newsletters

A corporate newsletter may be one of the only interactions a person has with an organization—therefore making a credible impression important. Early work in credibility research maintained that a story's credibility is synonymous with a story's believability (Hovland & Weiss, 1951). Additionally, source credibility theory helps explain how audiences ascribe credibility to people and/or organi-zations (Berlo, Lemert, & Mertz, 1970; Hovland & Weiss, 1951; Newhagen & Nass, 1989). Hovland and Weiss (1951) found that statements made by high-prestige sources tended to lead to audiences ascribing believability to those pro-nouncements and agreeing with those statements. The believability of the sponsoring source (e.g., news outlets, corporate entities, non-profits, etc.) or sponsor credibility also affects audience inclinations to assign credibility to the messages relayed through that source (Flanagin & Metzger, 2003). For example, a recent study (Lowry, Wilson, & Haig, 2014) found that "when websites are successful in convincing users that the website sponsor is credible, users will be more trusting and more willing" to attend to the messages on such websites and even interact with them (p. 84).

Scholars (Fogg & Tseng, 1999; Robins & Holmes, 2008) have established that well-designed publications, both online and in print, are seen as more cred-ible by readers. Effective design, therefore, is associated with surface credibility or the assigning of believability to an article based on how the information is graphically laid out. An experimental study that specifically examined image size found that an advertisement that contained a larger picture generated a "sig-nificantly more favorable attitude" than an advertisement with a smaller picture (Percy & Rossiter, 1983, p. 19). These findings speak to what is called the "amelioration effect," a term coined by Robins and Holmes (2008, p. 386). This happens when users are presented with the same message content, but the design has been changed. Those who see a message with a "higher aesthetic treatment" will perceive the message to be more credible than those who see the message in a "lower aesthetic treatment" condition (Robins & Holmes, 2008, p. 387).

Observers (Adatto, 1993; Birkerts, 1994; Ewen, 1988, Mander, 1978; Postman, 1985) have long noted how mediated visuals have affected how well individuals attend to content or text, voicing a concern that the increasing power of the image overwhelms critical awareness of nuance and complexity. This is what Ewen (1988) called an inundation of "stylistic information" that makes it difficult to see the "interconnectedness of facts" (pp. 264–265). Mander's (1978) critique specifically centered on television; that medium privileged the power of the visual, he said. "There is no need to do more than follow the images, hear the voices, [and] watch the cycle of realities" that television offered, he said (Mander, 1978, p. 199). Adatto (1993), speaking more widely of images in such arenas as cinema and art photography, said that the American propensity to dwell on visuals led to an "image-conscious sensibility" that resulted in message respondents being distracted "from the meanings that images convey" (p. 175). Stephens (1998) offered a more charitable view of the influence of visual communication and the power it can have in helping society advance through tumultuous times. Pointing to the late-20th-century signs of the early decline of print, he claimed that moving visuals may help society grapple with "scattered thoughts, unclarified contradictions … and indeterminacy" (Stephens, 1998, pp. 212–213). By the early 20th century, scholarly analysis of the advance of the mediated visual began to articulate its rise as part of a convergence culture within media systems. This development, said Jenkins (2006), led to images being produced by both institutions and individuals, across multiple platforms, sometimes leading to new relationships between fragmented audiences and various institutional actors (e.g., corporations, non-profits, activist groups, etc.).

Scholars have observed that newsletter design offers particular challenges, not the least of which is integrating pictures and text, as large blocks of text can be intimidating for a reader (Williams, 2006). Others note that, when images and words are combined in a skillful way, newsletters can offer one of the strongest forms of communication (Lester, 2014; White, 2011). Still, scholarly literature offers sparse observations on corporate newsletters and how visuals relate to those newsletters' credibility. Notably, Smith and Ferguson (2013) tracked how a coalition of fracking companies used newsletters (among other communication tactics) to make a case for state (and not federal) regulation of the fracking industry. While they pointed to how the messaging resonated with a sizable part of the public who distrust the federal government, their analysis did not include discussion of how visuals were used within those newsletters. Other related studies focus on newsletters across various industries. Downing (2007) examined how American Airlines used several different internal corporate newsletters to rebuild corporate morale after the September 11, 2001, attacks; however, his analysis discussed rhetorical imagery and did not delve into how visuals were used in those newsletters. Levin and Behrens (2003) examined Nike's attempts to portray itself as a "revolutionary" brand by using its external corporate newsletter to offer images of its retail products and research and development activities (p. 53). Kuiper, Booth, and Bodkin (1998) studied IBM's employee newsletter and its use of photography and found that women employees were significantly underrepresented in that newsletter's photos. These studies, however, did not address the perceived credibility of the sponsoring organizations. In all, the existing scholarly literature provides limited analysis on how the use of images in corporate newsletters may affect the corporation's credibility.

Hypotheses

Company–consumer identification's emphasis, indicated in the word "consumer," is tightly focused on the transactional, stressing how the purchaser of a product or service reifies a sense of identification with the corporation through consumption. While beneficial, the C–C identification line of inquiry largely elides the study of corporate communications directed toward audiences that do not have an overt consumer relationship with the organization. Additionally, what still needs to be better established is how the presence or absence of visuals—specifically, photographs—influences readers' perceptions of story credibility, sponsor credibility, and perceptions that the company is a human-like entity (i.e., a corporate person).

In an attempt to address these gaps and contribute an effects perspective to corporate persona messaging, this chapter focuses on the measurement of audience responses to articles from a corporate community-relations newsletter that does not communicate directly about corporate products or services. The corporate newsletter in question was Chesapeake Energy's *Community Ties*, a 4-page newsletter aimed at people who live in the Haynesville Shale (Ohio), Marcellus Shale (Pennsylvania and West Virginia), and Utica Shale (Louisiana) regions, and other shale regions in Oklahoma and Texas (Chesapeake Energy, 2014). These newsletters customarily featured employees involved in such activities as protecting wildlife and the environment, and volunteering in their communities (e.g., supporting athletic teams, rebuilding homes, and raising money for needy families). Besides long feature stories on such items, the newsletters also normally carried a section of small briefs on employee community activities and regularly offered a column called "Royalty Owners," which featured accounts of the families who had sold rights to CE so that the company could drill on their land.

As the literature on C–C identification and corporate persona messaging both point to the corporation's attempts to build a pertinent, relatable presence in citizens' lives, this investigation proceeded to test four hypotheses. These hypotheses predicted that there would be significant perceived differences about the extent of corporate credibility and the perceived presence of the relatable corporate persona if photographs were included in the newsletter stories. The hypotheses were:

H 1A: Readers who see images in corporate newsletter stories *will perceive the company that wrote the newsletter to be more credible* than readers who see stories without images.

Perceived sponsor credibility—in other words, how credible readers feel the company is that created the newsletter—was assessed using a validated sponsor credibility scale that included questions about credibility, integrity, reputation, successfulness, and trustworthiness (Flanagin & Metzger, 2003). Responses to the questions were measured using a 7-point Likert scale (1=Not at all to 7=Very).

H 1B: Readers who see images in corporate newsletter stories *will perceive the story to be more credible* than readers who see stories without images.

Perceived story credibility was assessed using a validated 5-item perceived credibility scale that measured the constructs of believability, accuracy, trustworthiness, bias, and completeness. These are the same constructs that have been used in a number of previous studies (Abdulla et al., 2005; Bucy, 2003; Flanagin & Metzger, 2000, 2003; Gaziano & McGrath, 1986; Johnson & Kaye, 1998; 2004; Johnson & Wiedenbeck, 2009; Meyer, 1988; Newhagen & Nass, 1989) to measure perceived story credibility. Responses to the questions were measured using a 7-point Likert scale (1=Not at all to 7=Very).

H 2: Readers who see images in corporate newsletter stories *will perceive the company that wrote the newsletter to be more like a responsible community citizen* than readers who see stories without images.

This hypothesis predicted that images used in corporate newsletters would have the effect of making the corporation appear to be more engaged in the local community. Perceived engagement was assessed by asking participants whether CE cared about the well-being of its local communities, acted like a fellow member of its communities, understood the needs of its local communities, acted responsibly in its local communities, was committed to progress in its local communities, and worked to better society. All responses were measured on a 7-point Likert scale (1=Strongly disagree to 7=Strongly agree). These questions were developed for this study based on CSR literature observations about the corporation as a responsible citizen within its local communities (Carroll et al., 2012; Coombs & Holladay, 2012; McMillan, 2007).

H 3: Readers who see images in corporate newsletter stories *will perceive the company that wrote the newsletter to be more like a corporate person* than readers who see stories without images.

This hypothesis predicted that images used in corporate newsletters would have the effect of conveying to readers that the corporation was a human-like entity. This was assessed by asking participants questions as to whether CE reflected who they were, whether they could identify with Chesapeake Energy, whether Chesapeake Energy cared about their values, whether they considered CE to be like them, and whether they considered Chesapeake Energy to be a corporate person. All of these questions were created based on observations in qualitative studies about the construction and conveyance of the corporate person (Cheney, 1992; Heath & Nelson, 1986; St. John III, 2014; St. John III & Arnett, 2014). A 7-point Likert scale was used (1=Strongly disagree to 7=Strongly agree).

Method

A pre-test was conducted with 10 students to determine that the experimental stimuli (articles and pictures) and the questions and instructions were clear. Results from the pre-test led to some changes to questions to enhance clarity. Following the pre-test, participants were recruited from six universities in the United States and 130 participants took part in the online study in March 2014. Participants were asked if they had ever heard of Chesapeake Energy; if so, they were excluded from the study so as to not introduce another variable. Each participant read three feature-length stories taken from a *Community Ties* issue; all stories were approximately the same length and were similarly designed. For example, an article titled "Big Giving" included three color photos of citizens taking part in initiatives that were funded by CE—elementary students decorating a new school parking lot and using a new covered performance stage, both of which were funded by CE. Another piece titled "Improving Lives through Service" showed a CE employee working one-on-one with an elementary student to improve the child's reading skills; another photo depicted three employees preparing meals for the homeless at a local rescue mission.

Participants were randomly assigned to one of two groups. There were 65 participants in each group. One group saw the newsletters with the original photographs in the articles, and the other group saw the stories but with the pictures removed. After reading each of the stories, respondents assessed the perceived credibility of each story. Additionally, after reading all three stories, they assessed the perceived credibility and community citizenship of CE and responded to questions about the perceived presence of the company's corporate persona.

Participants

The participants came primarily from the American Midwest (40%), the Northeast (39%), and the Southeast (13%). Sixty-one percent of those who participated were female and 39% were male. In terms of age, 14% were 18 years old, 24% were 19 years old, 21% were 20 years old, 15% were 21 years old, 21% were 22–25 years old, and 5% were 26 years of age or older. Eighty-three percent described themselves as Caucasian, 7% as African American, 7% as Asian, 2% as Hispanic, and 1% as Native American. Age, gender, geographic region, and race had no significant impact on any of the measures related to the hypotheses in the study. All tests were performed using a 0.05 significance level.

Reliability of scales used

Five different scales were used in the study to assess a number of constructs that measured perceptions of story credibility, sponsor credibility, Chesapeake Energy's community engagement, its corporate persona, and the respondents' propensity to trust. All of the scales had Cronbach's alphas of 0.7 or higher, which suggests they were reliable (Cohen & Cohen, 1983; Nunnally, 1978). See Table 8.1 for Cronbach's alpha values.

Table 8.1 Scales used and Cronbach's alphas

Scale	α
Story credibility	0.753
Sponsor credibility	0.871
Community engagement	0.948
Corporate persona	0.902
Propensity to trust	0.815

A detailed list of questions that comprised each of the scales can be found in Appendix A at the end of this chapter.

A 3-item validated propensity to trust scale was used to assess a participant's trusting nature (McKnight, Choudhury, & Kacmar, 2002; McKnight, Kacmar, & Choudhury, 2004). These items were measured on a 7-point Likert scale. Disposition to trust has been found to impact perceived credibility ratings in a number of studies (Collins, 2006; Gefen, 2000; Mayer, Davis, & Schoorman, 1995; McKnight, Cummings, & Chervany, 1998; McKnight et al., 2004). It was measured to make sure that differences in perceived credibility between groups was not merely due to one group having more trusting people in it than the other. In this study, no significant differences were found between the groups in terms of propensity to trust.

Findings

H 1A: Readers who see images in corporate newsletter stories *will perceive the company that wrote the newsletter to be more credible* than readers who see stories without images.

A t-test showed the group that saw the story images assigned a significantly higher level of perceived credibility to Chesapeake Energy than those in the group that did not see the images, $t(128)=4.64$, $p=0.00$. See Table 8.2 for the means and standard deviations of the groups.

H 1B: Readers who see images in corporate newsletter stories *will perceive the story to be more credible* than readers who see stories without images.

A t-test performed on the data showed there was a significant difference between the group that saw the images and the group that did not see the images in the newsletter $t(128)=6.12$, $p=0.00$. The group that saw the images rated the stories higher in terms of perceived credibility than those who saw the same

Table 8.2 Differences between groups in perceived sponsor credibility

Group	M	SD	N
Saw images	27.29	4.43	65
Did not see images	23.18	5.60	65

stories without the images. See Table 8.3 below for the means and standard deviations of both groups.

H 2: Readers who see images in corporate newsletter stories *will perceive the company that wrote the newsletter to be more like a responsible community citizen* than readers who see stories without images.

Participants in the group that saw the images were significantly more likely to report that they felt Chesapeake Energy was a responsible community citizen than those who did not see the images, $t(128)=4.22$, $p=0.00$. See Table 8.4 for the means and standard deviations for each of the questions.

H 3: Readers who see images in corporate newsletter stories *will perceive the company that wrote the newsletter to be more like a corporate person* than readers who see stories without images.

The group that saw the images was significantly more likely to perceive Chesapeake Energy as a corporate person than those who did not see the images, $t(128)=4.43$, $p=0.00$. See Table 8.5 for the means and standard deviations of the two groups.

There were also significant positive correlations between the corporate persona items and how the respondents rated both story credibility and organizational (sponsor) credibility (see Table 8.6). That is, the higher respondents scored these credibility items, the higher they scored questions about the company as being a relatable corporate persona.

Table 8.3 Differences between groups in perceived story credibility

Group	M	SD	N
Saw images	28.08	8.73	65
Did not see images	23.51	11.36	65

Table 8.4 Differences between groups in perceptions of CE as a responsible community citizen

Group	M	SD	N
Saw images	34.52	5.38	65
Did not see images	29.11	7.58	65

Table 8.5 Differences between groups in perceptions of CE as a corporate person

Group	M	SD	N
Saw images	27.70	6.07	65
Did not see images	22.16	6.90	65

Table 8.6 Significant positive correlations between credibility and relatable corporate persona

Engagement impressions	Sponsor credibility r	Sponsor credibility p	Story credibility r	Story credibility p
Reflects who I am	0.59	0.00	0.41	0.00
Is a corporation I can identify with	0.59	0.00	0.35	0.00
Cares about my values	0.56	0.00	0.45	0.00
Is like me	0.55	0.00	0.45	0.00
Is a corporate person	0.26	0.00	0.28	0.02

What of the corporate persona?

These findings show that those who saw images in the newsletter stories were more likely than those who did not see the images to rate the stories higher in perceived story and organizational (sponsor) credibility, perceived community engagement, and the perceived presence of a corporate persona. These findings support, in particular, previous studies that show visual elements can enhance perceived credibility (Fogg et al., 2003; Lowry et al., 2014; Robins & Holmes, 2008). Building sponsor credibility is particularly important because, when this type of credibility is present, people are more willing to trust and interact with a company (Lowry et al., 2014). However, this study is unique in that it not only examined the relationship of visuals to perceived credibility but also how those visuals related to perceptions of corporate citizenship at the community level and the perceived presence of a corporate persona. Those who read stories accompanied by images were more likely to see the organization as a good citizen as indicated in their responses to questions about the company's presence in its community. Additionally, those who read the stories with the images were more likely to indicate positive reactions to the concept that CE was a relatable corporate person.

Participants' propensity to trust was measured, as it has been found in previous studies (McKnight et al., 2002, 2004) to impact perceived credibility: the more trusting someone is, the more likely they will be to perceive something as credible. However, importantly for this study, no significant differences were found between the groups regarding propensity to trust, so variations found between the groups were not merely due to having one group with more trusting members in it than the other. As such, the findings here point to the importance of visual amplifiers for public relations messaging, especially regarding the establishment of source credibility and story credibility. This chapter provides evidence that both are also key to garnering positive readings of stories about the corporation's involvement in the community and to facilitating the perception that a company has an affinitive persona.

Additionally, the use of this particular convenience sample—college-age students who are not familiar with Chesapeake Energy—allowed this study to examine what company–consumer identification customarily ignores: how audiences who do not experience a direct product or service connection to the company react to that same company's attempt to present itself as a credible, community-engaged corporation that seeks to exhibit a relatable persona. It was important to measure *Community Ties'* CSR efforts because, as Yoon, Gürhan-Canli, and Bozok's (2006) research found, those who have very little or no knowledge regarding a specific company are more readily persuaded by CSR messages than those who are familiar with that company. As the respondents in this study similarly had no prior experience with CE, this work surfaces how respondents reacted to the messaging and presence (or absence) of the related visuals and not their personal experiences with CE, approximating how citizens in the actual communities that received the newsletters customarily have no direct product or service experience with CE.

As with any experimental study, there were limitations that caution against over-generalizing these findings. This study was conducted online, via a link sent to potential participants; therefore, there was a loss of control over the environment in which the study was taken which could have impacted the results, as there was no way to verify that the person who the link was sent to was also the person who took the study. Only students enrolled at four universities in the United States took part in the study; a larger sample size could have brought some variance to these findings; Caucasians were over-represented in the sample. Also, only those unfamiliar with CE were included in the study so as to minimize the number of variables. Only stories from CE's *Community Ties* newsletter were used; as a result, stories from other corporate newsletters could have brought some varied results. This study focused on photographs as the image variable, excluding other design elements in corporate newsletters (e.g., corporate emblems, infographics, and line art) that might have impacted perceptions of credibility, corporate citizenship, and the company's corporate persona.

This study found that Chesapeake Energy, a company that has faced extensive critical scrutiny because of the potential dangers of its fracking practices, uses to measurable effect its *Community Ties* newsletter to attempt to display how it is a relatable, credible, and human-like corporate entity. These findings indicate that the use of photography in corporate newsletters can help boost the perceived credibility of the stories and the organization. In addition, including pictures also allows readers to feel that the company is more involved in the local community. Significantly, those respondents who saw photos with the stories were more inclined to indicate that those stories provided evidence of a relatable corporate persona (i.e., one that is "like me" and "cares about my values").

Despite its limitations, this study provides a basis for attempting to measure how the corporate persona appears in daily life. Within CSR literature, there is extensive discussion of how the corporation attempts to display its connection to communities; scholars express varying perspectives on the constructive nature of these approaches. Coombs and Holladay (2012) maintained that CSR efforts can be beneficial to society if: (1) they simultaneously address organizational concerns and the priorities of the stakeholders; (2) they offer tangible (not just symbolic) benefits to stakeholders; and (3) stakeholders see justice (e.g., fairness, respect) in the organization's activities. However, McMillan (2007) claimed that corporations inherently have a difficult time achieving such empathetic stances because they are narcissistic. CSR efforts, she said, may attempt to project an engaging corporate persona, but they actually reflect a corporation's desire to pull stakeholders in as "raw material" for furthering the development of a corporation's "self-referential identity" (McMillan, 2007, p. 22). Boyd (2012) similarly critiqued CSR as displaying a propensity for corporate self-focus. He noted that corporations often construct a middle-class persona through CSR. In doing so, he said, they offer "themselves as typical organizational persons, potentially creating a distraction from their immense wealth and power" and their concurrent ability to manipulate audience perceptions (Boyd, 2012, p. 49).

As such, scholars have, at times, provided notable cautions about the power of the corporate persona; however, this same critical literature is quite narrow as regards effects research. In contrast, some corporate social responsibility studies, especially company–consumer identification, have pointed to the effects of the corporate persona. But C–C identification, as first discussed in Chapter 2, customarily examines effects based on consumer responses to product and service-centered images and messaging. In contrast, as discussed in that same chapter, much of public relations research on the corporate persona tends to align with a constructivist analysis that eschews examining effects. This chapter, however, points to how the presence of the corporate persona can potentially be tracked as an entity that is reified in the eyes of recipients. That is, one can likely measure the degree to which the corporate person is made real to recipients by tracking responses to messages and images which attempt to convey that the corporate person is a credible character who is engaged in its community.

Chesapeake Energy's projecting a credible, anthropomorphic image can help it articulate to the public why fracking, an industry increasingly in crisis, is beneficial to society. As a recent study revealed, most of the public expressed they do not understand what fracking is and are undecided about its future (Boudet et al., 2014). And, as Smith and Ferguson (2013) discovered, in the case of fracking in the Marcellus Shale, there is skepticism about how well public officials are equipped to regulate a business like fracking. Accordingly, there appears to be significant room for CE and other fracking organizations to emphasize their community presence—instead of focusing mostly on the bureaucratic, large-scale, policy-making arena—as a route toward building acceptance and local policies that would allow for their continued operation. But, beyond the ramifications for the fracking industry, the findings in this chapter suggest that there are, indeed, effective and measurable approaches that a company can use to credibly build a more human-like appeal to its constituents.

Clearly, as previous chapters of this book have shown, public relations has the ability to relay to audiences that the corporation has a character and a personality that individuals may feel an association with. In this chapter, we see that the effects of this approach can be measured. But this is a case that examined a relatively static and traditional communication vehicle—the newsletter—to gauge the contemporary presence of the corporate persona. In the last 10 years, social media has offered a new platform for the corporate persona to present itself. The next chapter examines the effects of the conveyance of the corporate persona in that arena, pointing to how this construct may speak to individuals in the online environment.

Appendix A

Scales used in the studies in Chapter 8.

Perceived credibility scale questions

How believable did you find the story to be?
How accurate did you find the story to be?
How trustworthy did you find the story to be?
How biased did you find the story to be?
How complete did you find the story to be?

Sponsor credibility scale questions

Chesapeake Energy is a credible company.
Chesapeake Energy is a company with high integrity.
I consider Chesapeake Energy to have a positive reputation.
Chesapeake Energy is a successful company.
Chesapeake Energy is trustworthy.

Propensity to trust scale questions

I usually trust people until they give me a reason not to trust them.
I generally give people the benefit of the doubt when I first meet them.
My typical approach is to trust new acquaintances until they prove I should not trust them.

Community engagement questions

Chesapeake Energy cares about the well-being of its local communities.
Chesapeake Energy acts like a fellow member of its communities.
Chesapeake Energy understands the needs of its local communities.
Chesapeake Energy acts responsibly in its local communities.
Chesapeake Energy is committed to progress in its local communities.
Chesapeake Energy works to better society.

Corporate persona

Chesapeake Energy reflects who I am.
I can identify with Chesapeake Energy.
Chesapeake Energy cares about my values.
Chesapeake Energy is like me.
Chesapeake Energy is a corporate person.

References

Abdulla, RA., Garrison, B., Salwen, M.B., Driscoll, P.D., & Casey, D. (2005). "Online news credibility." In M. Salwen, B. Garrison, & P. Driscoll (Eds.), *Online news and the public*, pp. 147–163. London: Lawrence Erlbaum Associates.

Adatto, K. (1993). *Picture perfect: The art and artifice of public image making.* New York: Basic Books.

"Anti-fracking groups rally in Albany, urge ban." (2013). *Wall Street Journal*, June 17. Retrieved from http://online.wsj.com/article/AP0f9d03bf7dac4f9f9b8f703ace2823a2.html.

Berlo, D.K., Lemert, J.B., & Mertz, R.J. (1970). "Dimensions for evaluating the acceptability of message sources." *Public Opinion Quarterly 33*, pp. 563–576.

Bhattacharya, C., Korschun, D., & Sen, S. (2009). "Strengthening stakeholder-company relationships through mutually beneficial corporate social responsibility initiatives." *Journal of Business Ethics 85*, pp. 257–272.

Birkerts, S. (1994). *The Gutenberg elegies: The fate of reading in an electronic age.* Boston: Faber & Faber.

Boudet, H., Clarke, C., Bugden, D., Maibach, E., Roser-Renouf, C., & Leiserowitz, A. (2014). "Fracking controversy and communication: Using national survey data to understand public perceptions of hydraulic fracturing." *Energy Policy 65*, pp. 57–67.

Boyd, J. (2012). "The corporation-as-middle-class-person: Corporate social responsibility and class." In D. Waymer (Ed.), *Culture, social, class, and race in public relations*, pp. 45–56. Lanham, MD: Lexington.

Brantley, S., & Meyerdorff, A. (2013). "The facts on fracking." *New York Times*, March 13. Retrieved from www.nytimes.com/2013/03/14/opinion/global/the-facts-on-fracking.html?pagewanted=1&_r=.

Bucy, E.P. (2003). "Media credibility reconsidered: Synergy effects between on-air and online news." *Journalism and Mass Communication Quarterly 80*(2), pp. 247–264.

Campbell, J. (2015). "N.Y makes fracking ban official." *Lo Hud*, June 29. Retrieved from www.lohud.com/story/tech/science/environment/2015/06/29/fracking-ban-new-york/29492515/.

Carroll, A., Lipartito, K., Post, J., & Werhane, P. (2012). *Corporate responsibility: The American experience.* Cambridge: University Press.

Cheney, G. (1992). "The corporate person (re)presents itself." In E.L. Toth, & R.L. Heath (Eds.), *Rhetorical and critical approaches to public relations*, pp. 165–183. Hillsdale, NJ: Lawrence Erlbaum.

Chesapeake Energy. (2014). *Community ties*. Newsletter. Retrieved from www.chk.com/media/publications/communityties/Pages/default.aspx.

Chesapeake Energy. (2015a). *Focused, disciplined, driven.* [Annual report]. Retrieved from www.chk.com/Documents/investors/CHK2015AR_Issuu.pdf.

Chesapeake Energy. (2015b). *Focused, dedicated, driven.* [CSR report]. Retrieved from www.chk.com/Documents/responsibility/CHK_2015CR_Summary.pdf.

Chesapeake Midstream Partners. (2011). Press release, December 28. Retrieved from www.chk.com/news/articles/pressreleases/12-28-11%20chkm%20marcellus%20acquisition%20press%20release%20-%20final%20(3).pdf.

Cohen, J., & Cohen, P. (1983). *Applied multiple regression/correlation analysis for the behavioral sciences* (2nd ed.). New Jersey: Lawrence Erlbaum Associates.

Collins, J. (2006). "An investigation of web-page credibility." *Journal of Computing Sciences in Colleges 21*(4), pp. 16–21.

Coombs, W., & Holladay, S. (2012). *Managing corporate social responsibility: A communication approach.* Malden, MA: Wiley & Sons.

Downing, J. (2007). "No greater sacrifice: American Airlines employee crisis response to the September 11 attack." *Journal of Applied Communication Research 35*(4), pp. 350–375.

Ewen, S. (1988). *All consuming images: The politics of style in contemporary culture.* New York: Basic Books.

Ewen, S. (1996). *PR! A social history of spin.* New York: Basic Books.

Fish, S. (1991). "Preparation for the year 2000: One corporation's attempt to address the issues of gender and race." *Howard Journal of Communication 3*(1/2), pp. 61–72.

Fitzpatrick, J. & Petersen, M. (2016). "Induced earthquakes raise chances of damaging shaking in 2016." *USGS Science Features*, March 28. Retrieved from www2.usgs.gov/blogs/features/usgs_top_story/induced-earthquakes-raise-chances-of-damaging-shaking-in-2016/.

Flanagin, A.J., & Metzger, M.J. (2000). "Perceptions of internet information credibility." *Journalism and Mass Communication Quarterly 77*(3), pp. 515–540.

Flanagin, A.J., & Metzger, M.J. (2003). "The perceived credibility of personal web page information as influenced by the sex of the source." *Computers in Human Behavior 19*, pp. 683–701.

Fogg, B.J., & Soohoo, C., Danielson, D.R., Marable, L., Stanford, J., & Tauber, E. (2003). "How do users evaluate the credibility of web sites? A study with over 2500 participants." Paper presented at the Designing for User Experiences Conference, San Francisco, CA.

Fogg, B.J., & Tseng, H. (1999). "The elements of computer credibility." Paper presented at the Conference on Human Factors in Computing Systems CHI '99, Pittsburgh, PA, May 15–20.

Gaziano, C., & McGrath, K. (1986). Measuring the concept of credibility. *Journalism Quarterly 63*, pp. 451–462.

Gefen, D. (2000). "E-commerce: The role of familiarity and trust." *Omega: The International Journal of Management Science 28*, pp. 725–737.

Heath, R.L., & Nelson, R.A. (1986). *Issues management: Corporate public policymaking in an information society.* Beverly Hills, CA: SAGE.

Hovland, C.I., & Weiss, W. (1951). "The influence of source credibility on communication effectiveness." *The Public Opinion Quarterly 15*(4), pp. 635–650.

Ihlen, O., Bartlett, J., & May, S. (2014). *The handbook of communication and corporate social responsibility.* Malden, MA: Blackwell.

Intergovernmental Panel on Climate Change (IPCC). (2013). "Climate change 2013: The physical science basis." Retrieved from www.ipcc.ch/report/ar5/wg1/#.UlB9Hn-TCSo.

Jenkins, H. (2006). *Convergence culture: Where old and new media collide.* New York: New York University Press.

Johnson, K.A., & Wiedenbeck, S. (2009). "Enhancing perceived credibility of citizen journalism web sites." *Journalism & Mass Communication Quarterly 86*(2), pp. 332–348.

Johnson, T.J., & Kaye, B.K. (1998). "Cruising is believing? Comparing internet and traditional sources on media credibility measures." *Journalism and Mass Communication Quarterly 75*(2), pp. 325–340.

Johnson, T.J., & Kaye, B.K. (2004). "Wag the blog: How reliance on traditional media and the internet influence credibility perceptions of weblogs among blog users." *Journalism and Mass Communication Quarterly 81*(3), pp. 622–642.

Kuiper, S., Booth, R., & Bodkin, C. (1998). "The visual portrayal of women in IBM's *Think*: A longitudinal analysis." *Journal of Business Communication 35*(2), pp. 246–263.

Lester, P.M. (2014). *Visual communication: Images with messages.* Boston, MA: Wadsworth.

L'Etang, J. (2006). "Corporate responsibility and public relations ethics." In J. L'Etang, & M. Pieczka (Eds.), *Public relations: Critical debates and contemporary practice,* pp. 405–422. Mahwah, NJ: Lawrence Erlbaum.

Levin, L., & Behrens, S. (2003). "From swoosh to swoon: Linguistic analysis of Nike's changing image." *Business Communication Quarterly 66*(3), pp. 52–65.

Lichtenstein, D., Drumwright, M., & Braig, B. (2004). "The effect of corporate social responsibility on customer donations to corporate-supported nonprofits." *The Journal of Marketing 68*, pp. 16–32.

Lowry, P.B., Wilson, D.W., Haig, W.L. (2014). "A picture is worth a thousand words: Source credibility theory applied to logo and website design for heightened credibility and consumer trust." *International Journal of Human–Computer Interaction 30*(1), pp. 63–93.

Luo, X., & Bhattacharya, C. (2006). "Corporate social responsibility, customer satisfaction, and market value." *Journal of Marketing 70*(4), pp. 1–18.

Mander, J. (1978). *Four arguments for the elimination of television.* New York: William Morrow & Co.

Margonelli, L. (2013). "The energy debate we aren't having." *Pacific Standard* March/April, pp. 30–34.

Marin, L., & Ruiz, S. (2007). "'I need you too!' Corporate identity attractiveness for consumers and the role of social responsibility." *Journal of Business Ethics 71*, pp. 245–260.

Masters, E. (2013). "Public radio's pro-fracking spin." *Extra!* July, pp. 7–8.

Matz, J., & Renfrew, D. (2015). "Selling 'fracking': Energy in depth and the Marcellus Shale." *Environmental Communication 9*(3), pp. 288–306.

Mayer, R.C., Davis, J.H., & Schoorman, F.D. (1995). "An integrative model of organizational trust." *Academy of Management Review 20*(3), pp. 709–734.

Maykuth, A. (2011). "Shale gas CEO: Anti-drilling activists 'extremist'." *Philadelphia Inquirer*, September 7, p. A-1. Retrieved from http://articles.philly.com/2011-09-07/news/30123374_1_marcellus-shale-coalition-natural-gas-drilling.

McKnight, D.H., Choudhury, V., & Kacmar, C.J. (2002). "Developing and validating trust measures for e-commerce: An integrative typology." *Information Systems Research 13*(3), pp. 334–359.

McKnight, D.H., Cummings, L.L., & Chervany, N.L. (1998). "Initial trust formation in new organizational relationships." *Academy of Management Review 23*(3), pp. 473–490.

McKnight, D.H., Kacmar, C.J., & Choudhury, V. (2004). "Dispositional trust and distrust distinctions in predicting high- and low-risk internet expert advice site perceptions." *e-Service Journal 3*(2), pp. 35–55.

McMillan, J. (2007). "Why corporate social responsibility? Why now? How?" In S. May, G. Cheney, & J. Roper (Eds.), *The debate over corporate social responsibility,* pp. 15–29. Oxford: University Press.

Metze, T., & Dodge, J. (2016). "Dynamic discourse coalitions on hydro-fracking in Europe and the United States." *Environmental Communication 10*(3), pp. 365–379.

Meyer, P. (1988). "Defining and measuring credibility of newspapers: Developing an index." *Journalism Quarterly 65*, pp. 567–574.

Moreno, A., & Capriotti, P. (2009). "Communicating CSR, citizenship and sustainability on the web." *Journal of Communication Management 13*(2), pp. 157–175.

Nazari, K., Parvizi, M., & Emami, M. (2012). "Corporate social responsibility: Approaches and perspectives." *Interdisciplinary Journal of Contemporary Research in Business 3*(9), pp. 554–563.

Newhagen, J., & Nass, C. (1989). "Differential criteria for evaluating credibility of newspapers and TV news." *Journalism Quarterly 66*, pp. 277–284.

Nunnally, L.J. (1978). *Psychometric theory* (2nd ed.). New York: McGraw-Hill.

Park, C., MacInnis, D., & Priester, J. (2007). "Brand attachment and management of a strategic brand exemplar." In B. Schmitt, & D. Rogers (Eds.), *Handbook of brand and experience management*, pp. 3–17. Cheltenham: Edward Elgar.

Percy, L., & Rossiter, J. (1983). "Effects of picture size and color on brand attitude responses in print advertising." *Advances in Consumer Research 10*(1), pp. 17–20.

Phillips, M. (2016). "Why Oklahoma can't turn off its earthquakes." *Bloomberg.com*, November 7. Retrieved from www.bloomberg.com/news/articles/2016-11-08/why-oklahoma-can-t-turn-off-its-earthquakes.

Postman, N. (1985). *Amusing ourselves to death: Public discourse in the age of show business.* New York: Penguin Books.

Rich, J.L. (2016). "Drilling is just the beginning: Romanticizing rust belt identities in the campaign for shale gas." *Environmental Communication 10*(3), pp. 292–304.

Robins, D., & Holmes, J. (2008). "Aesthetics and credibility in web site design." *Information Processing & Management 44*(1), pp. 386–399.

Serini, S. (1993). "Influences on the power of public relations professionals in organizations: A case study." *Journal of Public Relations Research 5*(1), pp. 1–25.

Smith, M., & Ferguson, D. (2013). " 'Fracking democracy': Issue management and locus of policy decision-making in the Marcellus Shale gas drilling debate." *Public Relations Review 39*(4), pp. 377–386.

Stephens, M. (1998). *The rise of the image and the fall of the world.* New York: Oxford.

St. John III, B. (2014). "Conveying the sense-making corporate persona: The Mobil Oil 'Observations' columns, 1975–1980." *Public Relations Review 40*(4), pp. 692–699.

St. John III, B., & Arnett, R. (2014). "The National Association of Manufacturers' commmunity relations short film 'Your Town': Parable, propaganda, and big individualism." *Journal of Public Relations Research 26*(2), pp. 103–116.

St. John III, B., & Pearson, Y. (2017). *Crisis communication and crisis management: An ethical approach.* Thousand Oaks, CA: SAGE.

United States Geological Survey (USGS). (2016). "Wastewater disposal likely induced February 2016 magnitude 5.1 Oklahoma earthquake." Press release, October 24. Retrieved from www.usgs.gov/news/wastewater-disposal-likely-induced-february-2016-magnitude-51-oklahoma-earthquake.

Vlachos, P.A. (2012). "Corporate social performance and consumer-retailer emotional attachment: The moderating role of individual traits." *European Journal of Marketing 46*(11/12), pp. 1559–1580.

White, A.W. (2011). *The elements of graphic design.* New York: Allworth Press.

Williams, R. (2006). *Design workshop.* Berkeley, CA: Peachpit Press.

Yoon, Y., Gürhan-Canli, Z., & Bozok, B. (2006). "Drawing inferences about others on the basis of corporate associations." *Journal of the Academy Of Marketing Science 34*(2), pp. 167–173.

9   Through the social media window

Tracking the affinity of the corporate persona

In her 2011 book, *Alone Together*, Sherry Turkle discussed the advance of affordable, portable technology as an intimate, yet disassociating, force in Americans' lives. She found that, as Americans increasingly rely on texting and social media sites like Facebook to communicate, they correspondingly distance themselves (and become even unskilled at) face-to-face communication. Sites like Facebook are a disruption to established ways of knowing the quality of a relationship, she said, observing that "we recreate ourselves as online personae and give ourselves new bodies, homes, jobs, and romances" (Turkle, 2011, p. 11). But individuals are not the only ones who have the potential to create an online persona—corporations have the opportunity to offer a human-like entity on social media. Dimitry Ioffe, CEO of the digital marketing firm TVGla, points out, in a *Frontline* program called "Generation Like," that companies want to engage in some kind of relatable approach (usually conversation) that is designed to get a social media user to trust the corporation's product. In this case, the corporate brand is like a person engaging with the user. "You want to trust in any conversation that you believe what that person on the other side is telling you," Ioffe said, making such an interaction "no different between a brand and your best friend" (*Frontline*, 2014). Teenager Ceili Lynch felt personally connected with Paramount's *The Hunger Games* movies. Fueled by the opportunities to win prizes, she was sometimes spending up to 5 hours a day liking and sharing various items on the movie's online page and re-tweeting related promotional material becoming, as author Douglas Rushkoff noted, "part of the marketing campaign itself" (*Frontline*, 2014). After viewing how she was presented on *Frontline*, Lynch was sanguine about its depiction of her life as so deeply affiliated with a corporate brand (and the corporate entity behind it), maintaining that the way she acted reflected what associations are like in today's world:

> I get the impression that a lot of older people think, based on my interview, that it's only a few pockets of people who do this thing, tweeting and sharing, who like something so much they're willing to put so much effort into it. But actually there are so many fans and people who will do that kind of thing not just for *The Hunger Games* but their favorite bands,

singers, movies, books, TV shows. Anything out there now people will support online.

(Lavelle, 2014, para. 7)

There is no debate in modern society that the Internet has acted as a modern-day backbone for making associations with others in our society; in many ways, its presence parallels the society-building connectivity that was offered by the American railroads, especially after the successful connection of the first trans-continental railway at Promontory Point, Utah, in 1869. And, much like public relations' part in promoting the expanding presence of the railroad (as seen in Chapter 5), PR has similarly played a significant role in amplifying the import-ance of the Internet. By the late 1990s, public relations interest in the power of the Internet was becoming apparent, with the discussion of websites as PR vehi-cles appearing in materials of the *Public Relations Society of America* (PRSA), the *International Association of Business Communicators* (IABC), the *Inter-national Public Relations Association* (IPRA), and in *PRWeek* and *PR News*. But many of the assessments of the Internet contained in these publications in the waning days of the 20th century were halting. An executive vice president at Hill & Knowlton bemoaned to one PR trade publication that corporations were not proactively using the Internet to get their news out. Instead, he said, too many corporations found themselves "chasing after the American consumer," some of which were actually using the Internet to put up false stories to influ-ence public opinion ("Internet," 1997, p. 34). This reactive stance toward the online world was apparent in PRSA's *Strategist* publication when, in 1998, it published a long piece on anti-business (or corporate hate) sites. The authors suggested that traditional media monitoring was an optimal way to guard against such web action, because "new media may feel new, but the old rules apply" (Grady & Gimple, 1998, p. 27). A writer for IABC's *Communication World* claimed that the new technology of the world wide web was "calling the shots," but finished his 4-page article with a similar backward-looking claim by insist-ing that television is "the global messenger" (Lane, 1998, p. 21). Watson (2015), in a scholarly review of the IPRA regarding new technologies and the Internet, found that this mid-90s time period reflected the practice's ambivalence or inability to articulate how the Internet might inform public relations practice. Still, by 2004, Hendrix observed that the PRSA Silver Anvil Award winners compiled for his case study textbook, drawn from the late 1990s up to 2002, were now strikingly different as "all the organizations represented in this text-book now have their own web sites" (2004, p. 5). The increasing amount of web activity pursued by public relations professionals, however, did not necessarily equate to re-conceptualizations of the field's activities. *PRWeek* pointed out that the Internet "makes so many other parts of life easier, better, or quicker" but elided talking about public relations aspects, saying that the Internet "failed to get us out of the either/or situation of dry, text-only accounts of breaking news and issues on one hand and vapid, surface-level television reports on the other" (Creamer, 2004, p. 12). This statement, much like that which Watson found in earlier IPRA articles, reflected a certain inattention at the start of the 21st century to how the Internet could likely reconfigure public relations strategies and tactics.

PRWeek's and Watson's discrete observations pointed to a key factor that hindered public relations' ability to conceptualize broader use of this emergent technology: a well-established media relations orientation. Prior to the rise of the Internet, the public relations industry had customarily attempted to gather the attention of various publics, and thereby build associations, through the dissemination of client-related news. For decades, the field established itself as a conveyor of client information through news releases, video, news briefings, or special events (or sometimes just highly visual stunts) that could be seen as useful, important, or novel news by the journalistic outlet, which would in turn relay it to the public. During the Internet's rise in the mid- to late 1990s, corporations tended to approach online communications with a traditional media relations bent, engaging in "shovelware" practices (i.e., simply placing existing content online without tailoring it for the Internet). The advent of social media by the mid-2000s, however, led to a wider realization that the opportunity to place corporate news as stories on platforms like Facebook called for understanding that such platforms are "part of an entirely different media ecosystem" (Allagui & Breslow, 2016, p. 28), which could allow the sharing of a client's news among, and within, various social media networks. One public relations professional observed that placing corporate news on social media is "about taking a traditional PR resource (such as a press release or bylined article) and transforming it into a fully integrated digital asset" (Morgan, 2014, p. 17). Although these observations reflected an increased sensitivity for a more intimate touch through social media, the past decade has still revealed some reluctance by organizations to convey a more personal approach through that platform. Instead, older approaches have not been abandoned but adjusted. For example, several studies showed that, through the mid- to late 2000s, corporations, non-profits, and government agencies simply encapsulated their own news and then relayed it directly through media like Facebook and Instagram. But original news content on their social media sites was often minimal, with the accounts merely linking to existing information on an institution's own site or other locations (Chewing, 2015; Waters, Burnett, Lamm, & Lucas, 2009; Waters & Williams, 2011). Still, some organizations tried to make connections with audiences that went beyond a direct dissemination of news and/or message points. For example, book publishers in the United Kingdom used Twitter not only to disseminate product-related news, but offer "interactive content such as competitions, games and votes" (Thoring, 2011, p. 157). The New England-based burrito chain Boloco used social media to place their CEO in conversation with followers concerning their kudos and complaints, supplementing their exchanges with links to videos (e.g., footage of the CEO's family going to a New England Patriots game), which showed how the CEO and his company were connected to the region (Winters, 2012). Within a few years, corporations' attempts to use social media became even more multifaceted. For example, the mattress company Casper hired "journalists in-house to launch an editorial site focused on the science of sleep, while simultaneously creating word-of-mouth marketing across traditional advertising and social media platforms" (Roy, 2016, p. 7). That same year, *PR News* singled out Bayer for a social media award because of its use of multiple modalities (Twitter, conferences, tours, blogs) to heighten its presence among various stakeholder groups and to promote an appreciation campaign for science mentors ("Bayer wins," 2016). Almost two decades into the 20th century, it was becoming apparent that public relations professionals were increasingly knowledgeable about using online methods to interweave the product and service offerings of a client with news and other novel attention-getting techniques.

These examples show that public relations, while often working in concert with marketing, also offers clients additional openings for building allegiances with audiences that go beyond touting their brand, products, or services. As numerous scholars have pointed out (Dervin & Foreman-Wernet, 2013; Heath, 2006; Wehmeier & Schultz, 2011), public relations affords clients the opportunities to act in a sense-making role in society, offering businesses ways, for example, to transmit news that may shape public understanding about the role of the corporation in society. Barker, Barker, Bormann, Roberts, and Zahay (2016) found that effective social media: (1) featured audience interactivity; (2) offered a conversational style that was not overtly product-centered; (3) provided helpful information; and (4) appeared credible. As such, the advent of social media allows companies to engage in strategies and tactics that move far beyond the simple placement of news stories to pursuing storytelling approaches that are timely, pertinent and, at times, interactive with the user.

Curiously, despite these broader observations that point to the usefulness of social media as a way for a corporation to disseminate non-product or non-service-related news to audiences (and engage with them on the same), little has appeared in the scholarly literature about this aspect. The studies that appear closest to describing aspects of conveying a corporate personality on social media are mostly situated within the marketing field. They offer a corporate persona construct known as corporate brand personality, which this book examined in Chapter 2's review of the marketing perspective of the corporate persona. In an extensive examination of the concept, Franzen and Moriarty (2015) pointed out that individuals can interact with products and services based on the "projection of human traits onto a brand" (p. 233). As marketing consultant Brian Solis said, it was important to "bring to life the personality and character of the brand through conversations, social objects and stories" on social media (2010, p. 16). He urged marketing people to think of the corporate brand as a person that would cause people to assess its appearance, its sound, and how it would interact with them. As social media gained prominence, it became a vehicle for asserting the personal connection of the brand personality. One top executive for Bridgestone, blunt about the potential humanizing role of social media for corporations, said "The great news is that now you have an opportunity to create a personality for your business and lead the discussion instead of reacting to it, good or bad" (Karpus, 2015, p. 18). Especially pertinent for this chapter, marketing scholars

(Gensler, Volckner, Liu-Thompkins, & Wiertz, 2013; Puzakova, Hyokjin, & Rocereto, 2013) observed that corporations were humanizing their brands through social media by connecting them more closely to the stories that were shared within a particular network. In doing so, corporations affect a brand personality that "converse[s] with consumers at a personal level, as if they were just another individual in the consumers' social network..." (Gensler et al., 2013, p. 250). Individuals can form as "brand communities" around this kind of appeal (O'Guinn & Muniz, 2009). In the social media realm, this can often be understood as being, in the example of Facebook, a "fan" who can influence fellow fans' connection to the brand and their intent to buy (Naylor, Lamberton, & West, 2012). The key, noted Killian and McManus (2015), was to use social media so that the corporation was managing relations, gathering news, and then creatively and entertainingly providing content.

In sum, the scholarly literature on corporations using social media to make a connection as a human-like entity is limited and reveals a persistent marketing influence. This is a notable gap, because, as one observer put it, by 2012 it was very clear that the rise of social media has offered "a world where conversation and dialogue have largely supplanted top-down, one-way messaging" (Brown, 2013, p. 7). At a minimum, there is a vital need to determine how the corporate persona may be perceived online because, as Swenson (2015) put it, "using content to build community and developing a relatable, aspirational corporate persona are incredibly important for communication scholars and practitioners, especially with the ever-growing popularity of social media channels" (pp. 158–159). Clearly, as it had done over the years in traditional print (newsletters, pamphlets), video (industrial movies and, more recently, for example, a show like *Undercover Boss*), and public presentations (speeches, open houses), the corporate persona has space to appear in social media. Therefore, this chapter examines how a corporate persona may be tracked as a perceived credible and relatable provider of information through Facebook and what such associations may tell us about the continuing presence of the corporate persona. One of the more promising avenues for determining if there is such an association is to examine how young millennials (aged 18–24) perceive a corporation's presentation of its own corporate news through the Facebook platform. Millennials indicate in surveys that social media is a leading source for news: a Reuters 2016 survey revealed that 28% of this age group indicated social media was the preferred news platform (Newman, Fletcher, Levy, & Nielsen, 2016, p. 7); the American Press Institute (API) found that 47% of millennials indicated following news was the main motivation for going on Facebook (API, 2015, para. 9). This tracks a 2016 Pew study which found that, among all U.S. adults, 62% get their news through social media, with 66% of Facebook users getting news through that platform (Gottfried & Shearer, 2016, paras. 1, 4). However, as this book shows, the presence of a corporate persona is not just about relaying news and information, it is about conveying a sense of who the corporation is in society in a relatable way, both in content (e.g., information about issues and activities that relate to individuals' values) and in approach (a first-person conversational style).

This chapter addresses these dynamics by offering findings from an experimental design that track how millennials, who read stories offered by a corporation about that corporation, view the story's credibility and the credibility of that organization. Moreover, this study also provides evidence of how millennials view that corporation's community engagement. Finally, it offers their perceptions of the quality of an anticipated relationship with that corporation and how much the corporation conveys a human-like corporate persona. This approach is similar to the study of Chesapeake Energy in Chapter 8. However, this study concerns an artificial company—Global Pictures—offering its own stories about community engagement through the Facebook platform.

Research questions

RQ 1: Among millennials, will there be significant differences in the *perceived credibility of news that comes from a corporation*, that is about that corporation, and that is written in a first-person, more personal style versus a third-person, more objective style? Will the number of shares, either low or high, affect the perceived credibility of the first-person versus the third-person presentation style?

This study used the same scales for sponsor credibility that were used in Chapter 8's study of the credibility of Chesapeake Energy's *Community Ties* newsletters (Flanagin & Metzger, 2003). Responses to the questions were measured using a 7-point Likert scale (1 = Not at all to 7 = Very).

RQ 2: Among millennials, will there be significant differences in the *perceived quality of an anticipated relationship with the organization*, based on whether news that comes from a corporation, that is about that corporation is written either in a first-person, more personal style or in a third-person, more objective style? Will the number of shares, either low or high, affect the perceived quality of an anticipated relationship when written in first-person versus the third-person presentation style?

In contrast to the study of Chesapeake Energy in Chapter 8, since Global Pictures is an artificial entity that represents a product (movies) that respondents are likely to be exposed to, additional anticipated relationship satisfaction questions were added based on scales developed by Huang (2001). This scale was used to further illuminate the perceived relatability of the corporate persona. Responses to the questions were measured using a 7-point Likert scale (1 = Not at all to 7 = Very). See Appendix B at the end of this chapter for these additional questions.

RQ 3: Among millennials, will there be significant differences in the *perception of an organization as being involved in the community*, based on whether news that comes from a corporation, that is about that corporation, is written either in a first-person, more personal style or in a third-person, more objective style? Will the number of shares, either low or high, affect the perception of an organization as being involved in the community when written in first-person versus the third-person style?

For this research question, this study used the corporate engagement questions that appeared in Chapter 8 regarding Chesapeake Energy's *Community Ties* newsletter (Carroll et al., 2012; Coombs & Holladay, 2012; McMillan, 2007) to determine respondents' perceptions of the company's community engagement. All responses were measured on a 7-point Likert scale (1 = Strongly disagree to 7 = Strongly agree).

RQ 4: Among millennials, will there be significant differences in the *perception of an organization as a corporate person*, based on whether news that comes from a corporation, that is about that corporation, is written either in a first-person, more personal style or in a third-person, more objective style? Will the number of shares, either low or high, affect the perception of an organization as being a corporate person when written in first-person versus the third-person presentation style?

Similar to the study in Chapter 8, all of these questions were based on findings in qualitative studies about the construction and conveyance of the corporate person (Cheney, 1992; Heath & Nelson, 1986; St. John III, 2014; St. John III & Arnett, 2014). A 7-point Likert scale was used (1 = Strongly disagree to 7 = Strongly agree).

Method

Undergraduate students were recruited as participants from two universities, one in the northeastern and one in the southeastern United States. The online study involved 202 participants, 57% of whom were female and 43% were male; 44% were Caucasian, 39% African American, 5% Hispanic, 4% Asian, and 7% "Other."

Each participant read three stories from a simulated Facebook account from the artificial company Global Pictures (see Figure 9.1). These three articles, each of which relayed a community engagement activity by Global Pictures, were based on articles from the websites of two Fortune 500 non-news companies in the U.S., slightly modified to not identify the actual company and to assure that all were approximately the same length and similarly designed. Since higher number of shares have been shown to have a positive effect on the credibility of product review websites (Kim, Brubaker, Kergerise, & Seo, 2010), surveys were administered to participants across four conditions: (1) a third-person-worded article with low shares; (2) a third-person-worded article with high shares; (3) a first-person-worded article with low shares and; (4) a first-person-worded article with high shares. Across the first 3 conditions, 51 respondents participated in each group; the fourth condition had 49 participants.

Care was taken to make sure the pages were designed in the same way, including the same numbers of likes across all four conditions; however, as mentioned above, numbers of shares were different (two sets of high, two sets of low) across the four conditions. Figure 9.1 shows the Facebook homepage created by the researchers, and Figure 9.2 is an example of one of the stories; all

Figure 9.1 Global Pictures Facebook page.

three stories were about some form of community engagement activity by Global Pictures. Articles offered news on the artificial company underwriting community dialogues on diversity, sponsoring recognition of teens who are active in their communities, and backing an energy conservation campaign. After reading each story, respondents immediately assessed the credibility of that story. After all three stories were completed, they answered questions about their perceived anticipated relationship with the company and their perception of the company as a relatable corporate persona.

Reliability of scales used

Six different scales were used in the study to assess a number of constructs that included perceived credibility of the story, sponsor credibility, community

Global Pictures New Pro-Social-Themed Series Highlights Teens Who Help and Lead Others

Global Pictures announces the debut of *The Helping Hand*, a brand-new docu-series that profiles in every episode a young activist who is making a positive change in his or her community and inspiring others to do the same. Each 30-minute episode, premiering June 2016 on Global Pictures' streaming service, will focus on a teen taking on issues ranging from poverty, to helping military families, to the environment.

The Helping Hand aims to inspire kids and teens to be active leaders in their communities by offering an insider's look at the personal stories of individuals who have been inspired to give back. Each episode will be capped by the profiled teen kicking off a "*Helping Hand* Challenge," an action or activity encouraging viewers to become a part of the movement by giving them ways to assist others in their own communities.

"*The Helping Hand* is another pro-social platform letting our audience connect to the issues they care about and to the work of friends and peers who are actively improving their communities," said Martha Goodridge, Executive Vice President, Public Affairs, and Chief of Staff, Global Pictures. *The Helping Hand* docu-series will provide a window in to how central the idea of helping others is to today's generation of kids and young adults."

The first teen featured in *The Helping Hand* will be Samantha Smalls, a 14 year-old from Boise, ID. At the age of 10, she was inspired by the film *The Blindside*, and the realization that there are kids who don't have a bed, to create "A Sleeping Place." With the help of her church, family and the generous contributions of local residents who donate funds, beds and their time, this non-profit organization has provided more than 700 families with bed frames, mattresses and bedding.

For more information or artwork, visit globalpictures.com.

Figure 9.2 Example Facebook story.

engagement, perceived quality of an anticipated relationship with the company, the perceived presence of the corporate persona, and propensity to trust. All of the scales had Cronbach's alphas of 0.7 or higher, which suggests they were reliable (Cohen & Cohen, 1983; Nunnally, 1978). See Table 9.1 for Cronbach's alpha values.

The questions used in Chapter 8 were also used in this study but with Global Pictures as the corporate entity. A new set of questions about perceived quality of an anticipated relationship was added into this study and can be found in Appendix B at the end of this chapter.

Table 9.1 Scales used and Cronbach's alphas

Scale	α
Story credibility	0.77
Sponsor credibility	0.92
Community engagement	0.95
Quality of the relationship with the company	0.87
Corporate persona	0.84
Propensity to trust	0.83

As was done in Chapter 8, a 3-item validated propensity to trust scale, measured on a 7-point Likert scale, was used to assess a participant's trusting nature (McKnight, Choudhury, & Kacmar, 2002; McKnight, Kacmar, & Choudhury, 2004). This scale was used to make sure differences in perceived credibility between groups was not merely due to one group having more trusting people in it than the other. No significant differences were found among the groups in terms of propensity to trust.

Findings

RQ 1: Will there be significant differences in *the perceived credibility of news that comes from a corporation*, that is about that corporation, and that is written in a first-person, more personal style versus a third-person, more objective style? Will the number of shares, either low or high, affect the perceived credibility of the first-person versus the third-person presentation style?

There were no significant differences among groups for the four conditions, as seen in Table 9.2.

There were five questions asked about sponsor credibility. All of the higher mean scores for sponsor credibility, though not statistically significant, split across two conditions. Three of those fell within the first-person, higher amount

Table 9.2 Total credibility ratings for each condition

Group	Mean	N	Std. deviation
1.00	68.3333	51	15.93696
2.00	68.5882	51	13.39579
3.00	68.7843	51	12.37144
4.00	69.6327	49	13.03792
Total	68.8267	202	13.66459

Notes
Group 1 = 3rd-person style, lower amount of shares.
Group 2 = 3rd-person style, higher amount of shares.
Group 3 = 1st-person style, lower amount of shares.
Group 4 = 1st-person style, higher amount of shares.

of shares: "Global Pictures is a credible company" (4.93), "Global Pictures is a company with high integrity" (4.89), and "Global Pictures is a successful company" (4.71). The other two fell within the third-person, higher amount of shares: "I consider Global Pictures to have a positive reputation" (5.17) and "Global Pictures is trustworthy" (4.62).

RQ 2: Among millennials, will there be significant differences in the *perceived quality of an anticipated relationship with the organization*, based on whether news that comes from a corporation, that is about that corporation, is written either in a first-person, more personal style or in a third-person, more objective style? Will the number of shares, either low or high, affect the perceived anticipated quality of the relationship when written in first-person versus the third-person presentation style?

There were no significant differences among the four groups (see Table 9.3). In this case, however, all of the eight questions with the highest means for the imagined relationship with Global Pictures fell within the first-person writing style with a high number of shares. Notable high scores were in response to "I would wish to keep a long-lasting relationship with the organization" (5.40) and "My relationship with the organization would be good" (5.33).

RQ 3: Among millennials, will there be significant differences in the *perception of an organization as being involved in the community*, based on whether news that comes from a corporation, that is about that corporation, is written either in a first-person, more personal style or in a third-person, more objective style? Will the number of shares, either low or high, affect the perception of an organization as being involved in the community when written in first-person versus the third-person presentation style?

Table 9.4 shows that there were no significant differences among the four groups regarding the perception of Global Pictures as being involved in the community. The highest mean score was for the statement "Global Pictures works to

Table 9.3 Mean scores for perceived quality of an anticipated relationship with Global Pictures

Group	1	2	3	4
Would meet my needs	4.45	4.62	4.60	5.00
Would have problems in a relationship (reverse-coded)	4.72	5.07	4.76	3.93
Would be satisfied	4.64	4.68	4.66	4.93
Would be a good relationship	4.58	4.70	4.70	5.33
Would not wish to continue relationship (reverse-coded)	4.52	5.00	4.77	4.33
Would be worthwhile to maintain relationship	4.52	4.78	4.63	4.93
Would want to keep a long-lasting relationship	4.56	4.66	4.61	5.40
Would wish I had never entered into relationship (reverse-coded)	4.94	5.25	5.07	4.40

Notes
Group 1 = 3rd-person style, lower amount of shares.
Group 2 = 3rd-person style, higher amount of shares.
Group 3 = 1st-person style, lower amount of shares.
Group 4 = 1st-person style, higher amount of shares.

Table 9.4 Mean scores for perception of Global Pictures as being involved in the community

Group	1	2	3	4
Cares about community well-being	4.78	4.86	4.75	4.91
Acts as fellow community member	4.47	4.70	4.63	5.04
Understands community needs	4.70	4.80	4.80	5.06
Acts responsibly in community	4.80	4.92	4.83	5.06
Is committed to community progress	4.72	5.05	4.85	5.02
Works to better society	4.96	5.19	5.01	5.10

Notes
Group 1 = 3rd-person style, lower amount of shares.
Group 2 = 3rd-person style, higher amount of shares.
Group 3 = 1st-person style, lower amount of shares.
Group 4 = 1st-person style, higher amount of shares.

better society" (5.19), for a third-person, higher-shares condition. However, the next two higher scores were for "Global Pictures understands the needs of its communities" (5.06) and "Global Pictures acts responsibly in its communities" (also 5.06), both for a first-person, higher-shares condition.

RQ 4: Among millennials, will there be significant differences in the *perception of an organization as a corporate person*, based on whether news that comes from a corporation, that is about that corporation, is written either in a first-person, more personal style or in a third-person, more objective style? Will the number of shares, either low or high, affect the perception of an organization as being a corporate person when written in first-person versus the third-person presentation style?

There were no significant differences in responses to the six questions about the perception of the corporate person. The highest mean scores were scattered across two of the four conditions. See Table 9.5 below.

Table 9.5 Mean scores for perception of Global Pictures' corporate persona

Group	1	2	3	4
Reflects who I am	3.72	4.00	3.77	3.81
Is a corporation I can identify with	3.86	4.33	4.06	4.28
Cares about my values	4.17	4.35	4.24	4.22
Is like me	3.80	3.94	4.00	4.12
Is a corporate person	4.03	4.13	4.28	4.46
Is a corporation I can feel a personal connection to	3.49	3.74	3.64	3.85

Notes
Group 1 = 3rd-person style, lower amount of shares.
Group 2 = 3rd-person style, higher amount of shares.
Group 3 = 1st-person style, lower amount of shares.
Group 4 = 1st-person style, higher amount of shares.

Additionally, as was seen in Chapter 8, there were significant positive correlations between how the respondents rated both story credibility and organizational (sponsor) credibility and the questions about the presence of the corporate persona (see Table 9.6). That is, the higher respondents scored these credibility items, the higher they scored questions about the company as being a relatable corporate persona.

What of the corporate persona?

One of the more interesting findings within this chapter is that attempting to measure the presence of the corporate persona through quantitative measures is a daunting but revealing endeavor. In this case, scales used about sponsor credibility were particularly meaningful: the correlations data revealed that the more a respondent found Global Pictures to be a credible site for the story, the more respondents saw Global Pictures as an organization that exhibited a corporate persona that was like them, reflected who they were, cared about their values, and that they identified with and felt a personal connection to. However, the data also indicated there were not any significant differences between first-person stories and third-person stories (nor amount of shares) regarding (1) *the perceived credibility of news that comes from a corporation,* (2) *the perceived anticipated quality of the relationship with the organization,* (3) *the perception of the organization as being involved in the community,* and (4) *the perception of the organization as a corporate person.* That is, key aspects of how the corporate persona has acted across the decades—as entities that offer value-laden messages, often in a first-person tone—was, when manipulated across groups, found to not affect respondents' perceptions in a statistically significant way.

Still, there were a few aspects of the study that suggested the impact of the first-person style. All the highest mean scores for the anticipated quality of the relationship questions (see Table 9.3) were in the first-person condition, and Table 9.4 shows that four out of the six highest mean scores for the presence of the corporate persona were in the first-person condition. Even with this tendency,

Table 9.6 Significant positive correlations between credibility and relatable corporate persona

Perceptions	Sponsor credibility r	Sponsor credibility p	Story credibility r	Story credibility p
Reflects who I am	0.59	0.00	0.41	0.00
Is a corporation I can identify with	0.59	0.00	0.35	0.00
Cares about my values	0.56	0.00	0.45	0.00
Is like me	0.55	0.00	0.45	0.00
Is a corporate person	0.26	0.00	0.28	0.02
Is a corporation I can feel a personal connection to	0.47	0.00	0.39	0.00

however, the differences among all four conditions (first-person versus third-person, higher shares versus lower shares) were not statistically different.

So, it is important to consider the data that points primarily to the correlation that the respondents made with source credibility and the corporate persona. That is, respondents read on Facebook a story about the corporation, offered by the corporation, and, *when they stated the corporation was credible, they tended to state it was a relatable corporate persona.* One of the lingering questions, however, is: since story credibility scores were also highly correlated with the perceived presence of the corporate persona, were respondents building perceived sponsor credibility as they read the series of three stories, or were they reinforcing what they inherently perceived as the sponsor credibility of such a corporate entity *on the Facebook platform?* As was pointed out at the beginning of this chapter, the moderating influence of Facebook as a platform for news is likely a confounding factor that should not be underestimated. In fact, the disproportionate influence that Facebook has as a gathering spot for news has led to criticism of the social media site. In early 2016, it was criticized for user-assisted algorithms that dampened the presence of conservative-leaning news on its "trending" topics feed (Nunez, 2016). By late 2016, Facebook was under increasing attack for not taking measures to prevent the spread of fake news in the wake of the 2016 U.S. presidential election (Dewey, 2016). In fact, PropOrNot, a collection of non-partisan researchers, found that a misleading story about Democratic presidential candidate Hillary Clinton's health reached 90,000 Facebook accounts and "was read more than 8 million times" (Timberg, 2016, p. A15). With only 18% of Americans saying they trust the news they get from national news organizations (Mitchell, Gottfried, Barthel, & Shearer, 2016, para. 2), there is a continued potential for news of all types—whether fake news or self-interested corporate news—to connect with social media audiences who have abandoned established news organizations. These criticisms reflect the reliance that Americans, especially millennials, have on Facebook as a news site, a predilection for the platform that may have favorably affected respondents' ratings on Global Pictures' source credibility and story credibility (which, this chapter found, also correlated with the increased perception of the corporate persona).

As this chapter reveals, determining how specific audiences view the corporation through the prism of the online world is a challenging task. Perhaps that is why one study found that, in examining 35 years of scholarship in *Public Relations Review*, scholars mostly investigated how corporations used the Internet as a media relations tool that offers "elite talk, by elites, for elites" with very little focus on who are the wider range of publics that can be reached (Verčič, Verčič, & Sriramesh, 2015, p. 148). Although public relations scholarship customarily emphasizes building dialogue and consensus among clients and multiple audiences, the authors found that social media studies in *Public Relations Review* customarily avoided examining audiences as distinct publics. Rather, they said, the studies emphasized the transmission aspect of social media messages to the point where the "public remains absent" (Verčič et al., 2015, p. 146).

But how individuals see a professed reality through social media is important, especially with millennials and the public at large turning to social media, like Facebook, as a critical news source (API, 2015; Gottfried & Shearer, 2016; Newman et al., 2016). This chapter offers information to help fill two gaps: a disturbing lack of research about how social media users actually perceive the information they receive through social media, especially corporate-related news offered by those self-same corporations, and the lack of research on how the corporate persona attempts to build a non-product/non-service-centered, human-like affiliation through social media. Findings here offer a first glimpse at how that kind of link may be made and discovers that attempts to talk more directly, in first-person, are slightly associated, though not statistically significant, with an individual's perception that a corporation is a human-like entity. This initial finding, then, reveals that merely making a rhetorical switch (articulating the corporation in first-person rather than third) within a concerted storytelling approach is not enough to develop a sense of affinity between the corporation and the individual. Instead, two other factors are essential: *the credibility of the organization telling the story* and *the credibility of the story*. Indeed, this is a core aspect of this book's exploration of the power of the corporate persona. As mentioned in Chapter 2, the corporate persona leverages influence best when it offers believable evidence within a story that resonates well with individuals' values, their lived experiences, and their surroundings (Fisher, 1989; Heath, 2013; Moffitt, 1994).

Second, it appears that the medium also looms large. Although this study did not directly address how Facebook's own credibility may have had second-order effects on the perception of a credible, relatable corporate persona, it is clear that studies tracking audiences' use of Facebook substantiate that many of them rely on that platform as a news site. Although this chapter and this book are not professing the old axiom that the "medium is the message" (McLuhan & Fiore, 1967), as earlier chapters showed, it is undeniable that corporations use media that inherently allow better opportunities to convey who they are, especially to audiences that do not have ready access to their products and services. The National Association of Manufacturers (Chapter 3) used pamphlets, videos, and speakers bureaus to build associations with customers who may never have directly bought a product from some of their varied corporate members. Norfolk and Western Railway (Chapter 5) and Standard Oil of California (Chapter 6) used their employee publications to speak against socialism and government overreach, counting on their employees and shareholders to share the corporations' messages with their families, friends, and larger communities. Chapter 8 showed that, more recently, Chesapeake Energy used a hard-copy newsletter with color photos of their employees volunteering in communities near their fracking wells, attempting to show its affinity with individuals in these communities who would never purchase a product or service directly from CE. At a minimum, this chapter reflects that corporations' sensitivity to choosing the right vehicle for conveying their corporate persona has never been more important, and, in Facebook's case, never more complicated to discern how the medium, in its own distinctive way, may amplify that persona.

As such, this finding also parallels what Akman and Hug (2016) have said about parts of Internet culture acting as real "objects" that have "positive and negative facades depending on how they are dealt with by the subject" (p. 231). This chapter revealed that the façade or corporate "face" of Global Pictures was seen as a more relatable corporate persona in conjunction with how well it was seen as offering a credible story on Facebook. Social media, therefore, would appear to be an ideal setting for a corporate persona who offers a compelling, believable story that resonates with the online user's needs. Ceili Lynch, the 16-year-old who, at the start of this chapter, discussed her intense social media activity in support of *The Hunger Games*, nevertheless said that social media had an unmooring effect. "…Social media kind of rips people apart," she said. "[W]e are all put into this arena where you're forced to try to survive on your own" (*Frontline*, 2014). Such a sense of unrooted individualism is tailor-made for the appeal of the corporate persona, a construct designed to ameliorate the challenges and discomforts of self-reliance by proposing ways that the individual can direct oneself. In the case of Ceili, it is earning badges that allow her to unlock news about a movie on social media, presented on a news site piloted by a corporate entity that knows what she cares about. Her interactions with the corporation online reveals the latest iteration of the power of the corporate persona, an entity that professes that it shares values and goals with the individual, while it attempts to guide that human toward a mutually prosperous end.

Appendix B

The scales used in this study are the same as shown in Appendix A in Chapter 8, with the following scale added:

Perceived anticipated relationship quality

Generally speaking, this organization would meet my needs.
Generally speaking, my relationship with the organization would have problems.
In general, I would be satisfied with the relationship with the organization.
My relationship with the organization would be good.
I would not wish to continue a relationship with the organization.
I would believe that it would be worthwhile to try to maintain the relationship with the organization.
I would wish to keep a long-lasting relationship with the organization.
I would wish I had never entered into the relationship with the organization.

References

Akman, J., & Hug, N. (2016). "Living parallel-ly in real and virtual: Internet as extension of self." In A. Novak, & I. El-Burki (Eds.), *Defining identity and the changing scope of culture in the digital age*, pp. 230–239. Hershey, PA: IGI Global.

Allagui, I., & Breslow, H. (2016). "Social media for public relations: Lessons from four effective cases." *Public Relations Review 42*, pp. 20–30.

American Press Institute (API). (2015). "How millennials get news: Inside the habits of America's first digital generation." March. Retrieved from www.americanpress institute.org/publications/reports/survey-research/millennials-news/.

Barker, M., Barker, D., Bormann, N., Roberts, M.L., & Zahay, D.K. (2016). *Social media marketing: A strategic approach* (2nd ed.). Cengage: Boston, MA.

"Bayer wins 2016 *PR News'* social media award for best Twitter community engagement." (2016). *PR Newswire* [news release]. June 7. Retrieved from www.prnewswire. com/news-releases/bayer-wins-2016-pr-news-social-media-award-for-best-twitter-community-engagement-300280802.html.

Brown, R. (2013). "Digital PR is dead: Social goes mainstream." In R. Brown, & S. Waddington (Eds.), *Share this too: More social media solutions for PR professionals*, pp. 3–10. West Sussex, UK: John Wiley & Sons.

Carroll, A., Lipartito, K., Post, J., & Werhane, P. (2012). *Corporate responsibility: The American experience.* Cambridge: University Press.

Cheney, G. (1992). "The corporate person (re)presents itself." In E.L. Toth, & R.L. Heath, (Eds.), *Rhetorical and critical approaches to public relations*, pp. 165–183. Hillsdale, NJ: Lawrence Erlbaum.

Chewing, L. (2015). "Multiple voices and multiple media: Co-constructing BP's crisis response." *Public Relations Review 41*(1), pp. 72–79.

Cohen, J., & Cohen, P. (1983). *Applied multiple regression/correlation analysis for the behavioral sciences* (2nd ed.). New Jersey: Lawrence Erlbaum Associates.

Coombs, W., & Holladay, S. (2012). *Managing corporate social responsibility: A communication approach.* Malden, MA: Wiley & Sons.

Creamer, M. (2004). "Media report shows the web has a way to go to becoming more than old media's bullhorn." *PRWeek*, March 29, p. 12.

Dervin, B., & Foreman-Wernet, L. (2013). "Sense-making methodology as an approach to understanding and designing for campaign audiences: A turn to communicating communicatively." In R. Rice, & C. Atkin (Eds.), *Public communication campaigns* (4th ed.), pp. 147–162. Thousand Oaks, CA: SAGE.

Dewey, C. (2016). "Facebook fake-news writer: 'I think Donald Trump is in the White House because of me.'" *Washington Post*, November 17. Retrieved from www. washingtonpost.com/news/the-intersect/wp/2016/11/17/facebook-fake-news-writer-i-think-donald-trump-is-in-the-white-house-because-of-me/.

Fisher, W. (1989). *Human communication as narration: Toward a philosophy of reason, value and action.* Columbia, SC: University of South Carolina Press.

Flanagin, A.J., & Metzger, M.J. (2003). "The perceived credibility of personal web page information as influenced by the sex of the source." *Computers in Human Behavior 19*, pp. 683–701.

Franzen, G., & Moriarty, S. (2015). *The science and art of branding.* New York: Routledge.

Frontline. (2014). *Generation like.* Broadcast transcript, *Frontline*, February 17. Retrieved from www.pbs.org/wgbh/frontline/film/generation-like/transcript/.

Gensler, S., Volckner, F., Liu-Thompkins, Y., & Wiertz, C. (2013). "Managing brands in the social media environment." *Journal of Interactive Marketing 27*, pp. 242–256.

Grady, D., & Gimple, J. (1998). "Virtual barbarians at the gate." *The Public Relations Strategist*, Fall, pp. 23–27.

Gottfried, D., & Shearer, E. (2016). "News use across social media platforms." *Pew Research Center*, May 26. Retrieved from www.journalism.org/2016/05/26/news-use-across-social-media-platforms-2016/.

Heath, R. (2006). "A rhetorical theory approach to issues management." In C. Botan, & V. Hazelton (Eds.), *Public relations theory II*, pp. 55–87. Mahwah, NJ: Lawrence Erlbaum Associates.

Heath, R. (2013). "The journey to understand and champion OPR takes many roads, some not yet well traveled." *Public Relations Review 39*, pp. 426–431.

Heath, R.L., & Nelson, R.A. (1986). *Issues management: Corporate public policymaking in an information society.* Beverly Hills, CA: SAGE.

Hendrix, J. (2004). *Public relations cases* (6th ed.). Belmont, CA: Wadsworth/Thomson Learning.

Huang, Y.-H. (2001). "OPRA: A cross-cultural, multiple-item scale for measuring organization-public relationship." *Journal of Public Relations Research 13*(1), pp. 61–90.

"Internet, promoted as PR dream, is nightmare for some companies." (1997). *O'Dwyer's PR Services Report*, April, pp. 1, 30, 32, 34.

Karpus, J. (2015). "Bridgestone's dealer network readying a social media program." *Tire Business*, July 20, p. 18.

Killian, G., & McManus, K. (2015). "A marketing communications approach for the digital era: Managerial guidelines for social media integration." *Business Horizons 58*, pp. 539–549.

Kim, H., Brubaker, P.J., Kegerise, A., & Seo, K. (2010). "To share or not to share, that is the question: Examining psychological effects of heuristic cues on users' attitudes on a product review website." Paper presented at the International Communication Association Annual Conference, June 21, Singapore.

Lane, C. (1998). "It's open season on the web, and technology is calling the shots." *Communication World*, March, pp. 18–21.

Lavelle, M. (2014). "What did 'Generation Like' think of 'Generation Like?'" *Frontline*, August 5. Retrieved from www.pbs.org/wgbh/frontline/article/what-did-generation-like-think-of-generation-like/.

McKnight, D.H., Choudhury, V., & Kacmar, C. (2002). "Developing and validating trust measures for e-commerce: An integrative typology." *Information Systems Research 13*(3), pp. 334–359.

McKnight, D.H., Kacmar, C.J., & Choudhury, V. (2004). "Dispositional trust and distrust distinctions in predicting high- and low-risk internet expert advice site perceptions." *e-Service Journal 3*(2), pp. 35–55.

McLuhan, M., & Fiore, Q. (1967). *The medium is the message: An inventory of effects.* New York: Bantam Books.

McMillan, J. (2007). "Why corporate social responsibility? Why now? How?" In S. May, G. Cheney, & J. Roper (Eds.), *The debate over corporate social responsibility*, pp. 15–29. Oxford: University Press.

Mitchell, A., Gottfried, J., Barthel, M., & Shearer, E. (2016). "The modern news consumer: Trust and accuracy." *Journalism.org*, July 7. Retrieved from www.journalism.org/2016/07/07/trust-and-accuracy/.

Moffitt, M. (1994)."A cultural studies perspective toward understanding corporate image: A case study of State Farm Insurance." *Journal of Public Relations Research 6*(1), pp. 41–66.

Morgan, C. (2014). "Supercharge your PR strategy." *Communication World*, April, pp. 15–17.

Naylor, R., Lamberton, C., & West, P. (2012). "Beyond the 'like' button: The impact of mere virtual presence on brand evaluations and purchase intentions in social media settings." *Journal of Marketing 76*, pp. 105–120.

Newman, N., Fletcher, R., Levy D.A.L., & Nielsen, R.K. (2016.) *Reuters institute digital news report 2016.* Retrieved from http://reutersinstitute.politics.ox.ac.uk/sites/default/files/Digital-News-Report-2016.pdf.

Nunez, M. (2016). "Former Facebook workers: We routinely suppressed conservative news." *New York Times*, May 9. Retrieved from http://gizmodo.com/former-facebook-workers-we-routinely-suppressed-conser-1775461006.

Nunnally, L.J. (1978). *Psychometric theory* (2nd ed.). New York: McGraw-Hill.

O'Guinn, T., & Muniz, A. (2009). "Collective brand relationships." In D. MacInnis, C. Park, & J. Priester (Eds.), *Handbook of brand relationships*, pp. 173–194. New York: M.E. Sharpe.

Puzakova, M.K., Kwak, H., & Rocereto, J.F. (2013). "When humanizing brands goes wrong: The detrimental effect of brand anthropomorphization amid product wrongdoings." *Journal of Marketing 77*, pp. 81–100.

Roy, B. (2016). "Social vs. traditional media: Has the battle already ended?" *PRSA Tactics*, April, p. 7.

Solis, B. (2010). "The social-media style guide: Eight steps to creating a brand persona." *Advertising Age*, May 10, p. 16.

St. John III, B. (2014). "Conveying the sense-making corporate persona: The Mobil Oil 'Observations' columns, 1975–1980." *Public Relations Review 40*(4), pp. 692–699.

St. John III, B., & Arnett, R. (2014). "The National Association of Manufacturers' commmunity relations short film 'Your Town': Parable, propaganda, and big individualism." *Journal of Public Relations Research 26*(2), pp. 103–116.

Swenson, R. (2016). "Building Betty Crocker's brand community: Conversations with consumers, 1940–1950." *Journal of Communication Management 20*(2), pp. 148–161.

Thoring, A. (2011). "Corporate tweeting: Analyzing the use of Twitter as a marketing tool by UK trade publishers." *Publishing Research Quarterly 27*, pp. 141–158.

Timberg, C. (2016). "Research ties 'fake news' to Russia." *Washington Post*, November 25, pp. A1, A15.

Turkle, S. (2011). *Alone together: Why we expect more from technology and less from each other.* Philadelphia, PA: Basic Books.

Verčič, D., Verčič, A.T., Sriramesh, K. (2015). "Looking for digital in public relations." *Public Relations Review 41*, pp. 142–152.

Waters, R.D., Burnett, E., Lamm, A., & Lucas, J. (2009). "Engaging stakeholders through social networking: How nonprofit organizations are using Facebook." *Public Relations Review 35*, pp. 102–106.

Waters, R.D., & Williams, J.M. (2011). "Squawking, tweeting, cooing, and hooting: Analyzing the communication patterns of government agencies on Twitter." *Journal of Public Affairs 11*(4), pp. 353–363.

Watson, T. (2015). "PR's early response to the 'information superhighway'; the IPRA narrative." *Communication & Society 28*(1), pp. 1–12.

Wehmeier, S., & Schultz, F. (2011). "Communication and corporate social responsibility: A storytelling perspective." In O. Ihlen, J.L. Bartlett, & S. May (Eds.), *The handbook of communication and corporate social responsibility*, pp. 467–488. Oxford, UK: Wiley-Blackwell.

Winters, C. (2012). "Top three social CEOs—what they can teach us." *O'Dwyer's*, September, p. 31.

10 Where to with the corporate persona?

In 1937, observing the increasing discontent that Americans felt toward business in the midst of the lingering Great Depression, Henry C. Link, director of the Psychological Corporation, said that Americans were inclined to embrace the welfare state, and to see government as the benefactor that could help them make it through tough times. He pointed out that business needed to appeal to the American character's penchant for self-reliance and, in the process, re-educate the populace about the benefits of the free enterprise system. He noted, however, that business leaders tended to make ineffective factual arguments, "unable to translate their ideas into an emotional appeal, *the only kind of appeal which has ever moved people in large numbers*" (quoted in Batchelor, 1938, p. 49, emphasis added).

As this book shows, however, by the mid-20th century in the U.S., business did come to a better understanding of this emotional aspect. In times of stress (e.g., increased government activity in the marketplace, concerns about society's acceptance of socialism, etc.), some industries embraced the storytelling ability of the corporate persona, attempting to establish that the corporation was a fellow traveler who shared Americans' values on a mutual journey of progress. Rather than focusing on data to convince the public, some corporations became more adept at marshaling facts and figures in a way that undergirded this claim of affinity. As such, this book establishes that the corporate persona construct may well arise in the future, particularly in the U.S., but perhaps also in other countries.

Why might that be the case? As regards the United States, there is significant evidence of economic disruptions that point to stressors on Americans' adherence to the free market paradigm. Chapter 7 provides several examples of socioeconomic stress in America, but there are more. The Russell Sage Foundation reported that inflation-adjusted household wealth declined 36% from 2003 to 2013 (Bernasek, 2014). The foundation went on to say this drop has been persistent—since 1984, household wealth has dropped 14% (Leonhardt, 2016). Since the Great Recession of 2008–2009, wages have gone up in the U.S., but only to pre-recession levels and still below where wages were in January 2000 (Green & Coder, 2016). One demographic researcher noted that this upward income trend was primarily due to increases in 2016 and that, otherwise, recovering wage losses has been "very long, very painful" (Zumbrun, 2016, p. 8). Other evidence indicates that the American Dream of advancement through the free market is in peril. A recent Stanford study revealed that only half of Americans born in the 1980s earn more than their parents; a consolidation of wealth by the top 10% of wage earners accounted for more than two thirds of this dynamic, and economic slowdowns accounted for the remainder (Chetty et al., 2016). Only 35% of Americans under 35 own a home (a record low), and home ownership overall is at 62%, the lowest percentage since the 1960s (Rampell, 2016, p. A13). More adults under 35 live with their parents than at any time since the 1880s (Fry, 2016). These various indicators offer a portrait of a marketplace where effective individual self-governing may have limited or no impact on one's ability to further one's life. Indeed, considering that the U.S. government receives less tax revenue than most modern industrialized nations (OECD, 2016), it is difficult to make the argument that an over-involved state is disrupting American free enterprise and one's ability to maximize oneself. Rather, the U.S. free market system, with the American welfare state in eclipse, reveals structural problems of wealth inequality and wage stagnation, which threaten the narrative of individual advancement through the marketplace.

There are several other indicators that can lead Americans to question the corporate vision of a better standard of living through free enterprise. In 17 U.S. states, more Caucasian Americans are dying than are being born, a result of the combination of lower fertility rates amongst Caucasians and an uptick in drug-related deaths (Sáenz & Johnson, 2016). Other researchers have found an overall increase in U.S. death rates that is associated with the rise in imports from China (Pierce & Shott, 2016). They suggest that related U.S. factory closings resulted in more Americans laid off who could not find new jobs; this led, especially for Caucasian adults, to depression, addiction and, in some cases, suicide (Ehrenfreund, 2016; Pierce & Shott, 2016). Indeed, the Center for Disease Control (CDC) reported in 2016 that, for the first time, the U.S. saw more deaths from heroin use (30,000) than from gun homicides (Ingraham, 2016, p. A21). Other recent reports, based on CDC data, reveal that Americans' "stress load" has increased significantly over the last 40 years, with fewer Americans in the middle and lower classes reporting good health, and the country's overall life expectancy declining for the first time in 20 years (Schanzenbach, Mumford, Nunn, & Bauer, 2016; Swanson, 2013).

The challenge for the continued use of the corporate persona is obvious—corporations would need to show, as they attempted to display in the mid-20th-century accounts in this book, that they bring benefits to Americans yet also walk a journey that reflects, at a minimum, a sense that they share in Americans' struggles. The first aspect, the material benefits of the corporation and free enterprise, has a certain degree of staying power. Indeed, Chapter 7 points to how a majority of Americans hold to capitalism as the preferred economic system, believing that it allows them to achieve the American Dream through hard work (McCoy, 2015; Newport, 2016). Relatedly, a 2015 Marketplace-Edison Research poll found that almost 80% believed that their own diligent efforts made more of a difference in bettering their lot in life, rather than luck ("What the," 2015), mirroring other research on the enduring belief in advancement through hard work (McCoy, 2015; Newport, 2016). Beyond this marketplace-friendly ideology, however, there are other compelling reasons for Americans to continue to be receptive to the idea that capitalism provides opportunities (along with products and services) that benefit all. Corporations, both in the U.S. and around the world, exist in an era that has recently seen 20 million people advance out of poverty, an increased global life expectancy by almost 20 years since 1960, and the introduction of "miracle drugs, vaccines, improved sanitation" and agricultural technology improvements (Gerson, 2016, p. A13). Additionally, the Stanford study (Chetty et al., 2016), when adjusted to include Americans born in the 1970s, points to about 63% of Americans out-earning their parents. "It's too soon to say the American Dream is fading," said Scott Winship, a researcher at the free-market-oriented Manhattan Institute; "Intergenerational advancement continues apace, but at a diminished rate" (Tankersley, 2016, p. A16). Allstate CEO Tom Wilson offered that corporations can and do show that they are committed to helping individuals through these challenging times. The company raised its minimum wage to $15 per hour, he said, because, "stronger, more prosperous communities with better-educated workers and customers also provide a much better economic and business climate" (Wilson, 2016, p. A17).

The evidence, however, is that corporations have also tended to ignore Wilson's observations, not heeding his call that corporations should demonstrably "get on with making the world a better place" (Wilson, 2016, p. A17). Rather, although it agrees with capitalism, the American public sees precious few recent examples of a corporate personality that asserts a common good with the individual. Granted, public relations practitioners have helped corporations make notable strides in showing how the company makes associations with the individual, but, as detailed in Chapter 2, these allegiances often hinge upon a connection with the corporation's products. For example, while it might make intuitive sense for baby formula company Similac to reach out with a "Sisterhood of Motherhood" initiative (*PRWeek*, 2016) and for H&R Block to reach out to K–12 educators with an "H&R Block Budget Challenge" curriculum (H&R Block, 2014), these companies speak to issues that are closely linked to their products, rather than attempting to make associations that more clearly resonate with wider prevailing American values. That is, such campaigns do not incorporate broader appeals to American values like progress through self-reliance, freedom, and self-direction—worldviews that can lead to individual receptivity to the free market. By not demonstrating such connections to enduring beliefs about Americanism, corporations contribute to more cynicism about companies, and society in general. Additional stories about recent corporate wrongdoings by companies like Wells Fargo (falsely creating new customer accounts), Exxon (hiding evidence of concerns about climate change), and Volkswagen (engaging in emissions tampering) only exacerbate such suspicion. Fewer than 20% of Americans voice trust in business (Norman, 2016), which is not surprising during a time when many have been struggling for decades and "tend to lose faith in society's institutions…" (Leonhardt, 2016). One economic columnist noted that there was a sensibility in the U.S. that continual advancement was *not* a given. "The arc of the political universe is long, and it doesn't have to bend toward progress or justice or anything good," he said, in a notable indictment of the American Dream (O'Brien, 2016, p. A10). In fact, older Americans, who have long been exposed free enterprise boosterism, revealed in the 2016 presidential election their sense of dissonance about the message of self-advancement through the free markets in contrast to the reality of their own personal economic misery. For example, one prominent labor economist notes that workers between the ages of 55 and 64 in 4 states that comprise America's "Rust Belt"—Michigan, Wisconsin, Ohio, and Pennsylvania—are experiencing the worst real-wage growth in America, earning income roughly equivalent to 1979 wages (Ghilarducci, 2016). Those same four states shocked most political experts and voted for Donald J. Trump, tipping the Electoral College to his favor.

While mainstream journalism and the political class discuss Trump's presidential victory as a protest vote by Americans against power centers in both the government and business, there is another aspect of the results that point to how the corporate persona may yet have come further into play. Trump's ascendancy reveals an unprecedented example of an embodied corporate persona. More than a brand personality, his continual assertion that his business is himself (e.g., through the licensing of his name to hotels and golf courses) reveals an inversion: rather than a corporation having a persona, he signifies that the persona can have a corporation, and that this can be relatable to the individual. While celebrities have long affected such an inversion—consider how Taylor Swift, Kobe Bryant, and George Clooney behave as personalities that are, in effect, their own businesses—the evidence for Trump's inversion is striking, as it asserts directly that his corporate persona joins the average American on his or her journey. When Trump stated at the 2016 Republican convention that "I am your voice," he claimed, much like the affinitive corporate persona messaging offered during the mid-20th-century U.S., that he walked the same road as the average person ("Full text," 2016, para. 30). During that convention speech, Trump also proclaimed, "I alone can fix [the country]," echoing mid-20th-century corporate persona messages that capitalism was the only way to a constructive society ("Full text," 2016, para. 35). Trump's particular inversion of a benevolent corporate persona resonated well with many Americans; they saw a persona that had a business background as an important qualification for leading the country. Envisioning Trump in the White House, one voter said, "A successful businessman will surround himself with the right people … when he goes to build one of his buildings, he doesn't pour the concrete himself" (Wan, Friess, & Hauslohner, 2016, p. A42). One letter writer to the *Washington Post* was more explicit, stating the country needed a businessman to guide the country back to capitalism: "We must reverse the trend toward socialism, and who better to make that change than a capitalist?" the letter said (Erdner, 2016, p. A21). Photographer Chris Arnade, who traveled extensively in the Rust Belt during the campaign, noted that Trump's message of benevolent paternalism appealed to those who felt frustration and anger about being treated as "back-row kids," left to struggle on their own to achieve the American Dream (Sullivan, 2016, p. C2).

As this book is being written, how Trump's particular inversion of the corporate persona will fully emerge is yet to be seen. What is known is that the fractures in the U.S. economic system weighed heavily in the 2016 presidential election and that related socio-economic changes already in motion will continue to challenge the corporate sphere. In 2014, more than half of the children under 5 in the U.S. were non-Caucasian (Wazwaz, 2015, para. 2). Estimates are that, by the end of 2016, the foreign-born population in the United States will reach almost 20% ("New Census," 2015) and that, by 2044, the U.S. is projected to become a Caucasian-minority country (ibid.). These trends foretell the likelihood of gradual cultural changes in the U.S. that would push for, at a minimum, adjustments to long-enduring Americanist values of self-reliance, individualism, and advancement through the marketplace. Additionally, from a global perspective, it is important to pay attention to such changes because economic disruptions and socio-demographic changes are not unique to the U.S. For example, the Brexit vote in the UK, the rise of far-right-wing sentiment in France, and disruptions in Germany due to immigrants from the Middle East and Africa all similarly put notions of prevailing values in flux. While it is beyond the scope of this book's exploration, the firmament in these countries may make it conducive for corporations (both native and global) to make assertions of shared values with targeted groups, all in an attempt to tamp down potential or existing crises that could undermine the corporations. In an era where large multinationals like Disney, BMW, and Microsoft are ranked at the top among "the world's 100 most reputable companies" (Smith, 2013), one must assume, at a minimum, that such global companies perceive they have much to risk if they do not display to countries in various states of turmoil that they are personable entities that demonstrate good, global corporate citizenship (Thompson, 2012).

What is public relations to make of this, especially if a corporate persona appeal is to be made in the midst of systemic economic dysfunctions *and* shifts in demographic patterns and notions of prevailing values? To address that question, some wider considerations of public relations are required. First, as L'Etang (2008, 2014) and Lamme and Russell (2010) have pointed out, public relations emerged and sustained itself across several periods and cultures that went far beyond associations with the competitive marketplace. Public relations, with this broader understanding, is an arena of intentional persuasive techniques that is often centered on re-affirmation of existing (or emerging) cultural dispositions among broad groups of peoples; it has appeared within religious settings, nation-building efforts, governance, and reform movements (Lamme & Russell, 2010; St. John III, Lamme, & L'Etang, 2014). Second, since at least the late 1940s, attempts to convey fundamental understandings of the societal role of the emerging public relations field have tended to elide "marketplace of idea" concepts, instead asserting that public relations, rather than primarily selling a product, service, or self-interested idea, attempts to influence society by acting in the public interest (Broom & Sha, 2013; Griswold & Griswold, 1948; Nielander & Miller, 1951). However, scholarship has also pointed to the need to address complexities that can problematize straightforward assertions of a public service role for public relations. Messina (2007) asserted that determining the public interest is virtually intractable for the PR person because, in doing so, the practitioner attempts to ineffectually transmute the narrow private interest of the client into a claim of pertinence to broader public interests and to act as a reifier of public interest that is actually more appropriate in the "interplay between the citizen and a representative [political] authority" (p. 38). In a more pragmatic sense, there are also concerns that public relations people must first serve their client organizations, inherently diluting any professional focus on public service (Edwards, 2016; Fitzpatrick & Gauthier, 2001; L'Etang, 2006) and that public relations practitioners do not necessarily have the training and skill sets to adequately identify or address items of public interest (Bowen, 2008; L'Etang, 2006; St. John III & Pearson, 2016).

Still, even with its limitations, the profession could well use the corporate persona construct in the U.S. to affirm common interests between companies and individuals in the face of the country's socio-economic fractures and changes. Coontz (2000) noted that the American mythos of individualism and self-reliance leads Americans to view events in the public sphere as matters of personality. "The choice," she said, "becomes either a personal relationship or none, a familial intimacy or complete alienation" (Coontz, 2000, p. 114). This does not mean, however, that organizations should think they merely need to project a "good guy" persona, striking a pose of being "energetic and efficient" while serving a "worthwhile purpose" and being a "good neighbor," noted Bernstein (1984, p. 53). Instead, a corporation should be allying its beliefs and aspirations to wider strains in the culture, "particularly [within] a society in ferment..." (Bernstein, 1984, p. 53). Given the U.S.' current (and projected) societal upheaval, such alignment of corporate beliefs and ambitions may well become more challenging in the decades to come. This challenge, however, is not unprecedented and not unremarked upon by public relations observers. As Harlow and Black (1947) pointed out in the mid-20th century, if a corporation is out of step with its society, the company "must step aside and accept the verdict of its fellow citizens" (p. 218). That is, the corporation must find some ways to "catch on" to the direction of public sentiment and not "fall for a moment behind the procession" (Harlow & Black, 1947, p. 218). Public relations practitioner David Finn (1961) similarly noted that, when a corporation is not in sync with the populace, the effective public relations person helps its executives look inward to see what is going wrong, rather than try to create a mask that everything is right.

While American corporations will surely need to be mindful of how disjoints in the public sphere may imperil their existence, the country's loyalty to mythical notions of self-made advancement, made possible through the helping hand of the free market, will likely persist in some form. The corporate persona has arisen as an adjunct to the American propensity for venerating the marketplace as the route for self-advancement. Chester Barnard, president of the Rockefeller Foundation, articulated this disposition:

> When I was a poor boy, I used to walk around among the finer homes and wonder how I could ever get the money to live that way. In that sense, I was envious, yes. But it never occurred to me to think that I ought to have the other fellow's money in order to do it. We were envious in the sense that we were *inculcated with the ambition* to attain that status for ourselves.
>
> (Goodfriend, 1954, p. 32, emphasis added)

Barnard's observation points to the distinctive claim of this book. That is, the corporate persona is not simply about legal or marketing considerations or about constructivist understandings that stress the polyphony of the corporate voice. Instead, it is about a corporation, through narrative, offering a re-affirmation of the bent for progress shared between the company and individuals. Corporations offer this story in times of stress so as to bolster associations with individuals and successfully navigate threats that may undermine the corporation's legitimacy or continued existence. As such, the corporate persona offers what author Pam Houston has called a "glimmer," a key that unlocks a story that resonates with the individual (Haupt, 2012). What helps make a glimmer work is that, when it is put within an effective narrative that resonates with individuals' values and knowledge, it can "stitch together the truths," said award-winning memoirist Angela Palm (2016, p. 193). Those truths, when asserted by an affinitive corporate persona, can prove very difficult to resist, because, as noted non-fiction author Elizabeth Greenwood said, we may say we are open to changes, but "our roots, our selves can't be extinguished" (2016, p. 238). The attempted linking of common values between corporations and individuals may well offer improved opportunities for corporations to learn how to contribute more effectively to the common good. There is also the very real possibility, however, that corporations can also offer what liberal critic Chris Hedges has called "seductive illusions" that leave individuals to "strike out at shadows," encouraging citizens to focus on self-governing rather than addressing systemic concerns (2016, para. 4). Hedges' warning points to the potential abuses that can come when an organization moves beyond Heath's (2006) courtship of identification to what this work points out is a Foucauldian *courtship of re-affirmation*. With this approach, the corporation emphasizes mutual values and aspirations, affirming a version of what Burke (1950) called a consubstantiation between rhetor and audience. When the corporation affirms such a co-existence, it is with the intent of offering insights on how to best self-govern and then thrive through the American private enterprise system. As Lasch (1984) pointed out, stressful times in an increasingly narcissistic society reveal that Americans, while ostensibly prizing individualism, look for a guide to help them traverse tough times. When that happens, said Sennett (1977), individuals tend to be attracted to appeals that address their insecurities rather than deal with logic and facts. The language of personality, he said, can outmaneuver rational analysis and constructive debate.

This book, then, invites further study and careful deliberation about the call of the corporate persona in the modern world. While it is an artifice, it is also, by its nature, imbued with a propensity to affect consonance with the individual. This, in turn, can make it difficult to ascertain the distinct ways it tries to assimilate the individual's worldview into its prerogatives. While Baudrillard (1983) discussed such a construct as being a simulation that is more real than real, Bruno Latour (1994) said that it was important to go beyond describing such mediating forces as distinguishable "things." They merit a more-considered recognition, he said: "They deserve to be housed in our intellectual culture as full-fledged actors. They mediate our actions? No, they are us" (Latour, 1994, p. 64). With this assertion, Latour offers a thought-provoking variation on Baudrillard: the corporate persona is more us than us. While such a claim appears to be problematic, this book reveals it is an assertion that the corporation has, at times, worked hard to affirm through conveying a human-like form. The corporate persona as an affinitive fellow being may well come into fuller flower in proportion to the economic and societal stressors that appear in the decades to come.

References

Batchelor, B. (1938). *Profitable public relations.* New York: Harper & Brothers.

Baudrillard, J. (1983). *Simulations.* New York: Semiotext.

Bernasek, A. (2014). "The typical household, now worth a third less." *New York Times,* July 26. Retrieved from www.nytimes.com/2014/07/27/business/the-typical-household-now-worth-a-third-less.html?_r=0.

Bernstein, D. (1984). *Company image and reality: A critique of corporate communications.* East Sussex: UK: Holt, Rinehart & Winston.

Bowen, S. (2008). "A state of neglect: Public relations as 'corporate conscience' or ethics counsel." *Journal of Public Relations Research 20*(3), pp. 271–296.

Broom, G.M., & Sha, B.-L. (2013). *Cutlip & Center's effective public relations* (11th ed.). Upper Saddle River, NJ: Pearson.

Burke, K. (1950). *A rhetoric of motives.* Berkeley: University of California Press.

Chetty, R., Grusky, D., Hell, M., Hendren, N., Manduca, R., & Narang, J. (2016). *The fading American Dream: Trends in absolute income mobility since 1940.* [Report]. Cambridge, MA: Harvard. Retrieved from http://scholar.harvard.edu/files/hendren/files/abs_mobility_paper.pdf.

Coontz, S. (2000). *The way we never were: American families and the nostalgia trap.* New York: Basic Books.

Edwards, L. (2016). "The role of public relations in deliberative systems." *Communication Theory 66*(1), pp. 60–81.

Ehrenfreund, M. (2016). "Economists link U.S. deaths to rise in imports." *Washington Post,* November 24, p. A24.

Erdner, G. (2016). "Reversing the trend toward socialism." [Letter to the editor]. *Washington Post,* November 13, p. A21.

Finn, D. (1961). "The price of corporate vanity." *Harvard Business Review 39*(4), pp. 135–143.

Fitzpatrick, K., & Gauthier, C. (2001). "Toward a professional responsibility theory of public relations ethics." *Journal of Mass Media Ethics 16*(2 & 3), pp. 193–212.

Fry, R. (2016). "For first time in modern era, living with parents edges out other living arrangements for 18- to 34-year-olds." *Pew Research Center*, May 24. Retrieved from www.pewsocialtrends.org/2016/05/24/for-first-time-in-modern-era-living-with-parents-edges-out-other-living-arrangements-for-18-to-34-year-olds/.

"Full text: Donald Trump's 2016 Republican National Convention Speech." (2016). *ABCnews.go.com.*, July 22. Retrieved from http://abcnews.go.com/Politics/full-text-donald-trumps-2016-republican-national-convention/story?id=40786529.

Ghilarducci, T. (2016). "Since Reagan, older workers in rust-belt states flipped from economic winners to losers." *Teresaghilarducci.org*. Retrieved from http://teresaghilarducci.org/news-events/431-november-2016-unemployment-report-for-workers-over-55#owag.

Goodfriend, A. (1954). *What is America?* New York: Simon & Schuster.

Green, G., & Coder, J. (2016). *Household income trends.* [Report]. Sentier Research. Retrieved from www.sentierresearch.com/reports/Sentier_Household_Income_Trends_Report_October2016_11_29_16.pdf.

Greenwood, E. (2016). *Playing dead: A journey through the world of death fraud.* New York: Simon & Schuster.

Griswold, G., & Griswold, D. (1948). *Your public relations: The standard public relations handbook.* New York: Funk & Wagnalls.

"H&R Block Budget Challenge offers $3 million in grants and scholarships, plus real-world personal finance skills." (2014). News release, *hrblock.com*, September 8. Retrieved from http://newsroom.hrblock.com/hr-block-budget-challenge-offers-3-million-in-grants-and-scholarships-plus-real-world-personal-finance-skills.

Harlow, R., & Black, M. (1947). *Practical public relations: Its foundations, divisions, tools and practices.* New York: Harper Brothers.

Haupt, J. (2012). "Q&A with author Pam Houston." *Psychology Today*, March 1. Retrieved from www.psychologytoday.com/blog/one-true-thing/201203/qa-author-pam-houston.

Heath, R.L. (2006). "A rhetorical theory approach to issues management." In C. Botan, & V. Hazelton (Eds.), *Public relations theory II*, pp. 55–87. Mahwah, NJ: Lawrence Erlbaum Associates.

Heath, R.L., & Nelson, R.A. (1986). *Issues management: Corporate public policymaking in an information society.* Beverly Hills, CA: SAGE.

Hedges, C. (2016). "American irrationalism." *Truthdig.com*, October 30. Retrieved from www.truthdig.com/report/item/american_irrationalism_201610305.

Ingraham, C. (2016). "Heroin deaths surpass gun homicides for the first time." *Washington Post*, December 9, p. A21.

Jansen, T. (2016). "Who is talking? Some remarks on nonhuman agency in communication." *Communication Theory 26*, pp. 255–272.

Lamme, M.O., & Russell, K.M. (2010). "Removing the spin: Toward a new theory of public relations history." *Journalism and Communications Monographs 11*(4), pp. 281–362.

Lasch, C. (1984). *The minimal self: Psychic survival in troubled times.* New York: W.W. Norton & Company.

Latour, B. (1994). "On technical mediation—Philosophy, sociology, genealogy." *Common Knowledge 3*(2), pp. 29–64.

Leonhardt, D. (2016). "A great fight of our times." *New York Times*, October 11. Retrieved from www.nytimes.com/2016/10/11/opinion/a-great-fight-of-our-times.html.

L'Etang, J. (2006). "Corporate responsibility and public relations ethics." In J. L'Etang,

& M. Pieczka (Eds.), *Public relations: Critical debates and contemporary practice*, pp. 405–422. Mahwah, NJ: Lawrence Erlbaum.

L'Etang, J. (2008). "Writing PR history: Issues, methods and politics." *Journal of Communication Management 12*(4), pp. 319–355.

L'Etang, J. (2014). "Foreword: The challenges of engaging public relations history." In B. St. John III, M.O. Lamme, & J. L'Etang (Eds.), *Pathways to public relations: Histories of practice and profession*, pp. xii–xviii. Abingdon, UK: Routledge.

McCoy, S. (2015). "The American Dream is suffering, but Americans satisfied: 15 Charts." *The Atlantic*, July 1. Retrieved from www.theatlantic.com/politics/archive/2015/07/american-dream-suffering/397475/.

Messina, A. (2007). "Public relations, the public interest and persuasion: An ethical approach." *Journal of Communication Management 11*(1), pp. 29–52.

"New census bureau report analyzes U.S. population projections." (2015). *Census.gov*, March 3. Retrieved from www.census.gov/newsroom/press-releases/2015/cb15-tps16.html.

Newport, F. (2016). "Americans' views of socialism, capitalism are little changed." *Gallup*, May 6. Retrieved from www.gallup.com/poll/191354/americans-views-socialism-capitalism-little-changed.aspx.

Nielander, W.A., & Miller, R.W. (1951). *Public relations.* New York: The Ronald Press Company.

Norman, J. (2016). "Americans' confidence in institutions stays low." *Gallup*, June 13. Retrieved from www.gallup.com/poll/192581/americans-confidence-institutions-stays-low.aspx.

O'Brien, M. (2016). "U.S. could be the next Argentina." *Washington Post*. December 26, p. A10.

Organisation for Economic Co-operation and Development (OECD). (2016). *Revenue statistic—Provisional data on tax ratios for 2015.* OECD.org. Retrieved from www.oecd.org/ctp/tax-policy/revenue-statistics-ratio-change-latest-years.htm.

Palm, A. (2016). *Riverine: A memoir from anywhere but here.* Minneapolis: Graywolf Press.

Pierce, J., & Schott, P. (2016). *Trade liberalization and mortality: Evidence from U.S. counties.* [Report]. The National Bureau of Economic Research. Retrieved from www.nber.org/papers/w22849#fromrss.

"PRWeek campaign of the year 2016." (2016). *PRWeek*, March 18. Retrieved from www.prweek.com/article/1387970/prweek-campaign-year-2016.

Rampell, C. (2016). "The economic wisdom of millennials." *Washington Post*, August 23, p. A13.

Sáenz, R.J., & Johnson, K.M. (2016). *White deaths exceed births in one-third of the United States.* [Report]. Carsey Research. Retrieved from https://carsey.unh.edu/publication/white-deaths.

Schanzenbach, D., Mumford, M., Nunn, R., & Bauer, L. (2016). *Money lightens the load.* [Report]. The Hamilton Project. Retrieved from www.hamiltonproject.org/papers/money_lightens_the_load.

Sennett, R. (1977). *The fall of public man.* New York: Alfred A. Knopf.

Smith, J. (2013). "The world's most reputable companies." *Forbes*, April 9. Retrieved from www.forbes.com/sites/jacquelynsmith/2013/04/09/the-worlds-most-reputable-companies-2/amp/.

St. John III, B., Lamme, M.O., & L'Etang, J.L. (2014). *Pathways to public relations: Histories of practice and profession.* Abingdon, UK: Routledge.

St. John III, B., & Pearson, Y. (2016). "Crisis management and ethics: Moving beyond the public-relations-person-as-corporate-conscience construct." *Journal of Mass Media Ethics 31*(1), pp. 18–34.

Sullivan, M. (2016). " 'Back-Row Kids' bring U.S. into focus." *Washington Post*, December 12, pp. C1–2.

Swanson, A. (2016). " 'Everybody outside of the top is suffering': How stress is harming America's health." December 13, *Washington Post*. Retrieved from www.washington-post.com/news/wonk/wp/2016/12/13/everybody-outside-of-the-top-is-suffering-how-stress-is-harming-americas-health/?utm_term=.2b4bdc8016bb.

Tankersley, J. (2016). "American Dream collapsing for young adults, study says." *Washington Post*, December 9, p. A16.

Thompson, G. (2012). *The constitutionalization of the global corporate sphere?* Oxford, UK: University Press.

Wan, W., Friess, S., & Hauslohner, A. (2016). "A question on Americans' minds: What does Trump's win say about us as a nation?" *Washington Post*, November 10, pp. A1, A42.

Wazwaz, N. (2016). "It's official: The U.S. is becoming a minority-majority nation." *US News and World Report*, July 6. Retrieved from www.usnews.com/news/articles/2015/07/06/its-official-the-us-is-becoming-a-minority-majority-nation.

"What the Marketplace-Edison Research poll found." (2015). *Marketplace.org*, October 23. Retrieved from www.marketplace.org/2015/10/23/economy/anxiety-index/what-marketplace-edison-research-poll-found.

Wilson, T. (2016). "Companies must be forces for good." *Washington Post*, October 3, p. A17.

Zumbrun, J. (2016). "Voter discord over wages isn't easily resolved." *The Wall Street Journal*, August 8, p. A2.

Index

For Product Safety Concerns and Information please contact our EU
representative GPSR@taylorandfrancis.com
Taylor & Francis Verlag GmbH, Kaufingerstraße 24, 80331 München, Germany

www.ingramcontent.com/pod-product-compliance
Ingram Content Group UK Ltd.
Pitfield, Milton Keynes, MK11 3LW, UK
UKHW020951180425
457613UK00019B/625